A GUIDE TO LIFE

Wisdom from the World's Cultures

CONTENTS

INTRODUCTION

What is wisdom? It's a question that has occupied great thinkers of all colours and creeds for millennia. Although it is hard to agree on a definition, most people accept that wisdom arises from reflection on experience, a process whereby what we learn from the past informs, and improves, our decisions in the present.

According to his compatriot, Plato, the Ancient Greek philosopher Socrates declared that 'the unexamined life is not worth living'; conversely, what we gain through such a self-appraisal makes life better.

Wisdom, then, underpins wellness, another concept that is difficult to pin down as it encompasses not just physical health, but mental and social health, too.

In a nutshell, to be well is to be healthy and happy across each of these dimensions. Each nation and its people have unique perspectives on how to achieve this, creating the catalogue of insights from which this book springs.

These insights cover a vast territory, ranging from rites of passage to exercise, from social mores to dietary advice, and from ancient customs to modern rituals. But for all their diversity, there are consistent themes, too: the importance of tolerance or, to put it another way, the celebration of difference; the health of families and the strength of communities as the foundations upon which our individual sense of wellness rests; the restorative power of nature.

Some insights on how to live well have already conquered the world: the practices of yoga and meditation, say, which have long since spread from the ashrams of Northern India to the boardrooms of Southern California.

Others have gone global more recently: in the last few years, the Danish concept of *hygge*, a sense of comfort or cosiness, has ignited the world's imagination; the same is true of the Japanese practice of *shinkrin-yoku*, now better known as forest bathing.

But many of the insights in the following pages are little known,

much less adopted, outside their culture of origin, which seems like a missed opportunity. For as well as providing a rich resource for anyone looking for inspiration to improve their own sense of wellness, they offer a fresh perspective on the countries from which they're taken.

Can you ever get under the skin of New Zealand without knowing a little bit about *kaitiakitanga*, the Māori notion of guardianship? What about decoding China if you're completely ignorant of the principle of yin and yang, or Italy if you don't understand the social significance of *la bella figura*?

We hope this book teaches you something about how to live a healthier, happier life, offering up a few tips you can put into action in ways big and small. Furthermore, we hope it inspires you to experience firsthand the wisdom of other cultures, which offer so much to those who approach them with open, enquiring minds.

AMERICAS

CANADA

This patchwork nation takes great pride in its diversity and differences. Its citizens know that tolerance is the route to harmony when your neighbours come from all around the world.

POPULATION
36 million

POPULATION DENSITY
4 people / sq km

World's highest consumption of macaroni cheese (1.7 million boxes per year)

A former prime minister once said that Canada has a cuisine of cuisines, 'not a stew pot, but a smorgasbord'. The motley of dishes gracing many dinner tables testify to a history that has produced a true rainbow nation (in 1971, Canada became the world's first country to establish multiculturalism as an official policy). Schoolchildren grow up surrounded by a gallery of different faces, and they're encouraged to cherish their background and heritage. Indigenous people had, of course, lived in this vast, rugged land for millennia before, in 1867, the British defined the modern, self-governing state of Canada we know today. Since then, through the use of immigration policies to populate the wilderness, Canada has welcomed generations of incomers, first from Europe, then the rest of the world. The result is a tapestry of people who share sensibilities, yet celebrate diversity.

AMERICAS

© Hero Images Inc./Alamy Stock Photo

© V J Matthew/Shutterstock, © RyersonClark/Getty Images

Clockwise from top: Ice hockey is Canada's national sport, played on outdoor public rinks everywhere; an Inuit woman on Baffin Island; the Confederation Trail runs the length of Prince Edward Island. **Previous page:** Fishing on Waterfowl Lake, Banff National Park.

TOP INSIGHTS for LIFE

FABRIC OF SOCIETY

The patchwork of Canadian society has been sewn together over the course of centuries, and the fabric holds firm despite its disparate materials. People take pride in the range of ethnicities, languages and cultures that coexist in one nation, but they stay humble about it rather than horn-tooting too much. This modest

"Canadians are the people who learned to live without the bold accents of the natural ego-trippers of other lands." - Marshall McLuhan, Canadian philosopher

belief in ethno-pluralism as opposed to assimilation into a single culture, or a so-called melting pot, might just be the most discernible difference between being Canadian and American.

MIND YOUR MANNERS

Canadians are mighty polite and it's not just a stereotype. Whether it's holding the door open for the person behind you or apologising profusely for an innocent mistake, good manners are ingrained in the nation's DNA. Canadians are connoisseurs of small talk, putting people at ease; a failure to engage is considered somewhat impolite. Such friendliness builds a sense of community, and on a more personal level, a warm, fuzzy feeling.

BE A GOOD SPORT

Hockey is much more than a national pastime. In small towns, hockey rinks are a meeting point for the community, and if the national team wins gold, the country takes to the streets. Canadians love sports, and even if you aren't well-versed in a game, you're certainly out for the party afterwards. Whether it's football or curling, Canadians also celebrate hometown heroes with passion. The cliché stands: it's not about who wins or loses, but how you play the game. At the tailgate party afterwards, hard feelings dissipate.

SHOOT THE BREEZE

You'd be surprised by the benefits of small talk. Studies show that it can make you smarter and happier. So turn to that stranger on the bus, train or plane next to you and ask how their day was. You'll find that even the most basic positive social interaction can brighten your mood – or that of others.

UNITED STATES

Like a golden retriever, this big, young country practically wags its tail with exuberance. There's a lot to learn from its all-in attitude to life.

POPULATION
329 million

RANK ON
WORLD GIVING
INDEX OF
CHARITABLE
BEHAVIOUR
#2

MILES OF ROAD
> 4 million

America is BIG. The third largest country in the world by both area and population, its fundamental bigness goes much further. Americans have big houses and big cars. They eat big burgers and drink big sodas. They've got big mountains and big plains and big lakes and big deserts. And they've also got big hearts: meet an American on a plane, the stereotype goes, and he or she will have invited you home for Sunday supper before the flight ends. You shouldn't generalise too much about such a big place, of course; what's true of an isolated New England fishing village may not be true of a multiethnic Chicago suburb or a Mexican-American border city. But regional differences notwithstanding, it's clear that there's a focus on living well, to the max, in the land of the free – a place where the pursuit of happiness is enshrined in the Constitution.

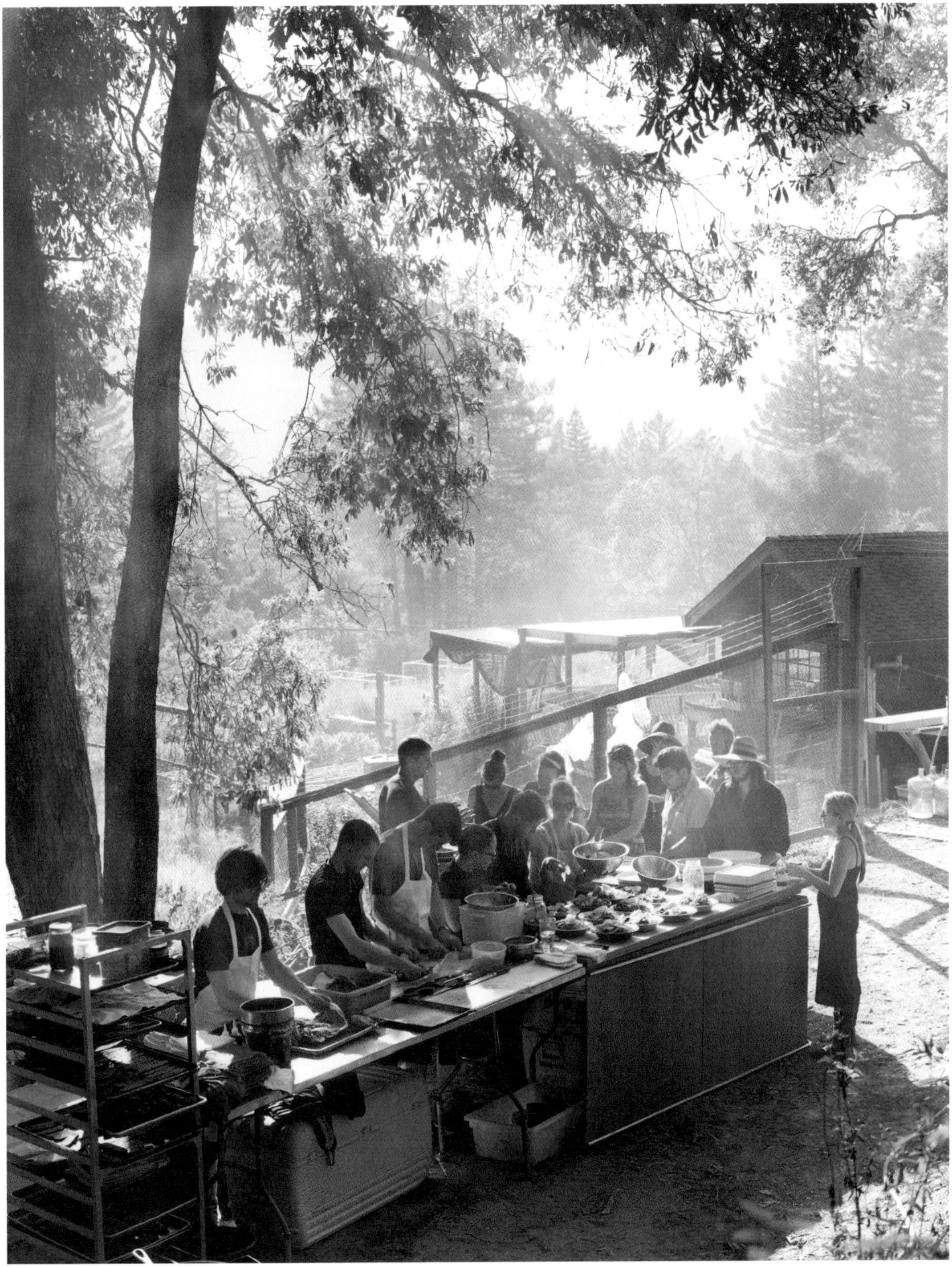

© Andrew Montgomery/Lonely Planet

AMERICAS

© Artur Debat/Getty Images

© Mark Read/Lonely Planet, © Justin Foulkes/Lonely Planet

Clockwise from top: Driving Route 66 between Chicago, IL and Santa Monica, CA is the a classic American road trip; a band performs in Key West, Florida; a hot dog, fresh from an LA food truck. **Previous page:** Cooking, eating and socialising together is a national pastime.

TOP INSIGHTS for LIFE

GIVING THANKS

On the fourth Thursday in November, American families gather to gorge on turkey and pumpkin pie, and to count their blessings. The Thanksgiving holiday is one of the country's best-beloved secular traditions, originating from the 'first Thanksgiving' of 1621, when English Pilgrim settlers and

The Constitution only guarantees you the right to pursue happiness. You have to catch it yourself. - Benjamin Franklin, one of the Founding Fathers of the USA

members of the local Wampanoag tribe shared a harvest feast. Some rightly point out that the holiday glosses over centuries of genocide against Native Americans. But the central idea – giving thanks – is something that benefits everyone; research suggests that gratitude can reduce anxiety, enhance empathy, improve relationships, and even extend life span.

FRONTIER SPIRIT

If there's an unknown horizon, Americans will head right for it. They've been doing it since the beginning: migrating over ancient land bridges, crossing the sea on rickety passenger ships, settling the vast prairies, rushing west for gold. Today, the US is one of the world's most mobile countries, with one in four citizens having moved within the country in the past five years. This restlessness is part of the national mythos, exhausting yet enlivening. Moving sparks imagination, spurs innovation, brings disparate groups into contact, brings boredom to heel. It's part of what makes the country such a thrilling place to be.

TREAT YOURSELF

Americans are not shy about their love of sugar, and shamelessly take their desserts way, way over the top.

GIVE THANKS, US-STYLE

Showing your gratitude is better with a side of sweet potatoes. So why not cook up a traditional Thanksgiving meal? Classic dishes include roast turkey with stuffing, cranberry sauce, green bean casserole, and the aforemen-tioned sweet potatoes. For dessert, pumpkin or pecan pie (or both!). Gather your friends and family and go around the table taking turns to say one thing you're grateful for.

GET BEHIND THE WHEEL

There are long drives and then there are *road trips*. How to have the latter? First, forget getting anywhere in a hurry. Take secondary roads rather than interstates; they're far more scenic. Stop at every roadside attraction, no matter how tacky. Eat every regional snack you see: boiled peanuts in the South, fry bread tacos in the Southwest. And play the radio, loud.

Think 20-scoop sundaes, milkshakes topped with an *entire piece of cake*, novelty chocolate bars the size of encyclopedias. Although eating too many of them isn't a good idea, these mega-desserts convey the American sense of delight in small indulgences, the importance of holding on to your childlike enthusiasms.

CHOOSE YOUR OWN FAMILY

The word 'ohana' means family in Hawaiian, but it's about so much more than the nuclear father-mother-sister-brother unit. *Ohana* includes your immediate relations, but also your extended clan, whether or not you share DNA. Your mum's best friend who you always called 'auntie?' *Ohana*. The college buddy you've been spending Christmas with for a decade? *Ohana*. No matter how you feel about your blood relatives, with *ohana* you'll always have family.

YOU TALKIN' TO ME?

'Nice weather, huh?' Yes, they're talking to you. Americans are famously chatty with strangers, smiling and striking up conversations everywhere from the supermarket to the subway. The level of friendliness varies by region – strongest in the South, somewhat fainter in the Northeast and Northwest. To outsiders, it may seem superficial or even disingenuous. But small talk helps knit together the fabric of a nation with so many different cultures.

HIT THE ROAD

From Jack Kerouac's *On the Road* to the movie *Thelma and Louise*, the road trip is a touchstone of American culture. Classic elements include a convertible (though any car will do), cheap gas station coffee, diner pie, and kitschy roadside motels. Is there any better stress reliever than watching the sun set over the open road?

LEAN IN & HELP OUT

Americans love to lend a hand. According to studies, the nation has the highest level of civic engagement in the world. Citizens join service organisations like Kiwanis or the Lions Club, hold bake sales to raise money for schools, serve hot food in homeless shelters, organise church charity drives... In many schools, students are expected to do 100 or more hours of volunteer work just to graduate.

Above: The concept of ohana – or extended family – originated in Hawaii.
Below: The ubiquitous stars and stripes symbolise the spirit of America.

AMERICAS

MEXICO

Life is good in Mexico. Maybe it's the diverse culture and cuisine; maybe it's the traditions dating back to the Aztecs; or maybe it's just the margaritas and sun-kissed beaches.

POPULATION
126 million

AVERAGE
WORKING
HOURS PER WEEK
> 43

VARIETIES OF
CHILI PEPPER IN
MEXICO
> 150

Mexico's contradictions don't make much sense until you dive under the surface. Mexicans work longer hours than anyone else – this is the home of the six-day working week – but, despite their toil, many people are poor. And yet, in the popular imagination, Mexico means margaritas now and work *mañana* (tomorrow), good times and endless beaches. So what gives? The keys to Mexico's happiness, not just for visitors but also for locals, are its values and traditions. Ask a Mexican what they cherish the most and they'll invariably say *la familia* (family), a concept that extends across generations and even into other realms; on *Día de los Muertos* (Day of the Dead), people celebrate and connect with deceased relatives, enacting rituals that often feature the country's celebrated cuisine. It's all part of a grand cosmic vision that recognises there are far more important things in life than material wealth.

AMERICAS

© Lindsay Lauckner Gundlock/Lonely Planet

© Kobby Dagan/Shutterstock, © PamelaViola/Getty Images

Clockwise from top: Sunshine, sea and a hammock strung between palms: the very epitome of *mañana*; Mexican street food is always a social affair; a carnival-goer at the Day of the Dead celebrations. **Previous page:** A carnival dancer by Oaxaca's Cathedral of Our Lady of the Assumption.

TOP INSIGHTS for LIFE

MAÑANA, MAÑANA

Yes, Mexicans are extremely hard-working people, but they still exhibit a laid-back attitude toward deadlines, business, personal affairs and even politics. And when you stop to think about this *mañana* mentality, it's a life-affirming, seize-the-day sort of perspective that says 'today is for living, tomorrow is for chores'. Sensibly, Mexicans want to dance, to drink, to laugh, and to love right now, without deferring their gratification – and the rest will wait until *mañana*.

"Solitude is the profoundest fact of the human condition. Man is the only being who knows he is alone." – Octavio Paz, Mexican poet

THE AXIS OF LIFE

La comida (food) is the axis around which Mexican life revolves.

Getting married? Better prepare a million tamales for your guests. Celebrating Day of the Dead? Your daughter will want a few *calaveras de azúcar* – skull-shaped sugary treats. Entertaining business contacts flying in from Amsterdam? Wow their taste buds in one of Mexico City's many world-renowned restaurants. Every state has culinary traditions that go back hundreds, if not thousands, of years. Many of the ingredients and techniques date back to pre-Columbian times, as do ancient agricultural methods such as *chinampa*, a form of floating farm devised by the Aztecs. When you consider all this, it's clear why Unesco features Mexican cuisine on its list of Intangible Cultural Heritage.

SWINGING BY

The Maya people are often credited with inventing the hammock. And what a wonderful, multipurpose device it is, providing comfort to crying children, protection from stinging ants, and, when the heat of the Mexican afternoon hits, the perfect siesta spot.

CONNECT WITH THE COSMOS

The Maya have a unique connection with the cosmos. To experience it, join the spring and fall equinox celebrations at the ruins of Chichén Itzá, where thousands gather to watch a shadow descend along the main pyramid's spine. This is said to be Kukulkan, the feathered serpent. If you miss it, don't worry – they do a laser show at other times of the year.

AMERICAS

CUBA

Cubans overcome life's challenges by sticking together through thick and thin, displaying a sense of humour whatever the circumstances, and revelling in rum-fuelled music and dance.

POPULATION
11.1 million

$1 buys
16 scoops of
ice cream

Cuba has eight
doctors for every
1000 people, one
of the highest
ratios in the world

The larder may be bare, the wardrobe thin and the 'new' car getting on for half a century old, but what Cubans lack in material possessions, they more than make up for in their capacity to cope, to joke, to share and to make do. Living under a socialist government for 60 years, a US trade embargo for 58 and food rationing since 1962 has given this people a strong sense of solidarity and survival. When the going gets tough, Cubans crack open the rum, sing and dance; when it gets tough for others, they help; and when there's no soap, cooking oil, eggs or bread, they search, queue and barter their way to a solution. Finally, when there's nothing to be done and a crisis looms, they'll deliver the *choteo* – an irreverent takedown of authority delivered with comic timing. The tease and the *chiste* (joke) is always part of conversation; it's ironic, infectious and lifts the spirit.

AMERICAS

© Mark Read/Lonely Planet

© 1001nights/Getty Images, © Mark Read/Lonely Planet

Clockwise from top: Catching up with friends on Havana's esplanade at sunset; street performers in Trinidad, Cuba (right) and Havana (left) keep the Cuban beats pumping. **Previous page:** Salsa singer at Patio de la Rumba, Havana.

TOP INSIGHTS for LIFE

LOVE THY NEIGHBOUR

Remember when neighbours used to help each other, look out for each others' kids, take good care of the elderly? In other words, be properly neighbourly. Cubans' warm-hearted consideration for their fellows is in evidence every day. For example, the people of Havana rushed to help the less fortunate in a district struck by a rare tornado in 2019; for the first time, thanks to 3G on cellphones, private business owners organised collections of aid and ferried it to the disaster zone. Fidel Castro spoke of selflessness and altruism for the national good; it's embedded in the psyche in Cuba.

"Cubans are masters at making the best out of any difficult situation... In Cuba, 'resolver' means to survive, to overcome all obstacles with inventiveness, spontaneity, and most important, humor." - Cristina García, Cuban-born journalist and novelist

GET THE JOKE

Cubans have long felt a need to vent about the absurdities of their situation. But they do it with a smile, delivering withering put-downs of authority with ease. This *choteo* is an expression of their *Cubanía* – Cubanness – and the ironic sense of humour filters through the dialogue of national life.

RUM, RHYTHM & GROOVE

Forged in the crucible of Spanish colonialism and immigration, and the arrival of waves of West African slaves, the entwined roots of dance and music run deep in Cuba's DNA. Whether they're playing melodic son, fast-paced salsa or body-shuddering reggaeton, Cubans don't need an excuse to party. Watch them swallow rum like water, swivel across the floor, and party like a pro.

MI CASA ES TU CASA

Book into a Cuban B&B for at least a week, and immerse yourself in daily life. You'll meet the extended family, learn what makes Cubans tick, and get a fast-track lesson in the country's unique culture. You'll pick up way more Spanish, too – all the better for understanding the *choteo*, *chistes* and *chisme* (gossip).

25

AMERICAS

JAMAICA

Shaped by its traumatic history, modern Jamaica is distinguished by a laidback way of living that sees everyone secure their own slice of paradise and appreciate the simple pleasures of life.

POPULATION
2.8 million

**AVERAGE HOURS
OF SUNSHINE
A DAY**
> 8

Jamaica has more
churches per
square mile than
any other country

With a global influence quite out of proportion to its size, this tiny Caribbean island is the home of reggae, Rastafarianism, sporting supremacy and a relaxed attitude to life that's epitomised in a thousand 'Jamaica No Problem' tourist T-shirts. But wellness here goes way beyond a big spliff and a determination not to sweat the small stuff. Jamaicans do practise professional-level nonchalance, but this is part of a national propensity to prioritise personal wellbeing over daily stresses, whether through a day off work for a dose of 'vitamin sea', or by enjoying musical therapy and an intense workout in the island's brilliant clubs and outdoor parties. Wellness is incorporated into the everyday as a matter of course rather than being fussed over and sought out – this is a place in which life is lived intensely, in the moment: mindfulness without the official label.

AMERICAS

Clockwise from top: Paddleboarding on Rio Grande; a tribute band at the home and grave of legendary reggae musician Bob Marley; a fresh crop of Jamaican marijuana. **Previous page:** Strolling the sands at Long Bay, Negril.

TOP INSIGHTS for LIFE

A GROUNDING IN GANJA

Jamaica decriminalised small-scale use of marijuana (ganja in local parlance) in 2015, but the 'holy herb' is much more than just a recreational drug for many Jamaicans. For followers of the Rastafarian faith, ganja is a sacrament, smoked

"He causeth the grass to grow for the cattle, and herb for the service of man." – Psalm 104:14 from the King James Bible

during meditations ('reasonings') and Nyabinghi worship sessions to enhance wisdom and spiritual clarity. Of course, not everyone reveres weed in this way: more than 50% of Jamaicans don't use ganja at all, and of those who do, many indulge just for pleasure (newly legalised ganja tourism is also a huge draw for visitors), but the healing effects of

the herb are also being harnessed here in earnest. Ganja tea has long been used to treat asthma and eye problems, but since decriminalisation Jamaica's medical marijuana industry has exploded. Local farms are producing high-quality organic herb under license, and making everything from edibles and cosmetics to concentrated cannabis oil.

BUSH BUSINESS

Most Jamaicans take a tandem approach to wellness, combining modern medicine with the island's *materia medica* of medicinal plants. Most people can reel off the ingredients for the 'bush teas' that simmer on the hob in many a Jamaican household: fevergrass, leaf of life, cerassee and the spectacularly named ram-goat-dash-along are used to treat anything from a cold to arthritis and high blood pressure. Fresh juices are also ubiquitous – soursop for nerves and fever, aloe for cleansing – while the battery of ingredients used to libate the libido is as long as your arm, with herbs like

COOK UP AN ITAL FEAST

Caribbean market stalls and groceries sell delicious Jamaican produce, from ackee and callaloo (get them tinned if not available fresh) to fresh breadfruit, yams and plantain. There are a host of online video tutorials demonstrating how to make a tasty ital soup, stew or curry, or a nutmeg-laced dairy-free carrot juice. Keep the classic reggae blasting as you cook.

JAMAICA ON SCREEN

Watch classic Jamaican movie *Countryman*, in which a fisherman dispenses livity lessons to a stranded American couple. Perfectly paired with a soundtrack of the Wailers' *Pass it On*, the scene where central character Countryman roasts fish and breadfruit over an open fire, and dispenses fresh fruits and fat spliffs, is a beautiful and gentle illustration of the Jamaican propensity for sharing the joys of island living.

chainey root and medina brewed up with Irish moss seaweed into fortifying 'front-end lifter' punches.

TAKING THE WATERS

Jamaicans (and most of the country's top spas) use bush baths – hot water infused with blends of herbs – to treat all kinds of ailments; and on an island where you're never far from the sea, a curative 'sea bath' (an extended non-swimming soak in the brine, often to alleviate back pain) delivers thalassotherapy JA-style. For many, the first response to aches and skin conditions is to bathe in a forest-wreathed freshwater mineral spring, or wallow in the mineral-rich thermal waters at Clarendon's Milk River Baths, Kingston's Rockfort or Bath in St Thomas.

ITAL IS VITAL

Long before veganism became a buzzword, Jamaica's Rastafarians (and a good quota of the wider population) have been extolling the benefits of an ital diet: fresh, unprocessed fruits, vegetables and pulses cooked without salt or animal products. Ital food is, unsurprisingly, said to underpin health and wellness, and boost what Rastas call 'livity': a person's essential life force. Though many Jamaicans eat strictly ital, and a host of restaurants and takeaways sell delicious ital fare, some followers of an ital diet interpret it quite loosely, incorporating fresh fish or eggs into their meals. It's safe to say, though, that ital cooking has filtered through to mainstream cuisine on an island famous for its fabulous fresh food and naturally health-enhancing produce – perhaps the best example of which are the Trelawny yams which Usain Bolt credits as fuelling his journey to become the fastest man in the world.

CREATIVE COMFORTS

'One good thing about music… when it hits, you feel no pain' – the Wailers' *Trench Town Rock* neatly encapsulates the relationship of many Jamaicans to their nation's marvellous musical output. Whether it's the raw sound of dancehall or the spiritual chanting of roots reggae, music is a kind of therapy here: it can uplift, commiserate, communicate, celebrate or call to arms, and the redemptive power of reggae – not to mention its killer basslines – resonates with audiences worldwide.

Port Antonio's Blue Lagoon, one of the most beautiful spots in Jamaica.

HAITI

The phrase 'fiercely independent' could have been invented for the Haitian people, whose self-reliance and communal approach to life and problem-solving sustains them in a quest for a better future.

POPULATION
10.8 million

% OF POPULA-
TION UNDER 24
> 50

Just over 2% of
the population
officially practises
Vodou

Being dealt a tough hand can some-times increase your determination to play the game even harder. Haiti, the only country in the world founded by a successful slave rebellion, was shunned from birth, and its people poorly used by a parade of self-serving political leaders. But this has helped to forge a nation where standing on your own two feet only happens with your neighbours' support, and community life is a cause for celebration. Haiti's roots in West and central Africa, and the sway of an-cestral Ginen, as the mother continent is known, still hold strong, not least in the spirits that live on through Vodou, the country's much misunderstood syncretic belief system. A true religion of the people, Vodou's inclusive, non-hierarchical approach to worship mirrors many Haitians' approach to life: honouring the ancestors and poking fun at power, accompanied by prayer, music and a generous offering of rum.

AMERICAS

Clockwise from top: Farmland in Haiti's Kenscoff Mountains; carnival masks in Jacmel; a cheerfully painted 'tap tap' ('quick quick') taxi. **Previous page:** Carrying crops in the Kenscoff Mountains.

TOP INSIGHTS for LIFE

BETTER TOGETHER

The countryside is the backbone of Haitian culture. Farming can be a tough life, but two concepts make things a little easier – the *konbit* and the *lakou*. A *konbit* is a communal work group, where a village gets together to clear land, raise a building or plant or harvest the season's crops. Back in the village, life centres around the *lakou*, a cluster of homes where multiple generations of families contribute to group living. The reach of the *lakou* even extends to when family members move to the city (or even abroad), but continue to support their relations back in the village.

"Little by little, the bird builds its nest."
– Haitian proverb

DIY PARTY

Brazil and Trinidad can keep their carnivals – Haiti has Kanaval. Two, actually: the official national event in the capital Port-au-Prince, and a people's affair in the southern town of Jacmel. The whole of Jacmel joins the parade and the entire country seems to come to watch. Participants dress as monsters and demons, jungle animals and characters from Haitian folklore, with giant papier-mâché figures taking centre stage – all made locally in this town famous for its art and artisans. Marching bands add to the fun and noise on one of the Caribbean's most singular days (and nights) out.

MOTHER TONGUE

Reflecting the country's roots, Haiti's national language, Kreyol, is made up of a melange of African tongues laid over the French spoken by the old colonial power. In everyday use, it's simple and direct, but it also lends itself to a range of proverbs that Haitians use to pepper conversation, from sardonic political comments to subtle philosophical points. This extends to a strong storytelling tradition, with life lessons often imparted through the exploits of Ti Malice the trickster and his hardworking but gullible companion Bouki.

AMERICAS

BARBADOS

As proud of their heavenly beaches as they are of their sporting heroes, Bajans know what matters most in life – and they're happy to share their tips over a shot of rum.

POPULATION
293,000

HOURS OF SUN-
SHINE PER YEAR
> 3000

NUMBER OF
RUM SHOPS
> 1500

Barbados is just 20 miles long and 15 miles wide, but its reputation belies its size – a consequence, in part, of the island's larger-than-life personality. A British colony for more than three centuries, and a fulcrum of the transatlantic slave trade, Barbados emerged from that dark chapter with a character that blends a British love of order with a West African spirit of spontaneity. Religion is a cornerstone of life – there are more than 100 denominations prac-

tising at over 300 churches (although Bajans candidly point out there are even more rum shops) – but one faith rules them all: cricket. The English might have invented the game, but Bajans have made it their own, contributing a list of all-time greats to the West Indies side, whose fortunes are always a topic of conversation at exuberant communal gatherings, whether that's playing dominoes on the front porch or dining with tourists at the weekly fish fry.

ONE TEQUILA
TWO TEQUILA
THREE TEQUILA
FLOOR

ONE LOVE
ONE BEER

AMERICAS

Clockwise from top: Informal cricket games between friends are a familiar sight across Barbados; a distillery worker at Mount Gay checks barrels of the amber liquor; a Bahan cricket supporter cheers on her team. **Previous page:** A bartender serves up cocktails at Mullins Beach Bar, St Peter.

TOP INSIGHTS for LIFE

SHARED PASSION

Sir Garfield Sobers, Frank Worrell, Malcolm Marshall, Desmond Haynes, Gordon Greenidge... Barbados has produced some of the West Indies' greatest cricket players; their achievements on the pitch remain a source of national pride and personal inspiration. At weekends during the dry season, you'll see Bajans playing cricket everywhere: on the road, in the field, on the beach. This tiny island has more than a hundred teams. And when the Kensington Oval hosts a first-class game in the capital, Bridgetown, the roars of the

"Free is how you is from the start." - George Lamming, Barbadian writer

crowd, the blowing of conch shells to herald a wicket or boundary, and the constant advice from 'experts' in the stands all combine to create one of the most enjoyable experiences in the sport.

AMBER NECTAR

If the buzz of the Kensington Oval reflects one dimension of the Bajan spirit, the vibe of a rum shop reflects another. Barbados is the birthplace of rum – Mount Gay Rum began distilling it in 1703 – and the amber liquor is an integral part of the culture. Depending on how they're defined, there are more than 1500 rum shops, many of them family-owned wooden shacks – social hubs where locals gather to drink, snack on cutters (sandwiches made from salt bread with a savoury filling), play dominoes, unwind and gossip.

FISHY FRIDAYS

Every Friday night the south-coast village of Oistins hosts its weekly fish fry, an institution for locals and visitors. Calypso, reggae and soca blast from the market stalls as crowds feast on fried swordfish, grilled breadfruit and macaroni pie, all washed down with Banks Beer. This no-frills event is a study in what matters most to Bajans – good food and drink, great company and music – and their willingness to share it with outsiders.

RUM-LOVER'S PARADISE

Hear the story of rum on a tour of Mount Gay Distillery, the oldest continuously running rum distillery in the world (www.mountgayrum.com/tour-mount-gay/). Guests can explore the plantation where it all began, gain an insight into the craft of modern rum-making and, most important of all, sample various strains of Barbados's signature drink.

AMERICAS

TRINIDAD & TOBAGO

Despite its diminutive size, Trinidad & Tobago is a cultural powerhouse that offers good lessons on how to celebrate community, unleash creativity and throw one hell of a party.

POPULATION
1.2 million

T&T is the highest-ranked Caribbean country in the UN's World Happiness Report

The limbo originated in Trinidad

The sister islands of Trinidad & Tobago exist in perfect equilibrium. Resource-rich Trinidad is famed for throwing world-class parties to a soundtrack of calypso and soca music, while laid-back, tourist-friendly Tobago, the location of the country's most beautiful beaches, moves to a much more relaxed rhythm. Due to a complicated history, the population of these islands is diverse, and their culture interweaves African, East Indian, South American and European influences. National holidays range from Carnival to Diwali; menus feature roti, curry and callaloo; and East Indian beats fuse with African melodies. A visit to this dynamic pair of islands reveals complexities and contrasts, but for all the variety on show in this corner of the Caribbean, one thing is universal: Trinbagonians value the importance of community above all else, both through everyday practices and festive traditions.

© Tim White/Getty Images

© Tim White/Getty Images

From top: Englishman's Beach on Tobago: the perfect spot for a 'lime'; the melodious steel pan drum originates in Trinidad.
Previous page: A dancer revels at the Trinidad & Tobago Carnival.

TOP INSIGHTS for LIFE

WHERE'S THE LIME?

To 'lime' is to hang out in the company of others, to relax, tell stories and enjoy food and drink together; the term itself is flexible and applies to a variety of occasions. A lime might refer to an all-night rager at one of Port of Spain's clubs, or it could simply be friends chilling out on a beach or a patio. Some limes are planned, while others are spontaneous. Some focus on dancing, others conversation. Are there any rules to liming? Not really, but if you're hosting one, make sure the drinks keep flowing (especially rum). Liming puts the focus on connecting with those around you – slow down, spend time with your people and celebrate the good stuff.

KNOW YOUR FETE

The best celebrations involve three essential ingredients: tradition, commitment and style, and Trinidad & Tobago's parties have these in spades. While the country has a festive atmosphere at any time, the shining jewel in the calendar is the famed Carnival in February, a pulsating explosion of sound and colour that attracts thousands of tourists each year. Festivities take place throughout the month of February, culminating in a massive celebration featuring steel pan band competitions, soca parties and parades. In T&T, fetes and festivals are creative outlets that bring people together, demonstrating pride in their history, identity and the islands' future.

MOVE TO THE BEAT

Trinidad & Tobago has long been a creative force in Caribbean music, producing genres as unique as the islands themselves – if you've ever visited the region, you've heard the cheery timbre of the steel pan drum, a Trinidadian original and the only acoustic instrument invented in the twentieth century. T&T is also the birthplace of calypso and the modern genre of soca, an energetic combination of calypso and East Indian rhythms sure to keep you dancing all night long.

MAKE THE TIME

Through its emphasis on limes and fetes, Trinidad & Tobago celebrates how people can bring out the best in each other, either by connecting at intimate gatherings or creating something grandiose and electric as a group. So make time for others – they make life richer (and a lot more fun).

AMERICAS

NICARAGUA

Nicaraguans have learned to live in the shadow of volcanoes, both literal and political, celebrating the natural riches of their country even as they build for a better, cleaner, safer future.

POPULATION
6 million

Lago de Nicaragua
is the largest
freshwater body in
Central America

By 2020, the country
plans for 90% of its
energy to come from
renewable sources

Visitors will likely see why the British and Spaniards both laid claim to Nicaragua, to the detriment of its native people: whether you're dipping your toes into warm, clear seas or paddling out to crashing waves, Nicaragua's beaches always deliver the goods. Surfers revere the big barrels of the Pacific coast while the clear waters of the Corn Islands on the Caribbean side are superb for snorkelling. The 'inland sea' of Lago de Nicaragua has a unique allure as well. Don't overlook the culture, though; the calendar is dotted with Catholic festivals, which showcase the irrepressible spirit of many Nicaraguans as they carve out time for celebration amid upheavals of both the natural and political variety. Nicaragua's next generation, some of whom fled to Costa Rica after protests against President Daniel Ortega turned violent, help to keep hope and faith alive in this naturally abundant country.

© worldroadtrip/Shutterstock

© Philip Lee Harvey/Lonely Planet, © oscar carbello/500px

Clockwise from top: Isla de Ometepe is known for its twin active volcanos; colonial León is full of architectural jewels; a happy market seller in León. **Previous page:** A horse and cart stop by the colonial-era veterinary surgery in León.

TOP INSIGHTS for LIFE

UNDER THE VOLCANOES

Nicaraguans live in the shadow of 19 active volcanoes – and some of them are real grumblers, forever threatening to pop. Situated in several national parks but close to working towns, their unpredictable schedules have given the people here a knack for making the best of whatever comes their way, and learning to cope with uncertainty (natural in this case, but sometimes political as well). The ever-present threat of an eruption hasn't diminished Nicaraguans' identification with the landscape's most prominent geological feature – on the contrary, the country proudly claims the nickname 'Land of Lakes and Volcanoes'.

MESTIZO MIX

The largest country in Central America is also one of its most multiethnic. Indigenous tribes on the Mosquito Coast have retained their language and culture, and the country's division under British rule on the Caribbean coast and Spanish rule on the Pacific side added even more spice to the mix. Add that to the Creole flavour of the East coast and it's clear that Nica is a kaleidoscope of the various influences in the region. In fact, the country's name is thought to have come from either a Nahuatl or an Arawak word, and though tensions over enforcement persist, Nicaragua was a pioneer in granting territorial rights to indigenous peoples.

CLIMATE CONSCIOUS

For a while, the country was an odd man out as a non-signatory of the Paris Agreement on climate change... for the reason that it didn't go far enough. Lacking any oil, Nicaragua has invested heavily in renewable energy and now gets over half of what it needs from clean, safe sources. But it's not stopping there: the government has set an aggressive target of 90% of energy from renewables in the near future. With the second-largest rainforest in the Americas after the Amazon, there's every reason for Nicaraguans to prize and protect the country's natural riches. It's signed the accord now, having made its point about the need for bolder action.

ASK A SEARCHING QUESTION

Can't get to Nicaragua for the festival of La Gritería on December 8th, a pre-Christmas holiday that celebrates the Immaculate Conception of the Virgin Mary? You can still take the festival's central question to heart; the evening call-and-response starts with ¿Qué causa tanta alegría?, or 'What causes so much happiness?' Give it some serious thought.

COSTA RICA

Peaceful, tree-covered and good for the soul, Costa Rica breaks the mould in a historically troubled region, leading the way when it comes to conservation, not to mention optimism.

POPULATION
5 million

% OF COUNTRY COVERED IN PARKS AND RESERVES
27

Tiny Costa Rica contains nearly 6% of the world's biodiversity

From a poor, neglected Spanish colony to a paradisiacal travel destination and environmental trailblazer, the story of Costa Rica's rise is replete with valuable lessons. Abolishing a standing army in the 1940s laid the groundwork for Central America's most stable democracy to flourish. Reversing a decades-long pattern of deforestation in the 1970s then restored the country's natural resources, allowing it to become one of the world's most popular and progressive destinations for ecotourism, with surfer-pleasing beaches, towering rainforest, volcano-heated hot springs and abundant wellness retreats. The affable Ticos have plenty of their own wisdom to impart, too. From the incredible fortitude of the indigenous tribes to the easy-going character of the Caribbean residents, and the longevity of the Nicoyan centenarians to the feisty spirit of Guanacaste's cowboys, you could spend a lifetime soaking it all up.

AMERICAS

Clockwise from top: The *Fiesta de los Diablitos* is one of the most important festivals in Boruca culture; be more sloth: the embodiment of *pura vida*; Costa Rica's eco-conscious attitude helps species like scarlet macaw thrive. **Previous page:** A secluded swim at Rincón de la Vieja National Park.

TOP INSIGHTS for LIFE

EMBRACING PURA VIDA

The ubiquitous phrase *pura vida* translates as 'pure life', and is used as a stand-in for 'hello', 'goodbye', 'thank you', and 'I'm doing well', or for expressing approval. Although *pura vida* is an apt descriptor of the laid-back lifestyle on the Caribbean coast, and makes many an appearance on T-shirts, souvenirs and business placards across Costa Rica, it did not originate here. In fact, the phrase was first employed by the protagonist of an eponymous Mexican film released in 1956. When Ticos watched *Pura Vida*, however, they connected deeply with the character's determination to remain cheerful despite life's challenges, and while its round-the-clock use can exasperate, the concept of *pura vida* is useful and uplifting.

"Nothing gets done without optimism." – Costa Rican diplomat Christiana Figueres, mastermind of the 2015 Paris Climate Agreement

PEACEFUL PROSPERITY

In a region where bloody coups and turf wars have been commonplace, Costa Rica has managed to sidestep such strife, reinventing itself as a bastion of peace and calm. This transformation can be traced back to a prescient move by former president José Figueres Ferrer, who abolished the country's standing army in 1948 and redirected defence spending towards education, healthcare and social security. To cap it all, the former military headquarters now houses the Museo Nacional de Costa Rica, complete with a butterfly garden... Subsequent leaders have championed conflict resolution instead of violence, and Costa Rica's peacekeeping spirit remains an inspiration worldwide.

NATURE FIRST

Costa Rica brims with eco-conscious citizens and businesses, and its government takes a nature-first approach to land management, having set aside more than a quarter of the country as national parks and protected areas. As a result, this little

BE THE SLOTH

When visiting Costa Rica, seek out the country's unofficial spokescreature, that adorable, slow-motion tree-dangler known as a sloth (oso perezoso in Spanish, or 'lazy bear'). Observe its subtle movements and vaguely satisfied countenance; take notes on how effortlessly it thrives in the treetops. Is it asleep or awake? No matter. The sloth is your teacher, and the lesson is *pura vida*.

GET THE BLUES

Costa Rica contains one of the world's handful of Blue Zones, areas where people frequently live to more than 100 years of age. According to researchers, these Tico centenarians from the Nicoya region have much to teach us when it comes a long, happy life, not least: have a sense of purpose, drink hard water, focus on family, eat a light dinner and work hard but avoid stress.

green nation has remained home to an estimated 6% of the world's biodiversity, including jaguars, tapirs, monkeys and sloths. Recreational hunting and traditional zoos are banned. Renewable resources like hydropower, wind, solar and geothermal energy supply most of the nation's electricity, and Costa Rica's leaders intend to become the world's first carbon-neutral country.

THROWIN' BOMBAS

Costa Rica's inventive citizens value the ability to string words together, particularly in the form of spoken poems referred to as *bombas*. Verses have four or six intermittently rhyming lines and are often 'thrown' at festivals or in cantinas, where they're used to critique politicians and social issues, or take the form of playful insults. Although *bombas* are strongly associated with the province of Guanacaste, and historically dealt with the *sabanero* (cowboy) culture of the northwest, they are ever-evolving and encouraged nationwide.

MOUTH MATTERS

Modern dental hygiene got its start not in Europe, but Mesoamerica,

where pre-Columbian dentists invented ways to fill cavities with jade and gold, remove tartar, treat halitosis and even whiten teeth. Like their native ancestors, Costa Ricans uphold high standards of tooth care and tend to take a toothbrush wherever they go. It's little wonder that the country has become a hub for dental tourism.

LITTLE DEVILS

From Costa Rica's indigenous Boruca tribe comes a 400-year-old tradition as entertaining as it is poignant: the *Fiesta de los Diablitos* (Festival of the Little Devils). The annual celebration near the Panama border welcomes the new year with tribesmen donning hand-carved masks, burlap sacks and banana leaf skirts to reenact the invasion of the Spanish, who are represented by a man in a bull costume. The mock-fighting is fuelled by *chicha* (a boozy beverage) and often gets rowdy, as devils are thrown into bushes and flung down hills. At the end, the devils pretend they're dead, and the bull retreats to the mountains. But there is one final act! The devils come back to life and set the bull on fire; so yes, while the Spanish won, the Boruca and their traditions live on.

Stepping into nature at Monteverde Cloud Forest.

AMERICAS

COLOMBIA

Freed from some of its demons, Colombia is a country on the rise. Its citizens' wellbeing rests on their devotion to family and church, leavened with a love of music and dance.

POPULATION
48 million

ANNUAL PUBLIC
HOLIDAYS
18

Colombia is one of
just 17 countries
classified as
'megadiverse'

Encompassing the soaring Andes and the steaming Amazon, Colombia also packs in Caribbean coast, ancient civilisations and colonial grandeur, all of which makes it arguably one of the most colourful countries on Earth, literally and figuratively. But despite the inherent drama, the people adhere to a traditional set of values resting on the twin pillars of family and church. The former come together frequently in service of the latter; Christmas, for example, is a drawn-out affair that features family reunions, shared rituals and, of course, extravagant parties. Non-religious parties abound year round, too; salsa is the quickening heartbeat of the nation. But for all its youthful exuberance, Colombian society cherishes its elders, whose wisdom – on, among other topics, folk medicine drawing on the country's cornucopia of plants – also informs the nation's understanding of what it means to live well.

Clockwise from top: Colourful facades in Cartagena; salsa is a way of life in Colombia; Colombian home remedies include euphorbia, used by traditional healers for the treatment of ulcers, cancers and tumours. **Previous page:** A view of Bogotá from the sacred mountain Monserrate.

TOP INSIGHTS for LIFE

NINE NIGHTS OF NOVENA

In a country where about 80% of the people are Roman Catholic, Christmas is celebrated with gusto throughout December. However, the festivities go up a notch over Novena de Aguinaldos, a series of nine prayers recited on consecutive nights from December 16th to 24th. The tradition has evolved into a social occasion that brings families and friends together to pray, celebrate life and share meals. The number nine represents the Virgin Mary's months of pregnancy before Jesus' birth. A different family member or friend hosts the novena each night, representing the journey from shelter to shelter that Mary and Joseph endured while seeking a place for her to give birth.

"No medicine cures what happiness cannot."
– Gabriel García Márquez, Colombian author and Nobel Prize winner

SWAY AND SPIN

This dance is popular in many Latin American countries but the western city of Cali is the self-proclaimed and widely recognised salsa capital of the world. You'll hear it playing in every corner here, from modest local bars to posh mansion clubs. The city has hundreds of registered salsa schools, and even some hostels offer classes (Colombians regard dancing as one of the best ways to stay physically and mentally healthy). Cali also hosts major salsa festivals, including Salsa y Verano in July, Festival Mundial de Salsa in September, and Feria de Cali in December.

GRANDMA'S REMEDIES

Diligently passed down by *abuelas* (grandmothers), go-to home remedies for common ailments include: aloe vera, to combat dandruff, conjunctivitis and even hair loss; calendula, applied to skin wounds; and the ever popular *aguapanela*, made by dissolving unrefined whole sugar cane in water or milk – for believers, it's considered *the* way to get rid of a common cold.

CLIMB A SACRED PEAK

Summiting Monserrate, a sacred mountain that rises from the centre of Bogotá, is a rite of passage for many Colombians. Join them as they troop up the 1500 steps to the church at its zenith, a feat that is seen as both a fitness challenge and a religious pilgrimage. Be warned: the steps are steep and oxygen is scarce, so the experience is taxing, if ultimately rejuvenating, for body and mind.

AMERICAS

ECUADOR

Living their lives in the shadow of grumbling volcanoes has given Ecuadorians a healthy respect for the planet — the state of which, as they acknowledge, underpins their wellbeing.

POPULATION
16.5 million

**VALUE OF
EXPORTED
COCOA BEANS**
US$600 million

Ecuador, including
the Galápagos, is
home to 47
volcanoes (active
and extinct)

With more than two dozen active volcanoes, regular seismic activity and a location directly on the equator, Ecuador is no stranger to the power of Mother Nature. As a result, Ecuadorians duly acknowledge her ability to either give life or take it away at any second, to the extent the government recognised nature under the constitution in 2008, enshrining its 'right to exist, persist, maintain and regenerate its natural cycles'. Cultur-

ally, this deep respect for the planet is reflected year-round at local festivals as well as national, multi-day extravaganzas in honour of the Earth's life-giving resources. The Inca sun festival, Inti Raymi, occurs every June, while the Fiesta del Yamor marking the harvest of Ecuador's staple crop, corn, happens every September. These celebrations are opportunities for family and friends to share their joy, but also show their reverence for the natural world.

AMERICAS

© Toni Massot / Alamy Stock Photo

© freedomnaruk/Shutterstock; © Barna Tanko/Alamy Stock Photo

Clockwise from top: Baños de Agua Santa sits in the foothills of the Volcán Tungurahua; Quechua women prepare corn flatbreads during Ecuador's Inti Raymi festival; Ecuadorian cacao is renowned for its quality. **Previous page:** Traditional costumes at Inti Raymi festival in Pujili.

TOP INSIGHTS for LIFE

CHOCOLATE PRIDE

Given its importance to Ecuador, it's no wonder that eating and drinking 'black gold' – chocolate, not oil – isn't an indulgence here. The ritual itself is rooted in a farming tradition that dates back centuries. Ecuador was the largest exporter of cocoa, the key ingredient of chocolate, until the beginning of the 20th century, and although it has lost that position, high-quality beans still bring in a fair chunk of the nation's revenue, accounting for more than 3% of total exports. Chocolate is a staple offering at events and holidays, where it is consumed with a true sense of national pride. Hard chocolate is commonly served after meals to relax and cleanse the palate, while hot chocolate often substitutes for morning coffee, a way to start the day on a high.

VOLCANO-HEATED HOT TUBS

Baños de Agua Santa (Baths of the Sacred Water) is a town in the central highlands that lies near the ever-threatening Volcán Tungurahua, one of South America's most active volcanoes. A fable recounts how the Virgin Mary appeared at one of the town's many waterfalls and, from that moment on, the area was blessed with natural hot springs, which heat a series of pools. People come here to recite the rosary while they soak away their troubles in the mineral-rich water; a trip to Baños is seen as both a religious pilgrimage and a rejuvenating break.

A FIERY FAREWELL

On the Fiesta De Año Viejo, Ecuadorians follow an ancient custom and symbolically burn away the disappointments and regrets of the old year, clearing the way for the new. People make effigies in the image of disliked politicians or unsavoury characters, then pin handwritten notes to these colourful dolls explaining why they deserve a fiery fate, as well as the maker's hopes for the coming year. At the climax of New Year's Eve, the effigies are thrown into the street to a chorus of cheers, then burned to ashes.

MAKE AN ECUADORIAN HOT CHOC

Boil two litres of milk, a cup of sugar, five tablespoons of Ecuadorian cacao and a cinnamon stick for five minutes. Dissolve one tablespoon of cornstarch into the mixture, then boil for five more minutes. In a separate bowl, beat two egg whites and three tablespoons of sugar until frothy. Serve the cacao hot with a tablespoon of froth on top. Enjoy!

PERU

Its name derives from the Quechua word for a land of abundance – and Peru is just that: a place rich in ideas on how to live in harmony with the planet and each other.

POPULATION
31.3 million

Amazonia covers
three-fifths of Peru

At its height,
the Inca Empire
stretched from
Colombia to Chile

Geographically, ecologically and culturally, Peru is as complex as the flavour of an artisanal pisco sour. Adventures abound in a land that alternates between mountain and plain, jungle and desert, and often past and present. You can climb the thigh-shredding Andes to the lost citadel of Machu Picchu, paddle a dugout canoe deep into the Amazon, fly over arid plains engraved with the enigmatic Nazca Lines, feast on ceviche in Lima or soak up the spiritual energy of Cusco, a hotspot for healing ceremonies. But whatever you do, you'll feel the presence of the great civilisations that evolved or arrived here, and whose beliefs and customs slowly intertwined to produce something unique. Chief among them are the mighty Inca, whose stress on living in harmony with the planet still permeates so many aspects of Peruvian culture, and seems shrewder than ever in a fast-warming world.

Clockwise from top: Q'eswachaka Rope Bridge, which has been rebuilt repeatedly for five centuries; ceviche is a classic Peruvian dish of cold, raw fish marinated in lime juice; dancers perform at Peru's International Spring Festival. **Previous page:** The 15th-century Inca city of Machu Picchu.

TOP INSIGHTS for LIFE

HAIL MOTHER EARTH

In an era of climate crisis and ecological turmoil, what sacred ritual could feel more relevant than *La Ofrenda a la Pachamama* (The Offering to Mother Earth)? The indigenous people of the Peruvian Andes have been worshipping this fertility goddess since the days of the Incan Empire. During this shaman-led ritual, symbolic offerings – coca leaves, flower petals, brown sugar, red wine and more – are enclosed in a piece of paper, which is folded, blessed and eventually burned with a prayer. It started as a way for peasant farmers to acknowledge their debt to Pachamama and thus attempt to rebalance the relationship between man and nature. Modern participants also take advantage of the goddess's undivided attention to air their hopes and dreams for the future.

THE SACRED PLANT

The coca plant is rich in beneficial minerals, essential oils and complex compounds, but sadly one of them overshadows all the rest: an alkaloid which, in its extracted, concentrated and powdered form, goes by the name of cocaine. But for millennia before the drug achieved notoriety, people throughout the Andes chewed and brewed coca leaves in their natural form (according to archaeological evidence, Peruvian foragers were using coca 8000 years ago). It's seen as a sacred plant here and it's easy to see why: chewing the leaves – the traditional method involves keeping a ball of them tucked between cheek and jaw – has a stimulating effect, boosting energy, suppressing hunger and thirst, and alleviating pain and altitude sickness – all valuable on, for example, a gruelling trek up to a lofty Inca citadel.

SUCCULENT CEVICHE

National dishes don't get much healthier than ceviche, which is the breakout star of the Peruvian diet. Consisting of chunks or slices of raw fish (or sometimes shellfish) flavoured with salt, onions and peppers, then 'cooked' in a marinade of lime juice known as *leche de tigre* (literally,

EAT PERUVIAN

Chef Gastón Acurio is the doyen of Peruvian cuisine. He has spent decades raising the country's gastronomic profile, building a global empire of restaurants in the process. In Lima, he runs the top-class Astrid y Gastón, a fixture on the World's 50 Best Restaurants list, as well as the La Mar and Tanta chains, which have spawned outposts in a dozen countries.

RENEW YOUR COMMU-NITY

Many Peruvian customs focus on the idea of renewal, particularly of the natural world. Can you take a leaf out of their book and apply this kind of thinking to your own community? Is there a green space that, with the help of many hands, could be given a new lease of life? Explore the volunteering options near you, or start a campaign that honours Mother Earth.

'tiger's milk'), ceviche is so popular that it has its own national day. Although there are many variations served throughout Peru, the classic version features corvina or cebo (sea bass), served with corn-on-the-cob and slices of sweet potato, often with a side of crunchy cancha (toasted corn kernels similar to popcorn). Since the 1970s, the appetite for ceviche has exploded around the world. You'll now find cevicherias (specialist restaurants) in many major cities, although there's nothing quite like eating this delicious, guilt-free dish in its place of origin.

LINES IN THE SAND

They might not have the instant impact of Machu Picchu, but the Nazca Lines inspire a deep sense of awe. Etched across 500 sq km of desert, they rank among the world's great archaeological mysteries. In total, there are about 800 ruler-straight lines, 300 geometric figures and 70 animal and plant designs, all created by removing dark, sun-baked stones to reveal the lighter soil below. Best appreciated from the sky, the patterns include a 180m-long lizard, a monkey with a curling tail, and

a condor with a 130m wingspan. Scientists think they were made by the Paracas and Nazca cultures that inhabited the area between 900 BCE and 600 CE. But why? Are the lines some sort of astronomical calendar? Sacred sites dedicated to the worship of water? Theories abound. Whatever their original purpose, they continue to be a thought-provoking testament to the power of human imagination.

BUILDING BRIDGES

Every June, four Quechua-speaking communities gather on the banks of the Apurimac River to renew the Q'eswachaka Bridge, the last Inca rope bridge in Peru. Inscribed on Unesco's Intangible Cultural Heritage list in 2013, the 37m-long bridge has been rebuilt repeatedly for five centuries. First, families twist together strands of grass to make thin ropes, which are then braided into strong cables. After stretching the cables across the gorge, weavers edge out as they replace the bridge's decaying fabric, eventually meeting in the middle. As well as honouring the past, this symbolic ritual unites the communities and strengthens their sense of a shared identity.

A market stall worker in Cusco.

AMERICAS

BRAZIL

Brazilians treasure the beauty of their country, celebrate its many colours and creeds, and revel in their renowned musical traditions, exemplified in that party to end them all, Carnaval.

POPULATION
209 million

DAYS OF
ANNUAL
VACATION
30

PARTICIPANTS IN
RIO'S CARNAVAL
> 6 million

Famed for throwing one of the world's best parties, Brazilians know a thing or two about living life at full throttle. Carnaval is but one well-known manifestation of the celebratory spirit that permeates nearly every aspect of Brazilian culture. Whether you spend the day on the shore, catch an impromptu samba jam, or join a neighbourhood street party, it's hard not to feel as if you're living life exactly as it's meant to be lived – in the moment, with all your senses switched on, your worries left behind, and not a care for tomorrow. Brazilians' all-in pursuit of pleasure transforms even a simple act such as going to the beach into an art: as if by magic, vendors will soon appear bearing everything you might need – chairs and umbrellas, ice-cold drinks, snacks – leaving you to simply sit back and enjoy. Living like a Brazilian means celebrating your life and cherishing your time among friends both old and new.

© Priscila de Lyra/500px

© PeopleImages/Getty Images

© MECKY/Getty Images

From top: Party people: samba dancers take the spotlight at Carnaval; throwing some capoeira moves on the sands at Ilha Do Mel.
Previous page: The world-renowned party beach of Copacabana.

TOP INSIGHTS for LIFE

BRAZIL'S BACKYARD

With over 7000km of coastline, Brazil has some of the most beautiful *praias* (beaches) on the planet. Every Brazilian has a favourite, and daydreams about beaches they're yet to visit – like the celebrated ones on the island of Fernando de Noronha or the white-sand stretches of Alter do Chão, located deep in the Amazon. Yet the beach is more than just a place to frolic in the waves or catch

> "*Happiness is the greatest thing that exists. But to create a lovely samba, you need a bit of sadness.*" – Vinicius de Moraes, Brazilian poet, lyricist and playwright

a few rays; for Brazilians, the beach is a communal backyard, a place to relax, hang out with friends and family, watch the sunrise, toast the sunset, eat, drink, play music, workout

– in short, somewhere to celebrate what the world has to offer in good company. So it's not surprising that 'praia' plays such an important role in the nation's psyche. '*E minha praia*' (that's my beach) is used in much the same way a Brit would say 'that's my cup of tea' – something that gives the speaker joy. And in places like Rio, locals are more likely to say '*tenha uma boa praia*' ('have a good beach') than 'have a good day'.

MASTERS OF FESTAS

Brazilians have mastered the art of throwing a *festa* (party). During Carnaval, nearly every city, town and village lets loose for a few days (or weeks) of merrymaking, with parties in the streets, costumed parades, and dancing until dawn to the sounds of samba, *pagode* and other Brazilian musical styles. The whole country turns upside down, as everyone, rich and poor, black and white, young and old, puts aside life's worries for a while. And although Carnaval comes but once a year, Brazilians have plenty of opportunities to let loose on

JOIN THE PARTY

If you want to celebrate life to the max, book a trip to Rio during Carnaval. It's fun watching the grand parades in the Sambódromo, but even more exciting to join the hundreds of street parties around town. Called *bandas* and *blocos*, these roving events feature live music and dancing, with vendors selling beer and cocktails along the way. Rio's tourism authority, Riotur, publishes the dates and times of street parties in the weeks before Carnaval.

TRY CAPOEIRA

One of the best ways to connect with Brazilian culture in your home country is by signing up for capoeira classes. Originating in Brazil, this exhilarating practice is part dance form, part martial art, and features music, singing and graceful but powerful moves, which embody the joy of the Brazilian spirit.

a more modest scale; the calendar is packed with festivals and events, and even small successes are celebrated here, which explains why Brazilians are renowned for their *joie de vivre*.

CONNECTING WITH ANCESTORS

Deeply rooted in Afro-Brazilian culture, Candomblé is a syncretic religion found in Brazil's Northeast, which the Nago, Yoruba and Jeje peoples brought here from Africa. The religion has a pantheon of over two dozen *orixás* (deities), each of which is also associated with a Christian saint; for example, Iemanjá, the goddess of the sea, is connected to the Virgin Mary. Conducted in the Yoruba language, Candomblé services take place at a *terreiro* (house of worship) and feature a trance-like dance. For its followers, Candomblé is a way of interacting with ancestors and respecting the divine power of nature. At big festivals, like the feast day of Iemanjá on January 1, believers dress in white and wade into the sea, making an offering of flowers in return for good fortune.

BITTERSWEET SAUDADE

Difficult to translate precisely, *saudade* refers to a sense of nostalgia, indescribable longing or deep regret. This spectrum of emotion can manifest itself in many ways, from the homesickness Brazilians living overseas feel when hearing their native language spoken on the street, to the sorrow of someone recalling a lost love. *Saudade* often goes hand in hand with a feeling of *alegria* (happiness), with the down times making the joyful moments all the sweeter.

CREATIVE PROBLEM-SOLVING

When faced with seemingly insurmountable obstacles, Brazilians sometimes resort to the *jeitinho* (literally, 'little way') – another untranslatable term that embraces the idea of finding a creative or improvised solution to solve a problem; an example might be gatecrashing a party as a way to get some free food and drink. The *jeitinho* is a deeply embedded part of society, and a useful philosophy for navigating whatever challenges life may throw your way.

The Festa de Iemangá pays homage to Candomblé's goddess of the sea and fertility.

CHILE

Chile is poetry. Chile is magic. Along this 4300km-long strip of a country, you'll find New Age energy centres, mystic indigenous peoples and vast mountain ranges fit for the gods.

POPULATION
17.9 million

NATIONAL
PARKS
41

AVERAGE AN-
NUAL RAINFALL
IN ATACAMA
DESERT
15mm

Variety is the spice of life, they say – and Chile has it in spades. In the north, the Atacama Desert contains one of the planet's largest reserves of copper; some people believe that this mother lode of metal draws the world's energy here. True or not, when you join a healing ceremony or sit in the hot springs near San Pedro de Atacama, there's no denying the power of this vast, austere desert. Things get greener further south in Chile's 'breadbasket', a fecund region full of farm-to-table restaurants and vineyards producing kick-ass red wines. Chileans embrace the concept of *la buena mesa*: good food, great company and wine glasses clinking. Down south is storied Patagonia, a realm of monster monoliths that make the heart pump and spirit soar; in the renowned Torres Del Paine National Park, the signature rock formation is even known as *La Escoba de Dios*, The Broom of God.

AMERICAS

© Pakawat Thongcharoen/Getty Images

© Anna Soelberg/Shutterstock, © Eric Lafforgue/Lonely Planet

Clockwise from top: Mother Nature in full swing at El Tatio Geysers; millenia-old stone moai gaze out at the setting sun on Easter Island; a vineyard in Casablanca valley, Valparaiso. **Previous page:** Learning to dance the *cueca* at the Casa de la Cueca.

TOP INSIGHTS for LIFE

POETRY AND ART

In Chile, you'll hear miners reciting lines from national poet Pablo Neruda, intellectuals in Santiago's universities serenading girls with verses from Vicente Huidobro, and radical feminists finding inner peace in the words of Gabriela Mistral. Great art isn't just found on the page, though. In places like Valparaiso, you'll see some of the finest street art in the Americas; in Santiago, museums house world-class collections of fine art; and across the ocean you have the enigmatic Moai sculptures of Easter Island.

"You shall create beauty not to excite the senses but to give sustenance to the soul."
– Gabriela Mistral, Chilean poet and Nobel Prize winner

Poetry and the arts have flourished in Chile, despite – or because of? – years of poverty and oppression.

NATURE WRIT LARGE

When you live in a country that extends from the driest desert in the world to the hulking glaciers of Antarctica, you can't help but marvel, and draw strength from, the majesty of nature. To their credit, the country's politicians have recognised this, and in 2018, Chile unveiled a new network of national parks that protect 10 million acres of Patagonia, expanding the country's parkland by nearly 40%.

EATING LOCAL

Many of the blueberries, plums and avocados that end up on the shelves of supermarkets in the northern hemisphere come from Chile's fertile Central Valleys, and it's also the source of the vast majority of the nation's fresh food. Chileans have been locavores since before the word emerged, their diet dictated largely by whatever can be grown or caught within a 20-mile radius, whether it's a bowl of fresh mussels, goat from the farm down the road or seafood stew served with a hearty broth of garlic, onions, oregano and paprika.

STAR THERAPY

In the modern world, we rarely see the stars at night. But in Chile's remotest corners, you can count millions of them – the country is home to some of the world's best observatories – and few experiences are as humbling. The country's best stargazing is found near the New Age centres of San Pedro de Atacama and the Elqui Valley.

AMERICAS

ARGENTINA

Argentines excel at the art of socialising. They'll make a family barbecue last all day – and they'll stay up half the night talking and drinking mate with friends.

POPULATION
44.7 million

YERBA MATE
PRODUCED EACH
YEAR
262,000 tonnes

Argentinians
consume an
average of 86kg
of meat per year

Argentina's economy is in near-constant flux. But one type of currency remains the same: time, and the way it's used to value the people you care about. Wherever you go in Argentina, social life is a big part of the culture. Getting together with family and friends is a priority, lighting up the *parrilla* (grill) for a leisurely barbecue is standard weekend practice, and passing around a gourd of mate is a widespread custom. From

properly greeting each other to hanging around the table for an hour or more after meals, Argentines dignify each other with their time. They share the same cup and shoot the breeze while their steaks cook slowly over a low fire, and when resources are scarce, they'll pool their money to pay for food and firewood. Argentines find any excuse to get together – and they think nothing of staying up until 4am for an extended conversation.

AMERICAS

© picture alliance/Contributor/Getty Images

© Jonathon Gregson/Lonely Planet, © rocharibeiro/Shutterstock

Clockwise from top: Carnival participants perform the ritual of worshiping Mother Earth in Salta; cooking meat on the *parilla*; sharing a cup of *mate* is a social tradition. **Previous page:** The road to El Chaltén in Los Glaciares National Park.

TOP INSIGHTS for LIFE

PASS THE GOURD

Sharing *mate* is a key social custom in Argentina. The tea-like infusion, made by pouring hot water over dried *yerba mate* leaves, is widely consumed in homes, offices, in traffic, on the beach – anywhere people get together. Everyone shares the same 'cup' (actually a hollowed-out gourd) and metal straw. One person in the group prepares the gourd and fills it with hot water from a thermos, passing it around to others; each person drains the gourd before handing it back. *Mate* is thought to have some health benefits, but sharing it is a social experience first and foremost.

SPIRIT OF ASADO

The *asado* (barbecue) is a staple of Argentine culture. More than a meal, it's a slow-paced event that lasts for a good part of the day – either for lunch or dinner, typically on weekends – and consists of several stages. When guests first arrive, there's a *picada* (a large board of cheeses, cold cuts and olives) served with red wine and soda, often followed by *choripán* (sausage sandwiches on grilled bread), *provoleta* (grilled provolone), and various cuts of steak and pork as they come off the *parrilla* (grill). The vibe is laid-back, social and inclusive: no one's in a rush. Bring an appetite and a bottle of Malbec to share.

REMEMBER THE PAST

Tango music is the soundtrack to life in Argentina. And while the lyrics vary, an overwhelming theme is nostalgia for the past, whether it be for one's mother or father, childhood home, lost love, or an unfulfilled dream. There's something poignant about this constant reminiscing: people live in the context of history, never forgetting about what (or who) came before them.

HELLO AND GOODBYE

When entering a home, a party or any kind of gathering, Argentines always greet each individual personally with a kiss on the cheek or a handshake. The same goes for goodbyes: you never skip them, and they must be extended to each person in the room.

PLAYING WITH FIRE

To learn more about the art of the *asado*, pick up the book *Seven Fires: Grilling the Argentine Way* (2009) by Francis Mallmann. The legendary Argentinian chef covers everything from grilling techniques and the importance of salt to table setting ideas and wine pairing suggestions – and, most importantly, a philosophical explanation of the patience and social spirit the occasion requires.

EUROPE

EUROPE

ICELAND

How has a tiny populace living on a windswept island near the top of the world managed to top the charts of lists ranking happiness, safety and equality on a regular basis?

POPULATION
343,000

POSITION ON
GLOBAL PEACE
INDEX
1st

WORLD RANKING
ON MEASURES
OF GENDER
EQUALITY
1st

In just a century, Iceland has transformed itself from one of Europe's poorest nations into one of its richest. Alongside that, Icelanders have become renowned for their progressive attitudes, while maintaining strong ties to their unique cultural heritage and protecting their awe-inspiring environment. Isolation has made them resilient, a small population has kept them connected to each other, and necessity has instilled a can-do mindset despite volcanic eruptions, the boom-and-bust cycles of the critical fishing industry, a much-mythologised banking crisis, the sudden explosion of tourism, and much more besides. It helps that there is so much to keep the locals warm in their sub-Arctic home – from geothermal waters to flickering auroras and a strong storytelling tradition, plus a streak of creativity a mile wide that finds form in literature, music and handicrafts passed down through generations.

EUROPE

Clockwise from top: Grass-roofed buildings, like these at Skogar Folk Museum, are part of Iceland's unique cultural heritage; navigating Jökulsárlón's icefield; Namafjall geothermal area at Hverir. **Previous page:** Sunset over Jökulsárlón's icefield.

TOP INSIGHTS for LIFE

THE WATER IS LOVELY

Iceland's warmth doesn't come from the sky. The mineral-rich geothermal water found here in abundance means winters are not just bearable, but often pleasurable. As well as being used to heat most houses, water suitable for long, reviving soaks can be found in fantastically varied places, from natural hot springs in remote fields to sleek modern spa complexes. The favourite spot for Icelanders is the beloved swimming pool, found in virtually every town.

"Better weight than wisdom a traveller cannot carry." – From the Hávamál (The Sayings of the Vikings)

The *heitur pottur* (hot pot) by the pool is a hot tub where locals congregate to catch up on the day. It's the steamy equivalent of a local pub or town square, and discussing the big issues clad only in a swimsuit strips most pretentiousness from conversation.

IT'LL WORK OUT OK

According to a 2017 poll conducted by the University of Iceland, 45% of the population live according to the unofficial national motto '*þetta reddast*', usually translated along the lines of 'it will all work out OK in the end'. This intense optimism may have been born of necessity – the country does, after all, have frequent obstacles thrown at it by Mother Nature – but it also breeds a self-belief that sees locals dive headfirst into challenges others may deem impossible. A case in point: a nation of 350,000 people producing a football team that made it to the 2018 World Cup (the smallest country to ever qualify).

A BOOKISH STREAK

Books matter in Iceland, which celebrates a literary legacy that stretches from medieval sagas and poetic eddas to contemporary Nordic Noir thrillers by way of a Nobel laureate (Halldór Laxness in 1955). Reykjavík is a Unesco City of Literature, and almost nowhere in the world are as many titles

FESTIVE GIFTS, ICELAN-DIC-STYLE

Why not recreate Iceland's Yuletide tradition of buying, giving and reading books? The main celebration is on Christmas Eve (24 December); after dinner, gifts (chiefly books) are exchanged, then Icelanders spend the rest of the evening reading at home. This is the culmination of the *jólabókaflóð* (literally, the 'Christmas book flood').

CHAIN OF POOLS

For travellers to Iceland, an itinerary can be formed around swims and soaks that tap into the quintessential pastime of getting into hot water. Sample Reykjavík's swimming pools, hike to Reykjadalur hot springs and soak in a steaming river. Check out the ethereal Blue Lagoon, set among black lava, and visit new design-driven bathing complexes such as GeoSea and Vök Baths.

published per capita as in Iceland; it is commonly claimed that one in 10 Icelanders will publish a book. A nation of storytellers uses literature to define and assert its identity, and to cherish and renew its language.

A LIVING LANGUAGE

Fewer than 400,000 people speak Icelandic, and due to geographic isolation and conscious preservation it has changed remarkably little in the past 1000 years; ancient texts are still largely intelligible to modern readers. In Iceland, creating new vocabulary for technological innovation is a national pastime. New terms are usually based on existing words in an effort to prevent loanwords from 'corrupting' the language; for example, the word for telephone is *sími*, from an ancient word for long thread, while computer is *tölva* – a fusion of *tala* (number) and *völva* (prophetess).

A SENSE OF BELONGING

The names of most Icelanders constitute a first name, plus the first name of their father (or, more rarely, mother) in patronymic form. Girls add the suffix -dóttir (daughter of) to their father's name and boys add -son (son

of) – hence Guðrún, daughter of Jón, is Guðrún Jónsdóttir, and her brother Sigurður will be Sigurður Jónsson. Because surnames only relate what a person's father is called, Icelanders don't bother with titles such as Mr or Mrs. Instead they use first names, even when addressing strangers. It makes for a notably democratic society when you're expected to address your president by their first name.

SETTING THE STANDARD

Throughout history, Iceland has been home to kick-ass women; for centuries, the women had to take care of farms and families while the men headed off to sea. Iceland had the world's first democratically elected female president, Vigdís Finnbogadóttir (elected in 1980), and the world's first openly gay head of government, Jóhanna Sigurðardóttir (elected prime minister in 2009). Today, the country is viewed as a pioneer of women's empowerment, and for the past decade it has topped the World Economic Forum's annual index measuring gender equality: it is the most gender-equal country to date, having closed over 85% of its overall gender gap.

Soaking it up: Iceland's famous Blue Lagoon geothermal baths.

EUROPE

SCOTLAND

This cold country has a warm heart. Journey here and be assured that you'll find the door wide open in welcome, and a dram of strong stuff placed in your hand before long.

POPULATION
5.4 million

**MUNROS
(MOUNTAINS
OVER 3000FT)
IN SCOTLAND**
282

**WHISKY
DISTILLERIES**
> 120

Scottish hospitality is the stuff of legend. Looking after travellers and providing them with food and shelter for the night has long been a sacred obligation in this wild country. Indeed, the world might be a better place if everyone was as convivial as the Scots: here, people invite strangers for a drink or give them a lift in the car within a few minutes of first meeting. In the rain-lashed Highlands, free overnight accommodation for intrepid hikers exists to this day. This is a people in love with their land: after all, what other nation makes a tradition of climbing all the mountains of a certain height? For all the chill of these latitudes, there is immense warmth in the Scottish way of life, from their ceildhs (social gatherings full of dancing and folk music) to their fiery whisky: a counter-reaction, perhaps, to the infamously inclement weather.

EUROPE

© Paul Harris/awl-images.com

© George Clerk 17625l/Getty Images, © Jakub Moravec/Shutterstock

Clockwise from top: Sunset on the Isle of Harris; whisky distilleries in Scotland are popular with visitors; indulging in a wee dram. **Previous page:** Edinburgh's Old Town thrums with life at dusk.

TOP INSIGHTS for LIFE

A WEE DRAM

A wee dram – a little glass of whisky – keeps the Scots going through many a bitter winter. Make no mistake, this is a whisky-obsessed nation, with more than 120 distilleries and a wider industry supporting 10,000+ jobs. Mentioning a wee dram also hints at the Scottish sense of humour, where understatement is key. It's not about getting drunk, though; it's a means of socialising and savouring Scotland's elemental essence – peaty soil, snowy hills and briny seascapes.

CRAZY CEILDHS

Originally, a ceildh simply meant a visit from family or neighbours, but the Scottish saw no need to stop at small talk. Perhaps because a visit from anyone was a notable event in a remote, sometimes hostile land, such gatherings became mini-festivals full of music, dancing and storytelling. Anywhere else, the tradition might have petered out with the advent of TV (invented by a Scot, incidentally), but to this day Scots properly switch on when the ceildh starts.

RICH IN WEED

Prevailing currents, constant water temperatures and development-free shorelines make Scotland a country rich in weed: seaweed. From wrack to dulse, the variety flourishing along its craggy coast is astonishing, and has been used as a nutrient-packed food, a poultice and a preventative against parasites among other applications. Now the secret is out: several companies harvest it for cosmetic products and healthy munchies.

MUNRO-BAGGING & BOTHY-GOING

Named after the man who catalogued them all, the Munros are mountains over 3000ft (914m). Working your way through all 282 of them has become a pursuit known as 'Munro-bagging'; the whole feat takes many years to complete, entailing scrambles and technical climbs. In between scaling summits, Munro-baggers and other hikers spend the night in the wilderness in free shelters called bothies, a testament to the nation's love of its rugged terrain.

BOUNTY OF THE SEA

It's easy to explore the health benefits of Scottish seaweed, even if you can't visit the country; several companies offer mail-order cosmetics and other products, such as the Hebridean Seaweed Company. If you can visit, plump for a stay at the elegant Isle of Eriska Hotel, where the spa treatments feature hand-harvested seaweed.

EUROPE

IRELAND

People had little of material value in Ireland for centuries, but the importance of community, a spirit of cooperation and joy in social interaction were, and still are, paramount.

POPULATION
5 million

BUBBLES IN A
PINT OF
GUINNESS
300

Sean's Bar in
Athlone dates
back to 900 CE,
making it Ireland's
oldest pub

It's no coincidence that you'll see Irish pubs all over the world – the convivial nature of Irish people, their love of a good story, live music and quick-witted banter is something that canny publicans have attempted to export for many years. In Ireland, however, it's simply a way of life, from the warm welcome for strangers to the bus driver's jokes, the tradition of staying up way too late to chat, sing and dance, and the absolute intolerance of airs and graces. Like many before, it'll make you realise there's far more to life than your possessions. Whether the island's history of suppression or its Catholic values are responsible, looking out for others is still a prime consideration for Irish people, and massive family gatherings, nights spent swinging around a dance floor or crying with laughter are the most valuable kind of all.

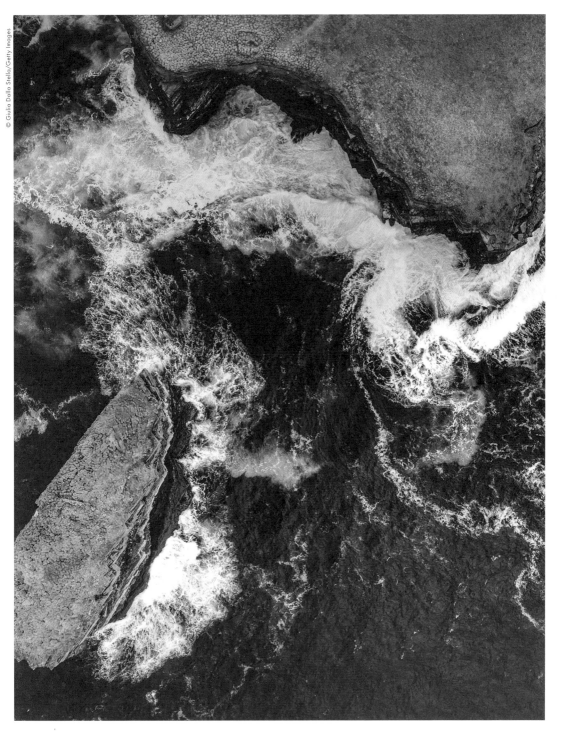

EUROPE

© BOULENGER Xavier/Shutterstock

left & right © Andrew Montgomery/Lonely Planet

Clockwise from top: Temple Bar in Dublin: a magnet for *craic*-seekers; a traditional Irish band plays in O'Donaghue's, Dublin; when in Ireland... have a pint of the black stuff. **Previous page:** Ireland's coastline is wild, craggy and beautiful.

TOP INSIGHTS for LIFE

WHAT'S THE CRAIC?

One of those nebulous concepts that's impossible to define precisely, having the *craic* is an integral part of Irish life, and can consist of anything from a night of rapid-fire ribbing in the pub to a wild party you can barely remember. It's an unspoken rule in Ireland not to take yourself too seriously or someone will be sure to enjoy a joke at your expense, and this sense of playfulness is so ingrained in daily life that in many parts of the country the standard greeting is simply, 'What's the *craic*?'.

THE CONCEPT OF MEITHEAL

The *meitheal*, a form of co-operative labour, has been used in Ireland for centuries, and was as much a social institution as a necessity for survival in times past. Neighbours helped each other cut hay or take in the harvest, working together in the knowledge that the favour would be returned one day. Fostering a sense of community and a feeling of belonging, the concept of *meitheal* is still widely used across Ireland, from small-scale seed meitheals where vegetable growers share seedlings, to state social services providing case coordination for vulnerable families.

SHARING THE SORROW

A time to process the death of a loved one, the Irish wake sees family, friends and community members keeping vigil over an open coffin in the home of the deceased. It's a tradition that allows mourners to share the burden of sorrow and say goodbye in a familiar environment. It's also an acceptance that grief is something to be acknowledged rather than hidden, and over time, this private yet public way of mourning can even help to overcome the fear of death itself.

> "To learn one must be humble. But life is the great teacher." – From *Ulysses*, James Joyce

ASK THREE TIMES IF YOU'RE IRISH

Irish people always decline an offer of hospitality at first. It's possibly a hangover from famine times and allows the host to be polite even if there's not enough food or space to go round. If you're asked a second time, it's safe to accept because you know the offer is genuine. If you're asked three times, it's almost rude to say no.

EUROPE

WALES

Welsh wellness springs from a deep connection to their homeland's often staggering scenery, plus the community spirit and ancient traditions that warm day-to-day life in the valleys and hills.

POPULATION
3.1 million

% OF COUNTRY
COVERED BY
NATIONAL PARKS
20

RATIO OF SHEEP
TO PEOPLE
> 3:1

Living amid some of the spectacular coastal and mountain scenery in the British Isles, if not the whole of Europe, the Welsh have good reason to boast about their lot. But they don't do that. Humble to the point of shyness in some eyes, Welsh people don't feel the need to brag to outsiders, but they readily and regularly celebrate their country's many positives with each other: the still-thriving, identity-defining language; the proud traditions of music and literature; the three national parks that make Wales such a world-class outdoor playground; the fertile ground that produces exceptional local produce; the ancient customs of the agricultural shows that are the highlight of the calendar, uniting towns and villages, and strengthening the bonds of community to the point where drivers think nothing of stopping the traffic on main roads for the sake of a friendly chat.

EUROPE

© Jax10289/Getty Images

© Gyvafoto/Shutterstock, Andreas Zerndl/Shutterstock

Clockwise from top: Vintage tractors at an agricultural show in Wales; the National Eisteddfod is a centuries-old celebration of Welsh culture; on Llanberis Path to the summit of Snowdon, Wales' highest mountain. **Previous page:** Mist over the Brecon Beacons National Park.

TOP INSIGHTS for LIFE

CWTCH CULTURE

Cwtch can mean anything from a hug with a loved one to a cosy nook in a house or public space where one feels safe. This cultural concept reflects the fact that when the Welsh let you in – into their homes, into their lives – they let you in with the most friendly, touching welcome imaginable. A *cwtch* evokes many things, depending on the specific context – childhood, a special place, a beloved person – but it always conjures up the feeling of a warm embrace, much-needed in a rain-prone land.

LESSONS IN LIVING WELL

The agricultural show – a phenomenon that occurs in every self-respecting town and village, plus some urban areas too – is Wales through and through, and more of a lesson in living well than a simple event. It usually features homegrown fruit and veg, handmade arts and crafts, a proud display of prized livestock, and a showcase of local businesses. Almost everyone in the area contributes somehow, and the preparations often start months in advance. Although it's an ancient tradition, the show also looks to the future, championing worthy causes and highlighting projects-to-be; but perhaps its most important function is as a grand exercise in community mindedness.

CELEBRATE WITH SONG

Song in the ancient Welsh sense of the word could refer to instrumental song (music) or vocal song (performed poetry in notoriously hard-to-master metre). The Welsh have remained mighty good at both. From the Eisteddfod – a celebration of music and literature dating back to the early medieval period – to the male voice choirs that surged in popularity from the 1700s onwards, Welsh song in all its forms has entranced listeners with its complexity and multi-voice harmony. You might not understand the words, but you can appreciate the sound, and the miracle of collaboration this art form represents.

GO TO THE SHOW

Outsiders are always welcome at any of the many annual Welsh shows, which take place mainly during the summer months of June, July and August. The biggest show is the Royal Welsh near Builth Wells, although generally the smaller the show, the more endearing it is.

101

EUROPE

ENGLAND

Making up the majority on an archipelago renowned for doing things differently, the English have always been unorthodox, and enjoy their own eccentricities. What better life lesson is there?

POPULATION
56 million

% OF POPULA-
TION LIVING
WITHIN 70 MILES
OF THE SEA
100

PUBS IN
ENGLAND
> 40,000

Since at least the 16th-century Act of Supremacy that severed ties with the Roman Catholic Church, and right up to the agonising wrangles over the UK's exit from the European Union, England has steered a unique course, often in a different direction to the rest of the continent (and, truth be told, sometimes against the wishes of Wales, Scotland and Northern Ireland, too). But never did you see a country more at peace with its peccadilloes and peculiarities; the

world gawps in disbelief as bare-chested Englishmen, fizz-free beers in hand, bellow their chants at football matches in the bleak midwinter. Hailing from a country that has played a major role on the world stage has given the English a deep, lasting well of self-belief, but also the confidence to mock themselves, and these contradictory traits find expression in everything from the stiffness of that famous lip to the self-deprecating, subtly revolutionary tradition of banter.

Clockwise from top: Don't forget the bucket and spade: trips to the seaside are quintessentially English; making friends at Colombia Road in London; a pint of ale in an English inn. **Previous page:** The fishing village of Port Isaac in North Cornwall.

TOP INSIGHTS for LIFE

THE ART OF BANTER

The diarist Samuel Pepys once described pubs – of which there are thousands, from ivy-wreathed countryside beauties to gritty inner-city locals – as the heart of England. And it is here where the English practise and perfect their banter, a way of talking about nothing in particular with friends or even strangers that spirals, with each pint of beer consumed, into a good-natured if spirited debate that sets the world to rights. Banter is a way to let off steam after a trying day; a way to air one's grievances with each other or, more likely, the state; a way to break down barriers in a country still riven by class; a way to slip the shackles of that traditional English reserve, and thus moan, mock and keep yourself sane, albeit temporarily.

TRIPS TO THE SEASIDE

Excepting the borders with Wales and Scotland, the sea laps England on all sides; it defines the nation and everyone goes there at some point in their lives. Such a trip has been synonymous with a sense of wellbeing since Victorian times, when the railways gave rise to a garish, fun-filled world of sandcastles, rock-pooling, donkey rides and Punch and Judy shows, not to mention a calorific cuisine of ice cream, sticks of rock (hard candy), pots of cockles and, of course, fish and chips eaten al fresco on the nearest bench, finger-numbingly cold wind be damned.

THAT STIFF UPPER LIP

A character trait associated with Brits in general but the English in particular is the ability to remain resolute in the face of adversity. Nothing reflects this stoicism better than the nation's response to WWII; to motivate the public, the government even produced posters bearing the slogan 'Keep Calm and Carry On'. This attitude extends from the public to the personal realm, too – the English still don't talk about their problems much, and woe betide the guileless person who, when asked if they're all right, responds with anything other than a variation of 'Fine, thanks'.

BANTER SKILLS

Assemble a group of friends and get the beers in. Start a conversation with something light-hearted. Let one comment feed off the next (and buy rounds to loosen tongues and build camaraderie along the way), addressing whatever is bugging you without allowing the debate to become eyeball-rollingly serious. Congratulations: you've just mastered the art of banter.

PORTUGAL

Legendary explorers, enigmatic poets and heart-stirring fadistas (fado singers) have shaped the psyche of this small, seafaring nation on Europe's southwest edge, where sorrow and joy often go hand in hand.

POPULATION
10.4 million

**ANNUAL
SEAFOOD
CONSUMPTION**
61.5kg per capita

**ANNUAL DAYS
OF SUNSHINE IN
LISBON AND THE
SOUTH**
> 290

Portugal is one of Europe's oldest countries, its borders unchanged since the 13th century, and age-old festivals blending pagan and Christian traditions are still a routine part of life. History is woven into the landscape, too, which bears traces of the Celts, Romans, Moors and Christians. As civilisations rose and fell, the Portuguese nurtured a quiet fatalism through music, poetry and other arts. The greatest works reflect on faded glories and loves lost, while also contemplating the vast oceanic horizon, for geography has had a profound effect on this coastal country. The sea and what lies beyond it have always caught the Portuguese imagination, and the nation boasts one of Europe's highest percentages of citizens living abroad. These expats often pine for their homeland, gripped by longing for its superlative seafood, magnificent weather and strong sense of community.

Clockwise from top: A street party during the Santo Antonio Festival in Lisbon; hand-painted *azulejos* (tiles) decorate the facade of Igreja do Carmo church in Porto; a Portuguese grilled sardine dish. **Previous page:** A vintage tram trundles up one of Lisbon's steep cobbled streets.

TOP INSIGHTS for LIFE

LOVE OF THE SEA

This is the birthplace of legendary navigators like Vasco da Gama, Pedro Álvares Cabral and Fernando Magellan, and even the country's remotest hinterlands are only a couple hours' drive from the coast. The Portuguese employ countless expressions related to the sea, like *há mais marés, que marinheiros* (literally, 'there are more tides than sailors', but the meaning equates to 'don't despair, other opportunities will come your way'). Not surprisingly, they're devout seafood lovers, and one of the largest consumers of fish in Europe – which might account for their long lifespans.

MUSIC OF MELANCHOLY

Portugal's soundtrack is *fado* (Portuguese for 'fate'), a melancholic music dripping with emotion. Fado, which has roots in North African rhythms, emerged from a working-class district of Lisbon in the 19th century. The soulful ballads are indelibly linked to Portuguese identity, often infused with a sense of *saudade*, that nostalgic, sorrow-filled longing for something that's no longer attainable. While celebration is also an essential part of the Portuguese spirit, *fado* reminds people not to forget the past, and to treasure what they've lost.

FEAST OF HOLY DAYS

In a country where more than 80% of people are Roman Catholic, religion remains a big part of life. Although church attendance has declined over the last few decades, the calendar continues to revolve around religious events. Parades and processions take centre stage on important Christian holidays, and every town and village is devoted to one or more saints, who are celebrated with fervour on their feast days. In Lisbon, San Antonio is the patron saint of good times in mid-June, when dozens of street parties happen around the city, Lisboêtas profess their love with sappy poems and gifts of *manjericos* (basil plants), and hundreds of couples get married. Up north, São João is the favourite, and Porto throws its biggest bash on 23 and 24 June, when believers and non-believers alike party hard.

LISTEN TO FADO

Spend an afternoon listening to a few *fado* albums. Check out classic songs by the famous Amalia Rodrigues, whose extraordinary vocal range is filled with all the sorrow of the world. Feel the raw power of her rendition, without regard to the lyrics, and let your mind wander freely, reflecting on your own joys and sorrows.

EUROPE

SPAIN

Lovers of siestas and aficionados of late-night revelry;
purveyors of fine food, yet recently declared the world's
healthiest people — the Spanish know how to live life to the full.

POPULATION
49 million

**BLOOMBERG
GLOBAL HEALTH
INDEX POSITION**
1st

**ANNUAL PUBLIC
HOLIDAYS**
at least 14
(national and
regional)

With its moody flamenco, jovial fiestas and colourful art, Spain has often been romanticised as a place of picaresque heroes and passionate heroines. In the 18th and 19th centuries, artists and writers were drawn to the country by the vibrant if exaggerated images of Iberian life depicted in operas, paintings and works of literature. Over 100 years later, the myth of impassioned Spanish culture is still alive and well.

But in our fast-moving modern world, Spain is also a place where people haven't forgotten how to relax and vary the pace. From the solemnity of Semana Santa to the ebullience of Seville's spring fair, from afternoon siestas hiding from the hot sun to the free-flowing football skills of FC Barcelona, Spain provides plenty of insights for those who want to know how to live life in the fast *and* the slow lane.

EUROPE

© joserpizarro/Shutterstock

© Mark Read/Lonely Planet, © Justin Foulkes/Lonely Planet

Clockwise from top: Seville's Feria de Abril celebrates local culture; the scallop shell is the symbol of the Camino de Santiago; a lunchtime tapas stop with wine. **Previous page:** The olive harvest over winter is an important time of the year in Spain.

TOP INSIGHTS for LIFE

ART OF THE SIESTA

Every country has its distinctive cadence, a rhythm that controls daily life. In Spain, that cadence revolves around the siesta, an afternoon repose when the sun burns too hot for comfort and anyone with a smidgeon of Iberian spirit finds a place to flop down, close their eyes and benefit from an energy-replenishing nap. In most towns and cities, the bulk of small businesses pull down their shutters soon after the lunchtime rush and don't open them again until early evening. The respite has its advantages. Come 8pm, recharged siesta-ers are ready to hit the town and party until the small hours. While the demands of modern life have

"He can who thinks he can, and he can't who thinks he can't. This is an inexorable, indisputable law." – Pablo Picasso, Spanish painter

eroded some tenets of the siesta, the tradition still has its adherents. Indeed, many medical professionals suggest that a power nap is not only inherently Spanish, but also good for your cardiovascular health.

LINGERING SOBREMESA

The anchor of the Spanish day is lunch, or *la comida*. The main meal is traditionally taken around 2pm and eaten slowly, accompanied by wine, conversation, family, and a welcome spot of post-lunch lingering popularly known as *sobremesa*. To digest the large amounts of food, it makes perfect sense to slacken the pace after your repast as you debate the merits of serrano ham over manchego cheese. The *sobremesa* begins with dessert and stretches, through coffee, liqueurs and perhaps a furtive cigar, into mid-afternoon. In today's busy world, it survives as a cultural hinge of Spanish life.

SPIRIT OF DUENDE

Duende is the soulful essence of Spain, a mysterious spirit that

PLAN YOUR OWN CAMINO

The Camino de Santiago is open to all-comers year-round. Walkers first need to choose a route (there are at least six, all converging on Santiago de Compostela). Next, choose your timing – May, June and September are good months weather-wise; high summer is hot and crowded. Finally, choose your companion(s) or decide to sally forth alone.

113

LONELY PLANET'S GUIDE TO LIFE

SEE FLAMEN-CO IN SEVILLE

The best place to see live flamenco and capture some of the spirit of duende is Seville. Replete with concert halls, *tablaos* (dinner shows), cultural centres and *peñas* (private clubs), there are enough venues here to fill a full week's itinerary. Furthermore, performances are guaranteed to be authentic and highly skilled.

enriches the culture with an energy that is at once dark and uplifting. The concept of *duende* is most commonly associated with flamenco, the ancestral music of the Roma people that, over time, got mixed with traditional Spanish folk dances to form the complex and spectacular art we know today. There is no simple way of encountering *duende*. Spontaneous and elusive, it hides in the anguished cry of a flamenco singer, a guitarist's percussive chords, or the frenzied stomp of a dancer's feet. Spanish poet Federico García Lorca once claimed that *duende* comes, 'not from the throat, but rises up inside of you from the soles of your feet'. Experience it during a musical performance and you're halfway to unlocking one of Spain's most precious secrets.

A TASTE FOR OLIVE OIL

You haven't really tasted olive oil until you've been to Spain. The country manufactures about half of the world's annual produce of the antioxidant-rich liquid and, while much is exported, the locals keep the best stuff for themselves. No Spanish restaurant is bereft of a bottle of extra-virgin

olive oil on every table, and many villages harbour small factories making high-quality *aceite* (oil) for local consumption. The Spanish even enjoy it for breakfast. Pan con tomate is the default *desayuno* (breakfast), a toasted bread roll topped with olive oil and crushed tomatoes – cheap, quick and good for you.

MOTHER OF ALL PILGRIMAGES

Religious processions are common in Spain, especially during Semana Santa (Holy Week) when penitents file into churches and monasteries clad in hooded costumes. But the mother of all pilgrimages is the Camino de Santiago, an epic multi-day journey on foot across northern Spain to the shrine of St James in Santiago de Compostela's cathedral. Practised since medieval times, the Camino has been enthusiastically revived since the 1990s and not just by religious pilgrims; modern hikers use the walk as a means of spiritual enlightenment, or as an escape from 21st-century culture. Whatever your motives, a trudge down the contemporary Camino offers a candid insight into Spanish culture old and new.

Hikers arriving at
the end of the
Camino de Santiago.

EUROPE

FRANCE

Few take 'art de vivre' to heart quite like the French. But then again, this is a home-grown expression spun from their deep-rooted passion for food, wine and fine living.

POPULATION
67.3 million

WORLD'S FIRST HAUTE COUTURE PERFUME
Chanel No 5
(1921)

ANNUAL CHEESE CONSUMPTION
27.2kg per capita

In a sophisticated world, the proudly traditional French venerate the very earth on which they make their stand: olive groves in sun-baked Provence, flower-dotted Alpine pastures, briny Breton oyster beds… The French dedication to the seasons, to natural flavours and fresh ingredients, has made the country into a culinary tour de force, and their language has given the world words like gourmet, haute cuisine and bon vivant. French mathematician René Descartes founded modern philosophy; Parisian literary salons spawned the Enlightenment; Coco Chanel dared women to don trousers and crop their hair. But despite the chic 'haute' prefix, French living is profoundly down to earth; it's about food shopping at the local market, taking two hours for lunch, celebrating neighbours at the annual Fête des Voisins, lingering over an aperitif with friends or around the family dinner table.

EUROPE

© Jag_cz/Shutterstock

© Matt Munro/Lonely Planet; © aprott/Getty Images

Clockwise from top: Sunrise on a vineyard in Chateauneuf du Pape; the town of Grasse has been synonymous with perfumery for four centuries; macarons are little parcels of French perfection. **Previous page:** Lavender fields in Provence.

TOP INSIGHTS for LIFE

FRENCH KISSING

Greetings are vital to the French. Not only do they deem it terribly rude not to extend a *bonjour* to everyone they meet, be it the baker in the village *boulangerie*, strangers on that early-morning run, or the guy in the autoroute toll booth, but exchanging kisses – from the cheek-skimming to the wildly exuberant – is also an absolute must. How many and which side first depends on where you are in France: two in Paris, three in Provence, four in the Loire Valley.

MODERN-DAY FLÂNERIE

Wandering at leisure while soaking up the city and seeking out the unexpected is a quotidian art that French urbanites have practised since the 16th century. Rather like deciding which direction to go by the roll of a dice, *flânerie* is all about the vagaries of chance and slow, mindful observation – of the foot-worn cobblestones, the couple on the café terrace, the tolling church bell, the kaleidoscope of city life. Try it.

UN CAFÉ & CROISSANT

Be it in a rural village or the cosmopolitan capital, the local cafe is French gold. It is a safe place to kick-start the day over *un café* and croissant, break for mid-morning coffee, catch up with the news, take time out with friends, debate, philosophise, people-watch on a sunny pavement terrace, sip a ritual aperitif at dusk or simply retreat for a moment to sit and contemplate the world.

BON APPÉTIT

Gourmet appetites know no bounds in France, where eating well – exceedingly well – is a birthright. The French enjoy a healthy obsession with food, gathering around a shared table to feast on the fruits of their bountiful land with three-course meals, and celebrating almost every known culinary item with its own tasty *fête*. Expect chestnut festivals, cheese festivals, snail festivals, garlic festivals, wild strawberry festivals, even feisty tripe festivals. Dare to join in.

LA SEMAINE DU GOÛT

France's Week of Taste in October is just that. Schoolchildren are served unusual delicacies – *andouillette* (tripe sausage) perhaps, smoky raclette cheese melted on a potato or a single oyster – to spark their culinary curiosity, teach them to eat wisely, and help them learn about the origins of food and the centuries-old *savoir-faire* (know-how) behind most artisan products. One to try at home.

AN OL-FACTORY AWAKEN-ING

Creating your own unique fragrance with a *nez* (nose or perfumier) in the French town of Grasse, synonymous with perfumery since the 16th century, is dizzying and revelatory: no other experience piques the sense of smell like this. Green amber, vanilla, lily of the valley, rose and civet (extracted from a cat's anal glands) are among the 127 floral, musky, woody, spicy or leathery essences to sniff.

LET THEM EAT CAKE

There is something infinitely comforting about devouring cake – a delicious nostalgia for a carefree childhood perhaps? *Patisserie* never goes out of style. Like French fashion designers, Parisian pastry chefs create new collections each season, dazzling sweet-toothed cake lovers with exquisite renditions of century-old classics, elaborate new techniques, and creative, contemporary combinations. Bite into an olive oil and mandarin orange or green tea and black sesame *macaron* by *haute-pâtissier* Pierre Hermé to understand what all the fuss is about.

HOLY TERROIR

A French term that roughly translates as 'land', *terroir* is the essence of France's famed food culture. Referencing a product's unique geographical, environmental and historical characteristics, *terroir* ensures creamy Roquefort cheese is only aged in subterranean caves near Roquefort-sur-Soulzon, or that grapes grown in pebble-covered vineyards in Châteauneuf-du-Pape go into coveted red wines, and that France's precious artisan producers continue to thrive.

THE POWER OF SCENT

The French perfume industry is one of the largest in the world, which explains why the naturally sexy French instinctively understand the seductive power of scent: the promised sophistication of Chanel No 5, the joyful fragrance of freshly cut grass, the feel-good smell of just laundered linen, the energising effect of a whiff of citrus... The routine spritz each morning really does linger all day.

TO YOUR HEALTH!

When the French raise their glass – no self-respecting meal is complete without wine – the ritual 'Santé!' or (more formal) 'À Votre Santé!' toast is pertinent. In medieval France, wine was used for medicinal purposes – a bottle of Côtes de Provence was prescribed for obesity, Châteauneuf-du-Pape for bloating and sweet Muscat de Frontignan baths for herpes – and Les Sources de Caudalie near Bordeaux is not the only modern French spa to offer dreamy *vinethérapie* (wine therapy) treatments like grapeseed-oil massages and red vine-extract baths.

A traditional
Savoyarde
cheesecake.

EUROPE

ITALY

Good living comes as second nature in a country known for la dolce vita; food, family and a healthy fear of the wind are just some of Italy's lifestyle secrets.

POPULATION
62.2 million

CENTENARIANS
> 14,000

Two-thirds of 18-
to 34-year-olds
live with their
parents

Descended from those original sybarites, the Ancient Romans, and famed for their inimitable style, warm-heartedness and good food, is it any wonder that Italians know a thing or two about living well? From their spectacularly diverse and fertile land, they figured out how to grow some of the best produce and turned it into a revelatory cuisine. Meanwhile, they embellished the country's natural beauty by littering it with great works of art and architecture, plus the world's highest number of Unesco World Heritage Sites. Italians also seem to have cracked longevity, with one of the highest numbers of people living to 100. So what is their secret? It might just be that time here goes a notch slower, allowing locals to perfect that dish, finesse that outfit and chat with their barista, because they understand far better than most *il dolce far niente* (the sweetness of doing nothing).

EUROPE

Clockwise from top: Bocce on the beach; *spaghetti al frutti di mare* in Cinque Terre; a cheese maker at a Parmesan dairy farm in Emilia-Romagna. **Previous page:** A tree-lined pavement in Ortygia, Sicily.

TOP INSIGHTS for LIFE

FOOD IS SACRED

Food is not just about sustenance in Italy – it's life itself. It's the basis of social engagements, a point of discussion at almost any gathering, and considered so sacred it has its own rules (ie commit the faux pas of adding cheese to your seafood and risk being shamed by all the Italians around you). The quality of ingredients is paramount, while the way you eat is as important as the food itself. Indeed, it was in Italy that the concept of Slow Food first found life, as an antidote to the fast food industry: the movement champions the use of local ingredients and techniques and promotes the simple pleasure of eating. This is

> *"At the table you don't get old."* – Italian proverb

something that they know a lot about: an Italian meal is never rushed and always made better by being eaten in company, because Italians know that eating well is essential to living well.

DOING NOTHING

Literally 'the sweet doing nothing', *il dolce far niente* encompasses everything from sipping wine at a little bar to going for a stroll at sunset or sitting on your terrace greeting neighbours and watching passers-by. It's the idea that doing nothing is an event in itself and as worthy of your time and attention as any work commitment. While the world hurtles forward at ever greater speeds, life eases to a gentler pace if you can dedicate yourself to the Italian style of doing nothing.

THE ITALIAN FAMIGLIA

Family has always been at the heart of Italian culture. Many live at home until their 30s (also for economic reasons). Those that don't generally speak to their families, or at least their mothers, on an almost daily basis. Additionally, the further south you go, the more the family becomes an extension of the individual; what you wear, who you date and even what mop you buy are subject to heated family debate. While this has its

EAT LIKE AN ITALIAN

Experience a *sagra* (local food festival) to really understand the importance and exceptional flavours of regional Italian cooking. Themed around a particular dish or ingredient, options are seemingly endless and run the gamut from gorgonzola in Gorgonzola (Milan) to truffles in Sant'Agostino Mirabello (Ferrara), fried fish in Santa Maria di Leuca (Lecce) and wild boar in Cameri (Novara).

TAKE A BREAK

Take a break from the daily grind by dedicating some time to that age-old Italian concept of *il dolce far niente*. This might entail wandering through the park on your way home or whiling away an hour or two over a good wine. Let your mind drift and your worries melt away as the mood takes you.

downsides (some say mother-in-laws are behind Italy's rising divorce rate), being close to your family can offer endless support, from helping to raise your kids to keeping you well fed.

LOVE OF CHIACCHIERARE

There's nothing Italians love more than a good *chiacchierata* (chat), with everyone from their friends and family, to the local barista. Parents call their kids just to ask what they ate for lunch, *nonnos* get together to shoot the breeze over a game of Briscola or Bocce, after-work *aperitivi* (pre-dinner drinks) are weekly occurrences, and a long discussion about apartment politics with your *portinaia* (doorman) goes without saying. Adopt this habit and you'll never get lonely, as it comes with a heartwarming sense of companionship.

AN ILL WIND

Among Italians many a malaise, from a cold to a headache, stomach ache or back pain, is attributed to the mysterious *colpa d'aria* (literally 'hit of wind'). It can happen by sleeping with your window open or having

seemingly innocuous air-conditioning blowing on the back of your neck. It's the reason why children are dressed like mini Michelin men, scarves are ubiquitous, as is a singlet worn beneath a t-shirt, and women often bring two bathers to the beach (so as not to lie in a wet bathing suit). Protect yourself from this invisible enemy and you just might avoid minor ills.

THE BELLA FIGURA

An intrinsic part of Italian culture is about making a good impression, known as a *bella figura*. On a personal level, it relates to everything from taking pride in your appearance to displaying manners and good etiquette. It means being well-dressed even if just popping to the supermarket, holding the door for someone (especially if you're a man), and bringing a gift when invited for dinner at someone's house. It's about care and attention to detail, which lends a sense of dignity and self-respect to those who practise it.

Watching the world go by outside the Massimo Theater in Palermo.

EUROPE

SWITZERLAND

Citizens of one of the world's most orderly yet creative nations, the Swiss execute every step in life – indeed, every life step – with enviable poise and resolve

POPULATION
8.3 million

ANNUAL CHOCOLATE CONSUMPTION
10.3kg per capita

AVERAGE TIME SPENT ON PUBLIC TRANSPORT
90min per day

Be it the famed efficiency with which its trains, cable cars and public transport run, the exquisite precision of its cuckoo clocks and luxury timepieces, or the ease with which its inhabitants speak four languages, Switzerland seems to have imposed order on the modern world. It's not surprising to learn that the Swiss gave the world Einstein, numbered bank accounts, the World Wide Web, the ultimate utilitarian knife and the unfussy Helvetica font. But what about absinthe and LSD? What about Velcro, the Red Cross, bobsledding and Toblerone chocolate bars shaped like the peak of the Matterhorn? So they're just as capable of the unexpected, too. The Swiss seek recreation and relaxation in the Alps, where Golden Age mountaineers conquered new heights and winter tourism was born in the 19th century, and where modern-day adventurers bottle fresh air and blast down ski slopes.

© ELEPHOTOS/Shutterstock

© White Smoke/Shutterstock/Shutterstock; © Adam Jones/Getty Images

Clockwise from top: A picturesque pitstop in the Swiss Alps; alphornists near the Matterhorn; the art of a Swiss chocolatier.
Previous page: A downhill skier races down the mountainside.

TOP INSIGHTS for LIFE

THE HILLS ARE ALIVE

In rural Switzerland, time-honoured traditions and ancient rituals make for a rich, uplifting pastoral calendar. Each spring, shepherds festoon their cows in bells and flowers and herd them up to higher pastures, where they spend summer chomping aromatic Alpine meadows full of wildflowers and succulent grasses. At sunset, the haunting echo of Betruf – an ancient prayer, sung by shepherds through cupped hands or a milk funnel, and said to confer protection against evil spirits – makes the mountainsides resound with song.

"Logic will get you from A to Z; imagination will get you everywhere." – *Albert Einstein, Swiss scientist*

LET YOUR HAIR DOWN

For all their poise, the Swiss know how to party. Festivals run the gamut from testosterone-fuelled to plain mad. Salvador Dalí-lookalikes rub facial hair with Garibaldi beards and hipster goatees at the Alpine Beard Festival in Chur; villagers smash cowpats with a golf club, spade or rubber boots at Reideralp's Chüfladefäscht (Cowpat Festival); and near the Swiss-Austrian border, pseudo Santas battle for the title of World's Best Santa Claus, competing in chimney-climbing and snowball-throwing contests.

FEEL-GOOD FOOD

Devouring more chocolate per capita than any other nation, the Swiss are aficionados of the feel-good power of a warm chocolate fondue or the sensory stimulation provided by a velvety square of milk chocolate laced with roasted hazelnuts, orange peel or piment. They were the first to combine chocolate with milk in 1875 and – most importantly for chocoholics the world over – developed 'conching', a process of mixing, stirring and aerating to remove any trace of bitterness from this magical substance, so we have them to thank for that irresistible melt-in-the-mouth sensation.

THE POWER OF SONG

No sound evokes the Swiss love for nature quite like the stirring call of an alphorn (traditionally used to call cows to milking) or the spiritual harmony of yodelling (the original mountain-to-mountain call). Listen to both at the Cor des Alpes in Nendaz in the Valais, Switzerland's biggest folk festival of the year, which draws alphornists and yodellers from all over the world.

EUROPE

AUSTRIA

There's no sea for miles in landlocked Austria, but who cares in a country where glacier-encrusted Alps and Mozart symphonies lift spirits, and nostalgia-laced coffeehouses gently stir the soul?

**POPULATION
8.8 million**

**The Alps cover
almost two-thirds
of Austria**

**Vienna ranked as
top city in Mercer's
Quality of Living
survey for 10
years running**

If you were to take a map and try to drop a pin on Europe's heart, you'd probably land on Austria – literally and metaphorically speaking. For such a dinky country, it has wielded immense cultural clout for centuries: Habsburg emperors held sway here for 600 years, propping up the arts scene and filling cities with lavish palaces, galleries, coffee houses and concert halls. This, in turn, attracted a maelstrom of genius in the form of Mozart, Beethoven, Strauss, Klimt and Freud. Still today, high culture, good living and a love of wilderness are all integral to what it means to be Austrian – be it a glitzy night at the opera, a decadent slice of cake or a thigh-burning Alpine hike. The Austrians walk a fine tightrope between urban and outdoors, culture and mountains, physical exertion and deep relaxation. And judging by quality of living surveys, they've struck the perfect balance.

EUROPE

© Justin Foulkes/Lonely Planet

© Anibal Trejo/Shutterstock, © Helen Cathcart/Lonely Planet

Clockwise from top: The headwaters of the River Lech; sweet treats in a Viennese *Kaffeehäuser*; a statue of Mozart, perhaps Austria's most famous son. **Previous page:** A streetlife scene in Salzburg.

TOP INSIGHTS for LIFE

CLIMB EVERY MOUNTAIN

Ever at ease when puffing up a sheer slope in mud-caked walking boots, the Austrians have a fundamental belief that *der Berg ruft* (the mountain calls). The bracing fresh air, the wide-open views of snow-capped three-thousanders and the challenge of pushing physical limits is good for the soul, they say. The Alps engulf almost two-thirds of the country, which though deceptively small on paper, soon reveal their enormity when you head uphill to be at one with nature. It's a pursuit that keeps folk here fit into their old age, with many 80-somethings considering a half-day hike over a mountain pass a mere *Sonntagsspaziergang* (Sunday stroll).

OBSESSED WITH JAVA

Where would Vienna be without its *Kaffeehäuser*? The Austrian capital's obsession with java has been going strong ever since Turks left behind sacks of 'magic' coffee beans when fleeing the city at the Battle of Vienna in 1683. The Viennese put their own spin on things: roasting the beans, adding milk, cream and sugar, and giving coffees their own fancy names. Today the city's *Kaffeehäuser* are still bathed in the nostalgic glow of *Gemütlichkeit* – broadly, a feeling of warm, friendliness and good cheer – that existed a century ago when Trotsky, Freud, Klimt and other great thinkers and coffee-drinkers frequented them to read, play chess, devour cake and put the world to rights.

ROCK ME AMADEUS

Said to boost memory, reduce stress, decrease blood pressure and make you brainy, classical music is Austria's cultural lifeblood. And the country where Mozart composed symphonies and Strauss taught the world to waltz has never lost its touch. Open and affordable to all, its ubiquitous concert halls regularly resound to the world's greatest orchestras. Not quite as highbrow but just as inherently Austrian is *Volksmusik*, the accordion-fuelled, yodel-rich folk music performed by dirndl-wearing gals and lederhosen-clad guys at jaunty summer festivals in the Alps.

BIG TALK OVER KAFFEE

For immersion into Viennese Kaffeehaus culture, hook onto one of the monthly Space and Place Coffeehouse Conversations, which revive the tradition of late-night debate. Expect to be paired off with a local and handed a menu of deeply probing 'life' questions. As founder Eugene Quinn explains, 'the Viennese hate small talk, but they are quite good at big talk'.

EUROPE

GERMANY

At first glance, German culture may not strike you as especially warm and fuzzy, but that's a misperception; comfort, in varying shapes and forms, is considered the key to contentment.

POPULATION
80.4 million

TREES IN
GERMANY
> 90 billion

BEER
CONSUMED AT
MUNICH'S
OKTOBERFEST
> 7 million litres

Germany has one of the world's biggest economies, but within living memory people didn't have much – so the Germans learned to appreciate the simple things in life. The deprivations of two world wars, and Communist rule of the former East Germany, taught them how to be frugal. And the influence of Protestantism, which originated here during the Reformation in the early 16th century, also inspires a pragmatic, down-to-earth outlook. Surprisingly for such a productive bunch, Germans on average clock fewer hours at work and get more holiday time than people from many other nations. Office life can be formal, but one thing's for sure: Germans know how to unwind. Their sense of wellbeing springs from the belief that happiness comes from a combination of good company, cold beer and a connection with nature. As the German saying goes, it's always important to see the forest for the trees.

EUROPE

© S. Borisov/Shutterstock

left & right: © Nikada/Getty Images

Clockwise from top: A traditional Christmas market in Frankfurt; *Prost!* Oktoberfest in full swing; enjoying a *gemütlich* picnic.
Previous page: Pausing for thought in a forest glade near Wolfach in the Black Forest.

TOP INSIGHTS for LIFE

THE CONCEPT OF GEMÜTLICHKEIT

Gemütlichkeit doesn't translate into a neat English expression; rather, it's the feeling of being at ease in the presence of others. A *gemütlich* experience could be, say, a quiet evening with your family or a candlelit dinner party with close friends. Embracing warmth,

> *"Gemütlichkeit is the relationship between time, beer and money." – Gerhard Polt, German writer, filmmaker and satirical cabaret artist*

cosiness and a sense of belonging, the concept has some similarities to the Danish term *hygge*, except that a *gemütlich* place will probably be somewhere that's not your own home, like a welcoming bar or cosy café. Some say there's no better way to experience a sense of *gemütlichkeit* than by visiting a Christmas market. Social acceptance is the heart of it, but good food, drinks and a comfy, laid-back vibe are also vital, as is remembering that it's not so much where you are, but who you're with, that counts.

LET THEM EAT CAKE

When the clock strikes 4pm in Germany, it's time for *kaffee und kuchen* (coffee and cake), a wonderful afternoon ritual, often taking place on the weekends with family and friends. In the morning, Germans will often buy a few slices at the bakery or farmers' market, and meet later to scoff them around the kitchen table. Alternatively, they might just plan a cafe rendezvous wherever the cake counter's selection makes the mouth water. No occasion in the workplace, like a colleague's birthday, passes without the appearance of a cake in mid-afternoon, which allows everyone to step away from their desks, and provides an excuse for everyone to take a break and catch up over a sweet treat.

LAZY SUNDAYS

In Germany, all businesses and offices close on Sundays, which forces people to disconnect. Take a leaf out of their book by leaving the grocery shopping and leftover errands for another day. Use the time for something *gemütlich* instead, like a picnic in the countryside or a walk in the woods. Nothing recharges the batteries like a few hours in the company of Mother Nature.

FAIRY-TALE WORLD

Winding from the town of Hanau to the city of Bremen, this 600km road trip is all about the Brothers Grimm, Jacob and Wilhelm, and passes through towns where they lived and places that inspired them. It's a world of fairy-tale castles, medieval villages and enchanted forests – and there's nowhere better to experience *waldeinsamkeit*.

INTO THE WOODS

Have you ever experienced a strange, almost sublime feeling when alone in a forest? That's *waldeinsamkeit*. Translated as 'solitude in/of the forest', it reflects the Germans' belief that there is no better stress-buster than getting out into nature on your own. Early uses of the term appear in German Romantic poetry in the 19th century, which waxed lyrical about the special pleasure of such seclusion – part of a wider literary movement that put a cultural and philosophical emphasis on nature, individualism and imagination. Ever since then, going into the woods – and Germany has plenty of them – has been associated with a species of tranquillity that can't be found elsewhere.

RAISE YOUR GLASSES

It's the nation's rallying cry – *prost!* In a country known for its high beer consumption, clinking glasses is an important element of drinking culture. Germans toast often, sometimes with every bottle opened or cork popped. Whether sitting with pals or strangers at the local beer garden, there is etiquette to be observed.

You must clink glasses with every single person while maintaining eye contact with them (failing to do so is a curse of seven years of bad sex!). As well as the standard exclamations of 'Prost!' or 'Cheers!', you can also say, 'To good health', or 'Here's to you!' Toasting may just take a fleeting moment, but it conjures up a lasting convivial atmosphere.

A SENSE OF SECURITY

Another untranslatable German word, *Geborgenheit* expresses the state of wellbeing that arises from a sense of security. That security manifests as different things for different people, but it might mean cuddling with your significant other, or getting stuck into one of your mum's home-cooked meals, or more broadly, any situation where you feel like you can drop the mask, let your hair down and be yourself. For Germans, who are known to be formal in the workplace, letting loose is essential to achieving personal balance.

The Bastei Bridge in Saxon
Switzerland National Park.

EUROPE

BELGIUM

A country of cult comics, Trappist beers and melt-in-the-mouth chocolate, Belgium has a trick or two to teach us about succumbing to temptation and the benefits of a good belly laugh.

POPULATION
11.6 million

CONSUMPTION OF CHOCOLATE PER CAPITA
6kg

BELGIAN BREWERIES
224

While it often gets a bad rap for EU bureaucracy and the flat-as-a-pancake landscapes of Flanders, the truth is there's a lot to like about anything-but-boring Belgium. As the Belgians themselves will attest, the way to the country's heart is through its stomach. There's insanely delicious chocolate for starters, and an entire world of fruity, refreshing ales to explore. Every street corner seems to have stands dishing out crisp, skinny, mayo-doused *frites*, or waffles slathered in cream, strawberries and syrup. The ethos? Life's short, so just go ahead and indulge. But food isn't the only thing used to enliven daily life. There's that famous Belgian self-deprecating sense of humour putting a light-hearted spin on things, not to mention a passion for comics (Asterix, Tintin and The Smurfs were born here) and a host of wacky festivals, all designed to keep the inner child fiercely alive and kicking.

Clockwise from top: Oranges at the ready: paraders at the Binche Carnival prepare to lob fruit into the crowd; the chocolate praline was invented in Belgium more than a century ago; the Manneken-Pis statue in Brussels. **Previous page:** Browsers at Bruges Fish Market.

TOP INSIGHTS for LIFE

THE BEST MEDICINE

Some might say that chocolate is the best medicine, banishing all ills for a brief ecstatic moment. One such fellow would be the Brussels pharmacist-turned-chocolatier Jean Neuhaus Jr, credited with the invention of the praline in 1912. For more than a century, Belgians have elevated chocolate to an edible art form. Detail matters: from the sourcing of grand cru beans to the purity of the cocoa butter and the delightful ribbon-wrapped packaging. Belgians believe chocolate makes life that bit sweeter and any old excuse will do to whip out the fresh-cream-filled pralines and caramel ganaches, most produced in small batches by the 2000 chocolatiers sprinkling the country.

HALLOWED BE THY BEER

If variety is the spice of life, Belgium has nailed it when it comes to beer, producing a cool 1500 kinds. Like black-habited hipsters dabbling with hops, monks spearheaded the country's craft brewing scene in the Middle Ages. Dry, chocolaty stouts, sour, spontaneously fermented Lambics, Trappist blond ales, smooth, sweet Duvels, funky cherry Krieks – the obsession here knows no bounds. And since 2016, you can raise a (perfectly matched) glass in the name of culture, with Belgian beer inscribed on the Unesco list of Intangible Cultural Heritage. Whether in solace or celebration, there's no finer way to mellow out than with a brew or two in a cosy pub or tavern.

HAVING A LAUGH

Forget the Grand Place and its stately guildhouses – the unmissable sight in Brussels for many is the Manneken Pis, a comically tiny statue of a boy taking a leak into a fountain, which neatly sums up Belgium's self-deprecating sense of humour. This don't-take-life-too-seriously approach shows up in all aspects of society: from the deadpan surrealist works of René Magritte to an unstoppable flow of weirder-the-better festivals, from the Binche carnival (orange-pelting parades) to Dinant's international bathtub regatta. Surreal? Bizarre? Bring it on...

POUR YOU

Belgians believe the good things in life should never be rushed and that the little details matter. So when you next crack open a beer, take their lead by pouring it to perfection at a 45-degree angle and gradually lifting the bottle to form a full, creamy, foamy head. Mastering this is a rite of passage and allows for deeper appreciation, apparently.

EUROPE

LUXEMBOURG

The world's only Grand Duchy is a well-heeled crossroads at the centre of Europe that has reinvented itself since the Second World War, ensuring its citizens enjoy an enviable quality of life.

POPULATION
605,000

Luxembourg
has the highest
minimum wage in
the EU

Second largest
investment fund
centre in the world
after the US

Outside the capital, where charming Unesco-listed historic buildings sit cheek by jowl with the high-rises of EU agencies, company HQs and financial conglomerates, Luxembourg is still a country where villages clustered around medieval castles mark the passage of time by the tolling of a church bell. Since its occupation in WWII, Luxembourg's tax laws have encouraged the flow of inward investment, drawing expats seeking economic opportunities from around the world (nearly half of the population are foreigners). But making a mint is just a means to an end in a country whose national motto is *'mir wëlle bleiwe wat mir sinn'* ('we want to stay what we are'); bordering Belgium, France and Germany, Luxembourg has defiantly retained its language, culture and cuisine despite its geography, and knows how to unwind with a good glass of wine, too (it has one of the world's highest rates of wine consumption).

From top: With its no-Sunday-shopping policy, Luxemboug offers an opportunity to relax and enjoy the company of family and friends; rows of vines in Remich, Luxembourg. **Previous page:** Browsers at Bruges Fish Market.

TOP INSIGHTS for LIFE

SMARTS, NOT SIZE

Not even 1000 square miles in extent, Luxembourg has nevertheless maintained its language and defended its identity not by throwing its weight around, but by being savvy. Neutral until just after WWII, when Nazi Germany invaded, Luxembourg moved quickly to help establish a more peaceful Europe in the aftermath of the war (it is one of six founder members of the EEC, the forerunner of the EU). Today

"Words are but dwarfs, examples are giants." – Luxembourgish proverb

its citizens have visa-free access to more than 180 destinations, which makes their passports the joint third most useful in the world. When you're smaller than Rhode Island, it pays to get along with others, near and far. Perhaps we could all learn something from that.

UNWIND WITH WINE

Viniculture has been a feature of southern Luxembourg since Roman times. With the Moselle River winding through beautiful countryside, the wines are truly delectable – and deeply appreciated. Although plenty of it gets exported, a study by the Wine Price Index found that the citizens of the Grand Duchy consume on average more wine per capita than the French or Portuguese. On the Route du Vin, even dedicated oenophiles may run into grapes they've never seen before. Maybe they're part of what accounts for Luxembourg's lofty rank in the UN's World Happiness Report.

NO SUNDAY SHOPPING

Shopping laws in Luxembourg still restrict most businesses' hours on Sundays, and also force them to close at a reasonable time during the week. Stores can apply to have one day of 24-hour service each year for a special occasion such as an annual sale, but most people prefer to guard against the creep of working hours.

DITCH THE TO-DO LIST

Whether or not you observe religious days of rest, it's a good principle to borrow. Pretend your local municipality has its own Sunday shopping laws, and you need to give one full day of the week up to nothing but leisure: no working and no ticking things off your to-do list in frantic fashion. It might just become a healthy habit.

EUROPE

THE NETHERLANDS

'Live and let live' could be the motto of the Netherlands; open-mindedness — to other cultures, to novel ideas, to new experiences — underpins Dutch culture.

POPULATION
17 million

The Netherlands
was the first
country to legalise
same-sex
marriage

NATIONALITIES
IN AMSTERDAM
176

With a cultural footprint disproportionately larger than its geographical one, the Netherlands is widely regarded as a bastion of liberalism. For centuries the country has provided a safe haven for those fleeing persecution, and each wave of new arrivals has added another facet to the character of this free-thinking, forward-looking nation. From a young age, Dutch children are taught about the importance of *verdraagzaamheid*

(tolerance), which entails respecting other people's attitudes, beliefs and individuality. The principle of freedom of choice has led the Netherlands to adopt progressive policies toward LGBTQI+ rights, euthanasia, soft drugs and more. Although there are cultural differences here – notably, between urban and rural regions – all Dutch people value plain speaking, a reflection of their belief that everything can, and indeed should, be talked about.

EUROPE

© photonaj/Getty Images

© Matt Munro/Lonely Planet, © Mark Read/Lonely Planet

Clockwise from top: A snowy forest walk near Utrecht; Roest's beach party presents a lively programme of club nights, live music, film and theatre; the red doors and window frames of the Roode Bioscoop facade in Amsterdam. **Previous page:** The traditional New Year's dive in Scheveningen.

TOP INSIGHTS for LIFE

TELL IT LIKE IT IS

The Dutch don't mince their words. This tendency to cut to the conversational chase, which outsiders might mistake for rudeness, stems from the influence of the 16th-century preacher John Calvin. Calvin never visited the Netherlands, but his branch of Protestantism took root here. Be straightforward, work hard, live frugally; although religious belief in general might be in decline (more than half the population have no affiliation), the tenets of Calvinism hold true for this nation of plain-speakers, particularly in the north. Straightforwardness of speech even has its own special word: *bespreekbaarheid*, which translates as 'speakability' and means that no topic is taboo.

"Human greatness does not lie in wealth or power, but in character and goodness." - Anne Frank, Dutch-Jewish diarist

GET GEZELLIG

The old friend whose company never fails to lift your spirits; the welcoming pub where you feel safe and stress-free; good times spent in the presence of your loved ones – all these scenarios reflect the concept of *gezelligheid*, which lies at the core of Dutch culture. With overtones of Denmark's *hygge* and Germany's *gemütlichkeit*, *gezelligheid* is ultimately untranslatable, although the words convivial, comfortable and cosy are often employed to describe it. In essence, it's a know-it-when-you-feel-it experience that might, for example, arise from a night out with friends that ends in the warm embrace of a wood-panelled *bruin café* (brown cafe); equally, a visit to your beloved grandparents could be just as *gezellig*.

SWEET FA

Tired of trying to be mindful? Perhaps you should give *niksen* a go instead. While mindfulness involves bringing one's attention to bear on the present, the latter – a Dutch verb that means

WALK ON THE WILD SIDE

The next time it starts blowing a gale, take a leaf out of the Dutch playbook and pull on a warm, waterproof coat rather than staying cooped up indoors. An ever-accumulating stack of research says that walking of any form is good for you, but a brisk one in a bracing wind stimulates a special sort of elation, re-establishing a connection to the elements.

TAKE TO TWO WHEELS

Amsterdam has suffered from its own popularity in recent years, attracting more visitors that it can comfortably handle. But the majority of them stay in the city centre. Escape the crowds by hiring a bike (tip: go for one without branding to blend in) and head for a less well-known neighbourhood such as bohemian De Pijp, a happy hunting ground for bruin cafés aglow with gezellig.

'doing nothing' – is a licence to let it go; not so much being in the moment as just, well, being. In our busy, always-on age, there's something startling about the notion of switching off completely. But some people claim it has the same stress-busting benefits as meditation, lauding niksen as an antidote to the modern scourge of burnout. In theory, it's easy to try – just plonk yourself down in a comfy chair and stare out of the window with no particular purpose in mind (no, you can't fiddle with your phone); in practice, it might not be so straightforward – after all, when was the last time you managed to do absolutely nothing for 10 minutes?

WALK IN THE WIND

In some cultures, the default response to a windy day is to hunker down and wait for the weather to take a turn for the better – but to the Dutch it's an opportunity to blow away the figurative cobwebs. Uitwaaien, which has no precise translation, is the act of going out for a walk in the wind, getting fresh air into your lungs and putting your thoughts in order. Also applied to a jog or a bike ride in blustery conditions, uitwaaien is

believed to be good for body and mind; it keeps the stresses and strains of daily life in check, lifting your mood in as little as five minutes.

TAKE THE PLUNGE

On January 1, tens of thousands of hardy souls gather at locations around the Netherlands to take part in Nieuwjaarsduik (New Year's Dive). Since the 1960s, the Dutch have plunged into the country's chilly seas and icy lakes to celebrate the coming year, clad in nothing more than orange hats and swimwear (and some of them don't even bother with that, preferring to brave the freezing water naked). The most popular mass dive happens at Scheveningen, a district of The Hague, where 10,000 people wade into the North Sea before warming up with cups of pea soup or hot chocolate. Risk of hypothermia aside, Nieuwjaarsduik is a grand exercise in social bonding, and sure to stir the blood; you'll certainly start the new year feeling f-f-f-fresh.

Explore Amsterdam on two wheels for the true Dutch experience.

EUROPE

DENMARK

Hygge may have captured the imagination of happiness-seekers the world over, but Denmark owes its place atop the world's lifestyle league tables to much more than a definition-defying concept of cosiness.

**POPULATION
5.8 million**

**TOTAL LENGTH
OF CYCLE
TRACKS AND
LANES
> 12,000km**

**28 Danish restau-
rants received
35 Michelin stars
in 2019**

Year after year, Denmark finds itself near the top of multiple official lists measuring happiness and quality of life. Can this compact country really be the Scandinavian utopia it's portrayed to be? Though most Danes would modestly say there is always room for improvement, signs really do point to 'yes', and it's not all down to *hygge*. The reality of Danish life is far less saccharine than that: here, a strong sense of

social responsibility is entwined with a deep and genuine trust of fellow citizens, institutions and public figures – honesty is assumed until it's proven otherwise. Add to this progressive attitudes toward work-life balance, green initiatives, a world-leading culinary movement, and the fact just about everything is beautifully designed, and it's little wonder that onlookers want a slice of the *smørrebrød*.

EUROPE

© ClarkandCompany/Getty Images

© Sarah Coghill/Lonely Planet, © Eugene Anball/500px

Clockwise from top: Foraging in the woods for seasonal produce; cycling is for the whole family in Denmark; a selection of smørrebrød (open-faced sandwiches) to go. **Previous page:** Al fresco dining on the Danish coastline.

TOP INSIGHTS for LIFE

WORK TO LIVE

Given that Denmark consistently ranks among the most productive countries in the world, one might imagine that it's a nation of workaholics, but not so. Working long hours is resolutely discouraged, and a general culture of flexible working ensures staff are able to spend time with family and friends, play sports or pursue hobbies. What's more, presenteeism gets short shrift: struggling into work stricken with flu wouldn't be considered heroic, but the height of bad manners. It really is true: a happy, healthy employee is an efficient one. Tell your boss.

"Enjoy life. There's plenty of time to be dead."
– Hans Christian Andersen, Danish author

TAKE TO TWO WHEELS

The Danes adopted cycling almost as soon as bikes were first brought to the country in the late 19th century. Seen as a straightforward way to get around (aided by Denmark's relatively flat topography), bikes also became a great leveller, as people from all walks of life cycled together, regardless of social status. The advent of motor vehicles saw their popularity dip for a time, but a concerted effort to introduce country-wide cycle infrastructure has made riding a bike in Denmark, well, as easy as riding a bike. Today, 90% of Danes own one, and they're used for over a quarter of all journeys under 5km. This integral part of the Danish identity brings with it a catalogue of proven benefits, too: fewer cars means less pollution and, in Copenhagen alone, cycling is directly responsible for 1.1 million fewer sick days every year.

THE LAW OF JANTE

Janteloven (The Law of Jante), or a version of it, is understood across all Nordic countries, but it was a Danish-Norwegian writer, Aksel Sandemose, who famously satirised the mindset in his 1933 novel *A Fugitive Crosses His Tracks*. In the fictional town of Jante, residents must follow 10 rules that

AARHUS EATING

For a taste of New Nordic food without breaking the bank at a Michelin-starred restaurant, head to Aarhus for its annual Food Festival (www.foodfestival.dk). Taking place each September, it's the largest event of its kind in northern Europe, and showcases local producers, as well as serving up plenty of opportunities to try mouth-watering produce from in and around the Bay of Aarhus itself.

159

FIRESIDE READING

Learning about *hygge* and how to incorporate it into your life can be a cosy endeavour in itself. Settle into the comfiest chair you can find to read Meik Wiking's *The Little Book of Hygge: The Danish Way to Live Well.* As CEO of the Happiness Research Institute, what he doesn't know about quality of life probably isn't worth knowing.

place the community above all else. Sandemose exaggerated for effect (the first rule coldly states 'do not think you are special'), and yet, even today, it's considered improper to boast about individual achievements. Many claim this entrenched attitude is holding Danes back. However, with the country leading the way in social equality, healthcare and welfare, it remains clear that the general philosophy of working together for the common good has its benefits.

HAPPINESS IN HYGGE

Not long ago, few people outside of Scandinavia would have known the word *hygge*, let alone how to pronounce it (it's *hoo-guh*, FYI). But it's become a global sensation, inspiring a bookcase-worth of how-to guides, and lighting up dollar signs in the eyes of scented-candle manufacturers the world over. To reduce it to a trend would be a serious disservice, though: *hygge* is a feeling, an atmosphere, not a product. At its heart, it's about slowing down to spend quality time with the people you love, and a warm, cosy, *hyggelig* moment could just as easily be experienced during

a simple picnic in the park as on a cold winter night, huddled around a roaring fire with a mug of hot chocolate – fluffy slippers optional.

SEASONAL FARE

Denmark's status as a culinary capital is world-renowned, but it's easy to forget that it's a relatively recent phenomenon. In 2004, a group of Nordic chefs joined forces to pen the New Nordic Manifesto, a set of guidelines for producing first-rate dishes using local produce in a sustainable way, while committing to the highest ethical standards. Eating the New Nordic way is about combining the freshest flavours into beautifully presented, healthy meals. The movement has spread far beyond the much-celebrated Noma, where the cuisine was pioneered by René Redzepi and Claus Meyer, and now serves as the inspiration for Michelin-starred restaurants and food trucks alike, both in Denmark and beyond.

New Nordic cuisine
champions local,
sustainable produce and
beautiful presentation.

EUROPE

NORWAY

The Norwegians' zeal for the great outdoors runs deeper than the fjords, and spending time in nature is more than a national pastime — it's in the very fabric of the culture.

POPULATION
5.3 million

% OF ELEC-
TRICITY FROM
RENEWABLE
SOURCES
97

WINTER OLYM-
PICS MEDALS
368

It's almost impossible to witness Norway's natural majesty and not be awestricken. The glacier-hewn landscape is at once inviting and intimidating, and has inspired people to hike, ski, write, sing and make art for almost as long as it's been inhabited. Like its Nordic neighbours, Norway has an egalitarian outlook, and its vast sovereign wealth fund – amassed only in the last 60 years – has been judiciously invested to fund public services for the benefit of generations to come. Though Norway's riches came from oil, almost all of its electricity is generated from renewable sources: the country (just like the tourist board slogan says) is largely powered by nature and, if domination in elite winter sports is anything to go by, so are its people. Environmentally conscious and civic-minded, Norway is looking forward to a clean, sustainable future.

EUROPE

© Henryk Welle/Getty Images

© Emma Wood/Alamy Stock Photo, ©V. Belov/Shutterstock

Clockwise from top: Get some perspective in Norway's Lofoten Islands; sledding with husky dogs; a Sámi woman in traditional attire at the Easter Festival held in Kautokeino. **Previous page:** Geirangerfjord and Seven Sisters waterfall.

TOP INSIGHTS for LIFE

BEST FOOT FORWARD

If you want to feel like a Norwegian, *gå på tur*. It literally means 'go for a walk' but don't be caught out; in Norway, this implies that you'll be embarking on a sizeable hike, usually in nature, just for fun. With a landscape so beguiling, it's unsurprising that outdoor activities are so popular here, but the country's changeable and sometimes severe weather can often prove challenging. According to the Norwegians, though, 'there is no bad weather, only bad clothes', and the environment is ours not to conquer, but to respect.

DUGNAD DAYS

With its roots in centuries-old agricultural practices, where communities would band together for arduous labour, *dugnad* is a kind of voluntary work in which everyone is expected to participate when the need arises. Especially common in the weeks leading up to Norway's National Day on 17 May, *dugnad* could take the form of planting a shared garden or even assembling office furniture at work. It isn't always met with enthusiasm but, apart from getting a job done, *dugnad* is often seen as a good opportunity to bond with neighbours and colleagues.

RAMPAGING RUSS

Russefeiring is a month-long fiesta of hijinks undertaken by teenagers in their graduating year, before their final exams. Mostly wearing red or blue overalls, the students complete dares and cause good-natured mayhem ahead of the final celebrations on 17 May.

SONGS OF SÁPMI

As the indigenous people of Lapland (Sápmi), the Sámi have an intimate knowledge of Scandinavia's frozen north which they communicate through a unique form of song, the *yoik*. Using haunting melodies, the singer conveys the spirit of an animal, place or situation. Sadly, centuries of oppression meant that the *yoik* disappeared from some regions of Sápmi entirely, but a new generation of Sámi are reviving their culture.

EASTER, SÁMI-STYLE

Learn more about Sámi culture at the annual Easter festival in Kautokeino, Finnmark. The Sámi move with the seasons, and lighter days and thawing snow ushers in the time for weddings and religious celebrations. You'll have the chance to hear many *yoiks* in the Sámi Grand Prix competition, as well as witness the reindeer-racing world championships, among other traditional events.

165

EUROPE

SWEDEN

With an enduring commitment to coffee breaks and a knack for knowing just how much is best, Sweden is the epitome of moderation – but with a side of something sweet.

POPULATION
10 million

% OF
HOUSEHOLD
WASTE SENT TO
LANDFILL
< 1

AVERAGE
LENGTH OF A
FIKA BREAK
13 mins

If your idea of living well is revelling in a state of maximum decadence, you probably won't glean many tips from traditional Swedish culture – it's not how things are done here. But the Swedes aren't left wanting; on the contrary, they endeavour to have *enough* of everything: enough for themselves, enough to share. The famed Scandinavian community-mindedness is just as strong here as in other Nordic nations, and manifests in a variety of ways – from high taxes translating into top-notch public services, to citizens engaged in bold, global initiatives to tackle climate change. Come Midsummer, though, community means dancing like a frog around the maypole, and gorging on strawberry cake and *snaps*. At least the aftermath is bound to be well managed: almost all of Sweden's household waste is recycled in some way, whether it's reforming bottles, generating energy or synthesising biofuels.

© phM2019/Shutterstock

left & right: © Matt Munro/Lonely Planet

Clockwise from top: Stockholm's Old Town; dancing around a Midsummer pole on Blidö in the Stockholm Archipelago; wildflowers gathered at Midsummer. **Previous page:** Embrace *flygskam*: with homes like this one in Ramkvilla, Småland, who needs to fly anywhere?

TOP INSIGHTS for LIFE

LIVING LAGOM

Going over the top just isn't the Swedish way. From the size and model of car you drive, to the length of time you spend at work, or even the amount of blueberry jam you daub on your waffle, the idea of living a life where everything is enjoyed in moderation can be summed up by the word *lagom*. Thought to have originated with the Viking-era phrase *laget om* (around the group), an expression describing how to share food and drink so that everyone receives just the right amount, the concept permeates right through Swedish culture, ensuring that everything is fair and 'as it should be'.

"Contentment is the only real wealth." – *Alfred Nobel, Swedish engineer and philanthropist*

DYING TO TRY DÖSTÄDNING

Far less depressing than it sounds, the pragmatic task of *döstädning* (death cleaning) is the act of assessing your possessions and paring them down so as not to be a burden on the family and friends you leave behind. There's no reason to wait until your twilight years to start preparations, though – *döstädning* can be undertaken at any age. Not so much a cultural phenomenon as a sensible approach to clutter, it's nevertheless a thoroughly Swedish approach to dealing with the affairs of later life: practical, effective and logical.

THE FLYGSKAM FACTOR

Swedes have been at the forefront of highlighting environmental concerns in recent years: Greta Thunberg's weekly 'skolstrejk för klimatet' (school strike for climate) demonstrations outside the Swedish parliament inspired a generation of young people around the world and, in tandem, *flygskam* (literally meaning 'flight shame'), gathered momentum. Championed by Swedes such as Olympic biathlete Björn Ferry, the premise is straightforward:

FEEL SOME FLYG- SKAM

You needn't go as far as chartering a sailboat to cross the Atlantic a la Greta (though you can if you want to), but the next time you're travelling, whether you're going to Ghent or Glasgow, give some thought to how you'll get there. Is taking the train a realistic option? The journey might just end up being as exciting as the destination.

DÖSTÄD-NING DECLUT-TERING

Whatever your stage of life, decluttering your home can be a genuinely cathartic exercise, and while the idea of *döstädning* might not seem particularly uplifting, Margareta Magnusson's lighthearted book *The Gentle Art of Swedish Death Cleaning* explains how purging your belongings can help to make life run more smoothly.

seek out more environmentally sustainable alternatives to flying wherever possible. And it seems to be working: in the space of just over a year, the number of domestic flights in Sweden fell by around 3%, while train journeys have risen by almost 5%, and the message is spreading fast. With more people demanding alternatives, travelling responsibly will only get easier.

DON'T JUST JOG – PLOG

Some wellbeing trends are little more than a quick-fix pick-me-up and, in the case of plogging, that's the intention: it's just jogging while picking up litter. Plogging pioneer Erik Ahlström began by stopping to collect rubbish on his cycle-commute in Stockholm. This quickly progressed to him taking a bag for rubbish when he went out jogging. Others joined him, and Plogga, as the official organisation is known, was born. It's since become a bona fide movement, with regular events taking place up and down Sweden and beyond. Participants enjoy a double dose of feel-good vibes – all the endorphins from a run, with the added benefit of doing something positive for the

environment. Best of all, it's free, and you can do it any time, anywhere.

LESS YAKKA, MORE *FIKA*

Finally, an indulgence! Okay, so they'll be all *lagom* about it (just the one cinnamon bun, please), but *fika* – having coffee and cake with friends or colleagues – is as much of a Swedish institution as Ikea. More than a simple tea break, it's a ritual of near-religious importance, and most people make time to do this daily, often twice. It's not necessarily long – 15 minutes is enough – but taking time out of the working day isn't just about getting another caffeine fix; it's been linked to increased happiness and productivity, too. Swedish studies have shown that *fika* breaks can help to reduce burnout, and that employees generate more creative ideas over an informal *fika* than during a traditional meeting. It's a science-backed breather; pass the *kladdkaka*.

Al fresco feasting at
Midsummer on Blidö.

EUROPE

FINLAND

Ever the strong, silent type, Finland quietly thrives on a habit of getting hot, but this land of fresh air, forests and lakes ensures there's every opportunity to cool down.

POPULATION
5.5 million

RANKING ON
UN'S GLOBAL
HAPPINESS
REPORT
1st

SAUNAS PER
FINN
0.54

Quietly topping the UN's Global Happiness Report for two years in a row, Finland has much to shout about, though the Finns are more likely to play down their success with self-deprecating humour than yell it from the treetops. An outstanding education system, social safety net and willingness to test progressive policies such as universal basic income mean the Finnish quality of life is envied around the world; and that's before we mention the surroundings. For every person in Finland, there are 4500 trees, so the tranquillity of a woodland walk is never far away. While small talk is generally eschewed, it would be wrong to imagine this to be a country solely of silent contemplation. Where else but Finland could have brought us the unmitigated joy of world championships dedicated to air guitar and – appropriately for the birthplace of Nokia – mobile phone throwing. And why not?

© wmaster890/Getty Images

© James Bedford/Lonely Planet, © Yoann JEZEQUEL Photography/Getty Images

Clockwise from top: A cottage in one of Finland's pristine pine forests; taking a sauna is a classic Finnish experience; cruising the Turku archipelago. **Previous page:** Bathing in Lake Saimaa after a sauna.

TOP INSIGHTS for LIFE

SWEAT IT OUT

Few customs have become so deeply ensconced in Finland's national psyche as taking a sauna. Though far from a rare indulgence – most Finns sweat it out at least once a week – some straightforward etiquette applies, whether in a traditional smoke sauna or a modern incarnation: get naked (no exceptions); shower; relax in the heat for as long as you can stand; repeat as desired. Water is ladled over hot stones to produce *löyly* (fragrant steam) and it's not unusual to be whipped with a *vihta* (a bunch of birch branches), believed to boost circulation. Studies suggest that saunas can improve cardiovascular health as well as conditions such as psoriasis and asthma. Besides that, it's simply a chance to unwind, and is all the more invigorating when combined with a refreshing dip in a lake or ice-cold plunge pool.

SILENCE IS GOLDEN

Many cultures recognise a version of the phrase 'silence is golden'. In Finland, they say '*puhuminen on hopeaa, vaikeneminen kultaa*' (speech is silver, silence is gold) and, generally speaking, it's looked upon as guidance to live by. Rather than exchange niceties unnecessarily, Finns generally tend to keep quiet but, far from being hostile, the attitude promotes learning to be at peace with your company and surroundings without feeling the need to interrupt the tranquillity.

A TRULY EPIC POEM

After years of painstaking work to document hundreds of Finnish folk songs, tales and mythology, philologist Elias Lönnrot combined them to create *The Kalevala*, a poem portraying Finnish culture and detailing events from the world's creation to gripping quests for marriage. Published in 1835, the masterwork is credited with helping to define the national identity, shape the Finnish language and galvanise the nation to gain independence from Russia. Today, it's considered Finland's national epic poem and painters, classical composers and even metal bands still look to it for inspiration.

RUSKA RAM-BLING

Earmark late September and early October for a pilgrimage to one of Finland's protected forests such as Koli National Park. The Finns call this colourful period *ruska*, and a trip to the forest now encourages visitors to appreciate the bright but fleeting rusts and ochres of autumn before the colours are replaced by the inky darkness of winter.

RUSSIA

Their country is often over-simplified and misunderstood, but beyond the stereotypes of stoicism and gruffness, Russians are realists with a deep vein of wisdom, self-sufficiency and intelligent scepticism.

POPULATION
142 million

OFFICIAL LAN-
GUAGES SPO-
KEN NATIONAL-
LY/REGIONALLY
1/35

% OF FOOD
GROWN IN DA-
CHA GARDENS
40

Ethnic Russians populate a vast swathe of eastern Europe and northern Asia, all the way to the Pacific coast opposite Japan. Yet the world's largest country is also a federation incorporating dozens of other nationalities, many with their own languages and beliefs. Autonomous republics and regions abound, including those for Muslim Chechens, Buddhist Kalmyks and shamanistic Tuvans – there's even a 'Jewish autonomous region' around Biro-

bidzhan. Still frequently viewed through a prism of Cold War demonisation, Russia's sheer diversity is often overlooked. It's a tough place to live. Siberian summers can top 35°C, yet temperatures drop below -50°C in February. Distances can be vast. And a brutal history has imposed a terrible series of invasions, wars, famines and political difficulties. Together, these have served to instill in the population a dogged strength and a huge degree of resilience.

© IRINA KROLEVETC/Getty Images

© Philip Lee Harvey/Lonely Plane, © danishc/Getty Imagest

Clockwise from top: Ritual shaman pillars on Cape Burhan on Olkhon Island; birch brooms and wooden pails at a Russian *banya*; a statue of a railway worker in Siberia. **Previous page:** In winter Siberia's temperatures can drop below -50°C.

TOP INSIGHTS for LIFE

SMILING IS SPECIAL

First-time visitors to Russia often wonder why the random people they encounter seem so gruff. Many jump to an entirely wrong conclusion. Russians certainly don't lack a rich sense of humour and the moment you've broken the ice with local friends, you'll find faces that beam with joy. However, most Russians believe that a smile should be sincere, not used as a token of meaningless politeness. Indeed, some consider that smiling at strangers is a sign of madness.

"The immensity of Russia, the absence of boundaries [is] expressed in the structure of the Russian soul." – Nikolai Berdyaev, Russian philosopher

NATION OF COTTAGE GARDENERS

Most dictionaries translate the Russian term *dacha* as 'a country cottage used as a second home'. However, a crucial aspect of most *dachas* is the garden plot on which each stands. Nothing better sums up the resilience of suburban Russians than their ability to be almost self-sufficient through cultivating fruit and vegetables in such gardens, with plenty being pickled for winter use and squirreled away in special bunker-like storerooms that are appended to many a Soviet-era tower block. The fact that Russia survived potential famine in the early 1990s was in large part due to *dacha* produce, and in 2003 a government law enshrined the right to grow one's own food in plots of up to 2.75 hectares.

EXTREME ECOPOLIS

This desire for self-sufficiency has been taken to an extreme at the lonely Siberian 'ecopolis' of the back-to-nature Vissarion sect. Followers of former policeman turned 'messiah' Sergey Torop teach themselves to make as much as possible by hand without resorting to monetary transaction. They shun

LEARN TO LOVE VODKA

Central to many Russian celebrations, vodka consumption is an art form. To ensure pleasure without pain or paralytic drunkenness, Russians always drink shots down in one. Breathe out heavily through the nose after consumption and ensure the right food combination, perhaps lining the stomach in advance with oily fish, raw egg, sunflower oil or – like the Ukrainians – cubes of pork fat.

BE WEATHER-POSITIVE

Russians say 'there's no such thing as bad weather, only bad clothing'. If you wear the right layers, even a typical Siberian winter's day of around -25°C feels pleasant. The Russians' weather-positive attitude is a transferable skill. So slip on your waterproofs and go for a walk in a heavy shower, lifting your face to the sky and giving thanks for the raindrops.

smoking, alcohol and processed food, tapping birch-tree sap as a refreshing cool beverage in place of bottled soft drinks. A central idea of the apocalyptic creed is that a global catastrophe will wipe out most of humanity, leaving the Vissarions as one of very few communities both remote enough and suitably skilled to survive in a world where modern society has collapsed.

BIRCHED IN THE BANYA

Few simple pleasures trump the joy of soaking in the banya (bathhouse). Though the central steam room is outwardly similar to a Scandinavian sauna (if perhaps a touch cooler and more humid) the banya is more than just a place to detox, the experience is also a way to warm up and socialise. Babies used to be delivered in the village banya's outer room; the traditional birch-wood fuel was believed to have antibacterial properties. Today, an important part of the banya ritual is to invigorate the skin by thwacking one another with veniki (leaf-on bundles of water-softened young oak or birch twigs).

CONSULT A QAM

Shamanic beliefs based on animistic spirit worlds are widely seen as archaic or New Age in the West. However, in several of the Russian Federation's more remote regions, especially Tuva, it would be perfectly normal to seek a consultation with a qam (shaman), much as one might visit a clinic. The shaman's first concern is a holistic reading of your soul and few Tuvans doubt the reality of the spirits evoked. A valued practitioner is believed to communicate and harmonise with such natural spirits, whether to aid health, bring rain, oversee funerals, tell fortunes or improve harvests.

SPIRIT OF GOGOL'S OVERCOAT

Russia has a magnificent literary and musical heritage, often grand in scale and tragic in theme. However, a very Russian sense of sardonic humour, added to a frequent need to circumvent censorship, means that there has long been an appetite for allegory and absurdism. Few writers have pulled off the genre so brilliantly as Nikolai Gogol in his 1842 short story The Overcoat – a cult classic.

A shaman tends the campfire at an internatinal gathering of shamans on the island of Olkhon.

EUROPE

LITHUANIA

Lithuanians' quiet determination not to conform has ensured their culture and traditions have weathered many storms, and living well here hinges on the rejuvenating power of nature.

POPULATION
2.8 million

**HEIGHT OF
TALLEST SAND
DUNE**
52m

**LENGTH OF
COASTLINE**
262km

The last country in Europe to de-nounce paganism, Lithuania has a history of refusing to conform. While the Baroque architecture of the capital, Vilnius, is a familiar kind of beauty, you needn't look far to see a subversive undercurrent: the self-declared artists' republic of Užupis, for example, and uniquely crafted church crosses hint at a rebellious spirit amplified, rather than dampened, during periods of occu-pation. Living well – and authentically

– has at times been a political act for Lithuanians. The rejuvenating power of nature has been a constant, though, and the country's pine-scented land-scape, rich peat mud and natural miner-al waters have long lured city-dwellers to seek traditional treatments for what ails them. Mud baths and amber mas-sages offer a Baltic boost in spa towns such as Druskininkai, Birštonas and the incomparably beautiful Neringa, on the windswept Curonian Spit.

EUROPE

Clockwise from top: Vilnius' Unesco-listed Old Town; a commemorative tile celebrates a peaceful protest against the Soviet occupation in 1989; Lithuania's Hill of Crosses. **Previous page:** Trakai Island Castle stands out against a winter landscape.

TOP INSIGHTS for LIFE

CROSS PURPOSES

Kryždirbystė, the Unesco-recognised art of making Lithuanian crosses, blends Lithuania's pagan and Christian heritage. Carved from oak or wrought in iron, the most poignant collection is found at the haunting Hill of Crosses. Since the mid-1800s, Lithuanians have come to this small hill near the town of Šiauliai to plant crosses as they remember and pray for loved ones. The Soviets repeatedly destroyed this collection but Lithuanians simply returned to plant more, and the site became symbolic of the people's determination to express their faith in the face of oppression. The pilgrimages continue today, and there are now over 100,000 crosses on the hill.

LITHUANIAN GOLD

Often called Lithuanian gold, Baltic amber has been prized for millennia, with archaeological evidence of amber craft in the region dating as far back as 3000 BCE. Market stalls, boutiques and museum shops ply amber jewellery all over Lithuania, but the fossilised tree resin has also been used in various treatments since ancient times. Today, proponents of the natural remedy say that amber in solid, powdered or emulsified form can help with ailments including anxiety, headaches, haemorrhoids, insomnia and acne. Three tonnes of the gem has even been used to create the world's first amber sauna, near the west-coast town of Palanga.

WISH UPON A TILE

In 1989, two million citizens of Estonia, Latvia and Lithuania formed the longest ever human chain to stand against the Soviet occupation. The Baltic Way stretched for 675km from Tallinn to Vilnius, where a tile has been laid to commemorate this powerful but peaceful protest. Marked with the word stebuklas (miracle), it is located in the city's Cathedral Square and has become a symbol of hope; it's said that by standing on the tile and turning round three times, your most ardent wishes will be granted, just as they were three decades ago for the Lithuanian people.

SOMETHING IN THE WATER

For a thirst-quenching experience, head to Birštonas and drink from the natural mineral water springs first noted in medieval times. Decorative pavilions were installed in the 19th century to ensure direct plumbing to the source: simply take a reusable cup to fill from the fountain and you could reap some of the reported health benefits, which devotees claim include a reduction in inflammation.

EUROPE

POLAND

Poland's vast natural spaces and diverse flora and fauna may be little known outside of the country, but its warm-hearted people will be only too happy to share.

POPULATION
38.4 million

% OF FOREST COVER
about 30

AMOUNT OF VODKA PRODUCED EVERY YEAR
260 million litres

The notion of living well in Poland may stereotypically extend to hearty meals and vodka toasts, but that's only part of the story. Though the great hospitality of the Poles means a guest never goes hungry (or indeed thirsty), the country's landscape ensures near-limitless opportunities for horizon-expanding outdoor pursuits, which its people embrace with passion. The rugged peaks of the Carpathian Mountains in the south call to be hiked in summer or skied in winter; the lakeland in the northeastern region of Masuria is ideal for kayaking; and abundant forests offer rich pickings for the experienced and novice forager alike. But for many Poles, spiritual fulfilment means more than this. Though religious belief is generally declining across Europe, Poland stands in contrast, with 86% of its citizens describing themselves as religious, making it one of the most devout countries on the continent.

EUROPE

© kpzfoto/Alamy Stock Photo

left & right: © Matt Munro/Lonely Planet

Clockwise from top: Foraging for mushrooms in Mazovia; St John's Chapel, carved out underground in Wieliczka salt mine; cakes on display in Kraków. **Previous page:** A Polish highlander wearing a hand-embroidered jacket.

TOP INSIGHTS for LIFE

GOD IN THE HOUSE

If you're lucky enough to be invited into a Polish home, you can expect to be given the VIP treatment: as the Polish proverb says, 'Gość w dom, Bóg w dom' ('Guest in the house, God in the house'), meaning there's no greater honour than to entertain. Arrive hungry, as your host will likely prepare a hot meal, and accepting seconds (or thirds) is regarded as complimentary rather than gluttonous.

"After slender 'boletus' the young ladies throng, Which is famed as the colonel of mushrooms in song." – From the epic poem Pan Tadeusz by Adam Mickiewicz

FEATHERED FRIENDS

Over 50,000 white storks (*bociany* in Polish) flock to Poland each year between April and August. The Poles believe that having one of the leggy birds' nests on or around your home brings good luck, and it's also thought they protect against lightning strikes. In fact, storks are so revered here that many Poles coax them to make a nest by creating special frames or placing a tractor tyre in a convenient place on their property. The village of Żywkowo, close to the Russian border, must be the luckiest in all of Poland: the birds outnumber the locals almost four to one.

MUSHROOM PICKING

Foraging for fungi is a national pastime. Come the autumn, Poles head to the forest to harvest nature's bounty; and so long as they don't cause damage to the environment in doing so, they're free to take as many wild mushrooms as they can gather. For the eagle-eyed picker, varieties such as chanterelles and porcini are up for grabs, and from a young age children are taught how to recognise the delicious from the deadly, as well as how fungi can be used in wholesome, traditional cuisine such as *pierogi*.

STORY OF A STORK

To understand more about Poles' reverence for these lanky, charismatic birds, take a flight of fancy and read Josepha K. Contoski's *Bocheck in Poland*. The prize-winning children's book follows the story of Bocheck as he tries to recover a golden anklet, so he can fulfil his father's wish and become a high-flying stork.

THE CZECH REPUBLIC

Educated yet understated, cultured but unpretentious, Czechs are famously open-minded, irreligious beer lovers. The Czech Republic has the lowest unemployment in the EU and is one of the world's top five countries for income equality.

POPULATION
10.7 million

% OF POPULA-
TION WITHOUT
RELIGIOUS
AFFILIATION
72

Czechs drink 140
litres of beer per
year (the highest
in the world)

The Czech Republic (shortened to 'Czechia' since 2016) is a Slavic, Central European nation that's a little more Germanic than Slovenia, more urban and less religious than Slovakia, and more grittily industrial than Austria. This was the land upon which Good King Wenceslas looked out in the popular Christmas carol, which glorifies redistributing wealth to the needy rather than a Bethlehem nativity. The historical Wenceslas (Vaclav 1, 907-935 CE) ruled over Bohemia, the northwestern region where a certain 'Bohemian' spirit still remains. However, despite centuries of achievement, Czech people tend to be self-deprecating, with a humour that underlines the plucky little nation's ability to survive. Thus in one classic gag, when faced with a shark, a Czech swimmer starts singing the national anthem *Kde domov můj* (Where is my home?). Disgusted, the shark turns away muttering: 'I don't eat the homeless!'

Clockwise from top: Prague's Charles Bridge and Old Town beyond; the Czech Republic is famous for its brewing history; a Czech *panelák* (giant housing tower block). **Previous page:** A forested path near Edmunds Gorge in Bohemian Switzerland National Park.

TOP INSIGHTS for LIFE

THE ORIGINAL PILSNER

The Czech Republic is one of the world's great brewing nations, and Czechs drink more beer per capita than anyone else. The very term Pils/Pilsener is synonymous with Plzen, the republic's fourth biggest city. Pouring beer with the right-sized head is considered an art form and the froth itself is said to have stomach-settling health properties. Beer even influenced Czech democracy: during the 1989 Velvet Revolution that brought an end to the communist 'People's Republic' of Czechoslovakia, the people's bars handed out the people's beer to the people – sustaining them as they marched around Prague, night after night, to demand a change of government.

BOHEMIAN TENDENCIES

Since the 19th century, 'Bohemian' in the English language has come to suggest behaviour that is socially unorthodox and sexually uninhibited. This nuance came via a French usage whose historical link to medieval Bohemia is far from provable, but nonetheless, it's hard not to be struck by the country's very open, casual attitude to (hetero)sexuality. This is especially clear in the multi-layered fiction of Czech author Milan Kundera. And with some of the world's highest levels of professed atheism, many Czechs thrive without any fear of divine retribution in choosing their own life path.

HAPPY IN PANELÁKY

While tourists in Prague will be dazzled by the opulent castle and the winding medieval streets, over 52% of Czechs live in functional apartments, most of them within giant blocks known as *paneláky* on 20th-century housing estates called *sídliště*. Such estates exist across the former Eastern Bloc countries, but some Czech cities have overwhelming proportions of them: the mining town of Most, for example, is 80% *paneláky*. As Czechs are generally extremely unpretentious people, there can be a certain inverted snobbery in living in a *panelák*. At least one ex-prime minister still does.

EUROPE

SLOVAKIA

Slovakians love nature – no wonder, given the proximity of forests and mountains to wherever you are in the country – and visitors inevitably end up falling for the nation's rural charms.

POPULATION
5.4 million

% OF COUNTRY
COVERED IN
FOREST
40

REGIONAL
VARIETIES OF
FOLK COSTUME
26

What really gets Slovaks going is the great outdoors – and they're blessed with plenty of it. You can walk from Bratislava in the west to the Ukranian border in the east almost exclusively via woods, hills and mountains, barely crossing a main road in the whole 750-odd km journey. Nearly half the population lives in the countryside and even in Slovakia's biggest city you're only a few miles away from lonely forests. Almost every Slovak has or aspires to have a *chata* (cottage) in the woodsy uplands because being close to nature matters so much. As a result of this, the country has a well-developed network of hiking, cycling and cross-country skiing trails, which benefit body and mind. This nation has also retained much of its folklore and many of its castles, so when you head into that unspoiled countryside, it's easy to believe you're travelling into the heart of a fairy tale.

© Juraj Kamenicky/Shutterstock

© kovop58/Shutterstock

From top: Hikers in the Western Tatras; an accordion-player entertains in Slovak folk dress.
Previous page: Folk architecture in Zdar under the Belianske Tatras.

TOP INSIGHTS for LIFE

FOLK FETISH

Slovakia has an unusually rich folklore tradition for its size. Experts have identified an astonishing 26 regions with distinctive folk costumes, and if you factor in the many folk festivals, characterised by the playing of traditional musical instruments such as the fujara, plus the *skanzenov*, or open-air ethnographic museums depicting times past, you have one of the world's most vivid montages of country living across the centuries. Rural life is not obsolete here, but real, relevant, thriving and to be enjoyed.

"...the three fundamental pillars of Slovak life; the family, nature and homeland." – Peter Karpinský, Slovak writer

FIRE UP THE OPEKAČKA

Slovaks have a passion for *opekačka*, or barbecue, in the great outdoors. Yes, you'll see the standard charcoal or gas-fired grill in many people's gardens, but deep in the forests and far up the mountains, you'll also find an abundance of the traditional open fire variety surrounded by a circle of stones, upon which Slovaks cook specially designed *špekačky*, or sausages on sticks. *Opekačka* is not just about eating meat and drinking beer, but about doing so with loved ones in a beautiful place.

MAGIC COTTAGES

Owning one house is rarely enough for an upwardly mobile Slovak; they will also want a *chata*, or mountain cottage, for weekend getaways. The *chata* is not just an aspiration for the privileged few, though: numerous public *chaty* dot mountain ranges such as the High Tatras, allowing nature-loving Slovaks to spend the night in the forests and mountains. Many are in off-the-grid locations only reachable by foot or bike, so they encourage physical activity and provide Slovaks with a break from our high-tech world.

GET FOLKSY IN THE COUNTRYSIDE

Forget the city; make a beeline for the countryside instead. That's where you'll gain a real insight into Slovakia's soul and learn how to cherish its rural charm. In particular, seek out one of the country's numerous folk festivals; try the big one at Východná, which takes place in early July in the shadow of the mighty Tatras.

EUROPE

HUNGARY

Equally fond of the relaxing and the rigorous, Hungarians are world-leaders when it comes to soaking in hot springs, sharpening their wits playing chess and riding horses like the wind.

POPULATION
9.8 million

THERMAL SPRINGS
> 1300

HUNGARIAN CHESS GRAND-MASTERS
57

In its day, the Hungarian Empire was one of the most formidable cultural and military organisations ever seen in the heart of Europe, and Hungarians remain proud of their country's historic achievements, bending the ear of anyone who shows even the slightest interest in them. This strong sense of patriotism has helped the nation to protect its language and heritage – and the people are also united by their pastimes and passions. Chief among them is bathing in the nutrient-rich thermal springs, which are scattered throughout this flat, landlocked country. When they're not unwinding in Europe's bathhouse capital, Budapest, or taking a dip in the world's largest bathable thermal lake, Hévíz, Hungarians are often to be found stimulating the old grey matter with a game of chess, at which they excel, or riding their beloved horses across the continent's greatest grassland, Hortobágy.

© Robert Fesus/Getty Images

© Sarah Coghill/Lonely Planet, © Will Sanders/Lonely Planet

Clockwise from top: Hungary is famous for its equestrian spirit; bathers play a game of chess in Budapest's Széchenyi Baths; a snack stand on Margaret Island. **Previous page:** A bathing house on Lake Héviz.

TOP INSIGHTS for LIFE

BATHHOUSE BASKING

Hungary is blessed with so many natural thermal springs that the exact number is hard to establish. Budapest alone has more than 120 of them; and you can multiply that by a factor of more than 10 countrywide. No wonder, then, that a dip in the piping hot waters has been the major pastime here for centuries, from the Romans to the Turks, then the Hungarians and their myriad international visitors, who converge eagerly on this spa-loving nation to luxuriate in the often elaborate bathhouses or *fürdők*. Now for the no-brainer: soaking regularly in natural, mineral-rich, 30°C+ water is good for you. Great, actually.

TAX YOUR BRAIN

Only a few places on the planet have produced more chess grandmasters than Hungary – and all of those places have much bigger populations. Per capita, then, Hungary rules supreme when it comes to this ancient, brain-taxing game, and it's also the home of the all-time top female player, the legendary Judit Polgár. Chess is a national obsession: Hungarians think nothing of producing their chequered boards on railway station platforms and spas even have floating versions. Chess is part of every school curriculum, too. Believed to teach you respect for your opponent as well as improving analytical thinking and sharpening concentration, it's celebrated as a powerful learning tool.

SADDLE UP

Hungary has produced a procession of famous horsemen and horsewomen (Attila the Hun, for example, and the legendary light cavalry force of the hussars). Perhaps it's the pull of the Alföld, otherwise known as the Great Hungarian Plain, but to this day something deep in the Hungarian psyche yearns to explore the world on horseback, both as a continuation of age-old tradition and a chance to be immersed in nature. It's not at all unusual for locals to invite visitors to join them on a ride, a time-tested way of getting to know each other.

TWO-FOR-ONE IDEAL

Take a portable chess set with you to one of the capital city's most popular spots, the Széchenyi Baths, and you can get a two-for-one deal on the experiences that are so key to Hungarian notions of wellbeing. It won't take long before a local takes you up on a game as you soak in one of the complex's numerous pools.

EUROPE

ROMANIA

From the old-growth forests of the Carpathian Mountains to the biodiverse wetlands of the Danube Delta, folklore-steeped Romania is as rich in ancient customs as it is in natural wonders.

POPULATION
21.5 million

BROWN BEARS
IN CARPATHIAN
MOUNTAINS
> 6000

SPECIES OF
BIRDS IN THE
DANUBE DELTA
> 300

Against the odds, bewitching Romania has reached the 21st century with much of its natural and cultural landscapes intact. The geography – the formidable, forest-clad ramparts of the Carpathians and the species-rich marshes of the Danube Delta, Europe's largest wetland – has helped, limiting human habitation. The mix of people who do populate this wild terrain – from ethnic Romanians, who trace their ancestry to the Romans, to Magyars, Rroma (Gypsies), Transylvanian Germans, Tatars and others – have learned how to fend for themselves. Such know-how proved vital in the 20th century, when communist dictator Nicolae Ceaușescu brought Romania to its knees. Three decades after his overthrow, this sense of self-reliance is as strong as ever in the countryside, where people work the land by hand, folk culture flourishes, and insights on how to live a happy, fulfilling life continue to be passed down.

© coldsnowstorm/Getty Images

© davidionut/Getty Images, © aaltair/Shutterstock

Clockwise from top: Romania is Europe's second-biggest producer of honey; a kingfisher takes flight on the Danube Delta; a wooden church in Maramureş. **Previous page:** A game of cards in Transylvania.

TOP INSIGHTS for LIFE

FARMING FOLK

Romania has retained an exceptionally rich folk culture, which continues to thrive in a country where more than half the population lives in rural areas. Many villages are cut off by the hilly terrain and poor roads, so they've learned how to be self-sufficient out of necessity. In these isolated outposts, traditional crafts such as wood carving, weaving and embroidery are alive and well, as are

"It is not the answer that enlightens, but the question." – Eugene Jonesco, Romanian playwright

customs and beliefs that seem to have stepped straight out of the Middle Ages. The heart of folkloric Romania is Maramureș, a remote region in the Mara and Iza Valleys where many people still pursue the sort of simple, sustainable lifestyles that have helped the country to preserve some of Europe's finest natural landscapes. In

particular, the low-intensity methods of farming employed here – which conservationists now advocate as a way to combat climate change – support, rather than suppress, biodiversity, producing a patchwork of wildflower-rich, butterfly-filled, wooden church-dotted meadows that lift the stoniest heart.

BEE MEDICINE

Apitherapy – using bee-derived products such as honey, pollen and royal jelly to promote wellbeing or treat illness – has a long history. The pioneering physician Hippocrates applied honey to heal wounds in Ancient Greece, the Romans believed that pollen had life-giving properties, and 'propolis' – a resin-like compound produced by bees – was once popular as an antiseptic in India, China and Egypt. In Romania, bees play a role not just in the ecosystem, but also in the economy; the country is the second-biggest producer of honey in Europe. Apitherapy plays a significant role in the alternative medicine scene, and in

GO CHURCH-HOPPING

Explore some of the last peasant villages in Europe on a time-travelling, church-hopping tour of Maramureș. Eight of these steepled wooden structures are World Heritage sites; a trip to see them will reveal a region that is a genuine living museum, where farmers still scythe the meadows, villagers wear elaborately embroidered, symbol-laden costumes, and folklore is not something confined to fairy tales.

SAVE THE BEES

Whether or not you're intrigued by apitherapy (or just fond of honey), there are good reasons to love bees. These insects are a vital link in the world's food chain, fertilising three out of four crops. But the global population has plummeted in recent years, and habitat loss – especially the destruction of wildflower meadows – is a major factor. Take action by dedicating a patch of your garden to native, bee-friendly blooms.

most towns you'll find a store selling products made from honey, beeswax and propolis for a wide range of prophylactic and therapeutic uses. There are also apitherapy-focused institutes in Bucharest aiming to professionalise this ancient approach to health and wellness.

SHANGRI-SPA

Although it is less well known for its thermal springs than neighbouring Hungary, Romania doesn't want for them – and the country has a spa scene stretching back to Roman times. In the geologically young mountains of Transylvania, warm, mineral-rich waters bubble up at every turn, and towns like Băile Tuşnad and Băile Felix have developed wellness scenes to capitalise on them. In the same region, bathers have been easing their aching bodies into the welcoming, salty waters of Sovata's Bear Lake – Europe's largest heliothermal lake, warmed all year by the sun's heat – for centuries. Elsewhere, there are more unorthodox treatments on offer, including speleotherapy – which involves breathing salty air in a cave – for respiratory problems at

the Praid Salt Mine, and slathering yourself in the dark, sapropel mud of Lake Techirghiol, which is said to soften and detoxify the skin.

SMELL OF HOME

For many Romanians, the aroma of a fresh cozonac, still warm from the oven, is quite simply the smell of home. This sweet bread is served at Christmas, New Year and Easter, but it's also a firm favourite at baptisms, weddings and other special occasions. Shaped as a loaf, this panettone-like delicacy is made from milk, yeast, eggs, sugar and butter mixed into a dough and then twisted around a filling of walnuts and cocoa, plus raisins, rum, cinnamon, poppy seeds, cream cheese and other variations, depending on the region (and, indeed, grandma's recipe), to create the distinctive swirled appearance of a slice. Strictly speaking, too much of this wicked cake might not be good for the heart, but the Romanians have no doubt that it's good for the soul.

Family farmers build
a giant haystack in
Maramureș.

EUROPE

BULGARIA

Through dark chapters of its history, Bulgaria's old ways have sustained it. Even as urban lifestyles prevail, recipes and beauty treatments outlast the centuries and rose petals are gathered by hand.

POPULATION
7 million

Bulgaria produces
about three
quarters of the
world's rose oil

DAIRY FARMS
> 28,000

With forest-cloaked mountains and piping hot springs, Bulgaria promises to invigorate body and soul. Hiking is almost a patriotic duty here: the Rila Mountains guard the country's holiest monastery while other ranges, like the Pirin peaks, are named after ancient Slavic gods. Down in the valleys, the May/June rose season has been celebrated for centuries with embroidered costumes and folk songs. Sounds idyllic, maybe, but the Bulgarian mindset is hardy, forged by centuries of oppression. Bulgarians defiantly maintained their language and customs through almost 500 years of Ottoman subjugation. Modern Bulgarians continue to revere their traditions: weaving and beadwork find expression in today's fashions, rose oil endures as a favourite beauty product, and even the young delight in pre-Christian festivals. And of course, grandma's classic recipes are still best.

Clockwise from top: An outdoor folklore gathering at the Ugar festival near the village of Bukovo; dairy cows in pasture; colourful *martenitsi* are exchanged in springtime to symbolise health and happiness. **Previous page:** A worker in a Bulgarian field of roses.

TOP INSIGHTS for LIFE

YOGHURT POWER

Read the ingredients on many yoghurts and you'll see Bulgaria in the fine print. *Lactobacillus bulgaricus*, the bacteria responsible for turning milk into yoghurt, was discovered by Bulgarian microbiologist Stamen Grigorov. It follows that Bulgarians are fanatical about dairy products, blending their famously rich yoghurt into *tarator* (cool cucumber and garlic soup), *snezhanka* (a salad with similar ingredients) and fruity desserts. Of course yoghurt provides protein, calcium and other minerals, and also a range of vitamins that include the B complex. Considering the significant proportion of centenarians in Bulgaria's Rhodope Mountains, we wouldn't rule out yoghurt's life-extending powers either; best order a large *ayran* (salty yoghurt drink).

RITE OF SPRING

For centuries Bulgarians have celebrated springtime with the same sociable tradition. Friends and families offer each other *martenitsi*, tiny red-and-white twine decorations. The receiver carries or wears the *martenitsa* until they see a stork or a tree in bloom, then the ornament is tied to the closest branch. These exchanges take place on *Baba Marta* (1 March), named for the mythical 'March Grandmother' whose moods usher in spring. The ritual links love and friendship with the natural world, and encourages observation of wildlife at a time when Bulgaria is awakening from its winter slumber.

SMELLING THE ROSES

History, health and beauty are intertwined in Bulgaria's most revered product. Roses have been cultivated since the middle of the 17th century, particularly in valleys surrounding the town of Kazanlâk. Following tradition, petals are plucked by hand at dawn. Rose oil is steam-distilled in big copper vats, and petals are infused to produce pure rose water. For Bulgarians, rose is a cure-all: it's an effective astringent, excellent at hydrating skin, as well as a classic fragrance.

THE GIFT OF GIVING

Is it better to receive gifts or to give them? On their name day (the feast day of the saint after whom they were named), Bulgarians offer gifts to friends and cook a meal for their family. It's a meaningful shift in perspective: closeness to others, and having the resources to treat them, are privileges worth celebrating.

EUROPE

ALBANIA

Closed off to the outside world for decades under a repressive regime, enchanting Albania has emerged with as firm a grip on its identity as ever.

POPULATION
3 million

**COUNTRY'S
NAME IN
ALBANIAN**
Shqipëria or 'Land
of the Eagles'

**CAFES PER
100,000 PEOPLE**
518

Until recently, Albania's crumpled mountains, fortress towns and sparkling beaches were just a rumour on most maps. But visitors venturing into this small yet varied country discover a place rich in history and unique in character; from Greeks, Illyrians, Romans, Goths, Byzantines, Bulgarians, Ottomans and Venetians to modern Italians and Serbs, every civilisation that has encroached on the Balkans seems to have left its mark here. But rather than erasing the local language and culture, these incursions seem to have reinforced the people's pride in their own customs and mores. Albanian cuisine has absorbed the influences around it, but the national identity has never faded. Come here to go *avash, avash* (slowly, slowly), to relish life's simple pleasures and to connect with locals… even as you stumble over the language, ranked a class 4 in difficulty for English-speakers (in other words, hard!).

EUROPE

© ollirg/Shutterstock

© Alla Simacheva/Getty Images

From top: The Catholic church of Theth is backdropped by the Albanian Alps; Skanderbeg Square in Tirana. **Previous page:** A boulevard in Tirana at dusk.

TOP INSIGHTS for LIFE

DESCENDANTS OF EAGLES

If you want to use International Sign Language to say 'Albania', it's easy: just make an eagle sign with your hands. You'll see the same majestic bird, double-headed, on the country's flag (and Albania does have a population of golden eagles, too).

"Slowly, slowly the lamb becomes a ram." - Albanian saying

Since the 11th century or so, eagles have been linked to its identity, and have helped this nation of only three million, which occupies an area about the same size as the US state of Maryland, keep its distinctive character despite decades of repression in the 20th century under communist dictator Enver Hoxha, and pretty much ceaseless control by other imperial powers before that. Turns out that knowing who you are is pretty powerful.

THE CULT OF BESA

Although it's sometimes connected to the grim tradition of blood feuds, *besa* (which means, loosely, to keep a promise or pledge out of honour) is a bedrock of Albanian culture. Its most famed practitioner is national hero Skanderbeg, a native Albanian who trained in the Ottoman army. Skanderbeg defected in 1444 to unite warring Albanian tribes against the Ottomans, persuading them to come together under a sacred *besa*; the truce held even after his death 24 years later, helping to keep the Ottomans at bay. Today, the concept of *besa* obliges Albanians to be hospitable to strangers (they may offer to give you a ride only if you swear not to try to pay them in return).

SLOW JOE

Yes, Scandinavians may drink more coffee per capita, but if you look around the streets of the capital city, Tirana, you'll find a cafe serving good Italian espresso on almost every block, one upside of many years of Italian occupation. Sip slowly, like the locals.

TIES THAT BIND

Novelist Ismail Kadare, who won the inaugural International Man Booker in 2005, wrote *Broken April* about a set of Albanian tribal laws known as Kanun, which were applied especially in the country's mountainous regions and contain the concept of a *besa*. Although the practice of blood feuds has mostly faded, Kadare's novel searchingly explores community ties that continue to bind.

GREECE

Olive groves and bountiful seas nourish Greek bodies, while philosophical wisdom sustains their souls. But Greece's superpower is togetherness, whether through music, dance or glugs of tsipouro (brandy).

POPULATION
10.7 million

INHABITED ISLANDS
227

STRINGS ON A BOUZOUKI
six to eight

Greece's contribution to world culture is as towering as Mt Olympus. The country is the birthplace of democracy (*demokratia*) and legendary institutions like the Olympic Games have Greek roots. Mathematics, science, philosophy and literature have benefited incalculably from Greece's great minds. Inspired by their homeland's illustrious thinkers – philosophical forefather Socrates, colossus of mathematics Archimedes, out-of-time lyric poet Sappho – modern Greeks strive for knowledge, kindling political debates in even the humblest village *kafenion* (traditional cafe). Curiosity and candour are instinctive here, a place that thrives on connectedness, strengthened by community-girding folk songs and raucous summer festivities. Travellers naturally seek Greece's good life on its beaches, but the country's larder is stocked from its knotty vineyards, olive groves and hilly interiors.

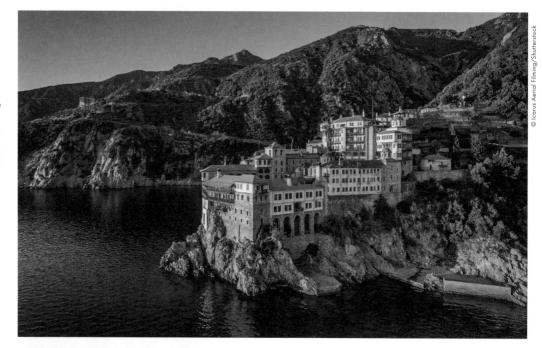

© Icarus Aerial Filming/Shutterstock

© Seagull_l/Getty Images,

© Sivan Askayo/Lonely Planet

Clockwise from top: Mt Athos has been an Orthodox spiritual centre since 1054; a kickabout in front of Plaka's Panagia Korfiatissa church; a plate of *dolma* (stuffed vine leaves). **Previous page:** An Athenian picks ripe tomatoes from the vine.

TOP INSIGHTS for LIFE

ETERNAL YOUTH

Even in old age, Ikaria's residents have a spring in their step. Inhabitants of the Aegean island enjoy unusually long lives, with one in three people reaching their 90s. Diets of fresh, unprocessed food, and disregard for hyper-connected, time-conscious modern living, are speculated to play their parts. But *panygiria* (festivals) truly keep Ikarians young at heart.

"What you leave behind is not what is engraved in stone monuments, but what is woven into the lives of others." – Pericles, Athenian statesman and general

Celebrating various village saints between May and October, these parties knit communities together through song and dance, shared meals and free-flowing red wine. When half of the year is dominated by joyous events to which the entire community is invited, it's no wonder that locals are inclined to live for almost a century.

A WARM WELCOME

Anyone who has been ushered into a Greek home (or guesthouse) and plied with coffee and a fat wedge of *spanakopita* (flaky cheese pie) is already familiar with the virtue of *philoxenia* (literally, 'friendship to a stranger'). Centuries ago, reliance on the kindness of strangers sustained travellers through perilous journeys. *Philoxenia* still carries an element of quid pro quo; generosity to others is a reflex, while the recipient of kindness has a duty to accept courteously.

ANTIOXIDANT SUPERFOODS

The antioxidant properties of Greek olive oils are outstanding. On the island of Corfu, The Governor olive grove even had their fragrant oils lab tested to prove their anti-inflammatory benefits and neuro-protective qualities. Also prized by Greeks (particularly

BIG FAT GREEK EASTER

Colourful community traditions have allowed Easter to thrive among believers and secular Greeks alike. Visit a small town to experience the electric atmosphere: on Good Friday evening, a procession follows a flower-covered bier around town, while Saturday's midnight mass fills churches with billowing incense. Try to score an invitation to a local family's Sunday dinner for roast lamb and egg-smashing games.

TAKE A VOLTA

On any warm summer evening in Greece, it can seem as though the entire town has taken to the streets. The *volta* (evening stroll) exemplifies the Greek love of the outdoors. Taking a walk has a stimulating effect on conversation; weather permitting, persuade your friends or family to join you in making a sunset stroll into a sociable routine.

among the long-living residents of Ikaria) is antioxidant-rich ironwort. A common ingredient in hot beverages across the Balkans, Greeks use it to brew 'tea of the mountain' and insist on its ability to stimulate the immune system. Mastic, a tree resin gathered on the island of Chios for thousands of years, is another folk-medicine favourite. Ancient Greeks swore by mastic's ability to cure digestive ailments, and modern scientists have found evidence of its effectiveness on gastrointestinal troubles as well as potential uses in cancer treatments. The healing properties of Chios Mastiha, clear firewater infused with mastic oil, are unconfirmed – but hearty enjoyment of a social drink is often its own medicine.

REVEL IN REMBETIKO

Music can be cathartic and a call to arms; *rembetiko*, Greece's blues, is both. The cradle of this musical style was 1920s Greece, when Greek refugees from Asia Minor poured into port towns like Thessaloniki following the Greek army's retreat from Turkey. Refugees expressed the themes of displacement, poverty and oppression in stirring songs accompanied

by traditional instruments like the *bouzouki* (similar to a mandolin). Because of its association with drug-taking, *rembetiko* gained a reputation as a dangerous counter-cultural force during the 1950s, but nowadays songs of nostalgia and loss are part of mainstream Greek culture, usually laced with optimism for a better future.

SPIRITUAL RETREAT

Pilgrims to Mt Athos, a cloistered community in northern Greece, follow ancient rules. Only male visitors are allowed to set foot on the peninsula, and all must navigate the paperwork of the Pilgrims' Bureau for a three-day stay in Athos' spiritual limbo. There's much about frozen-in-time Athos that seems uncomfortably outmoded – particularly if you're a woman, forced to keep a minimum 500m distance from the peninsula's shore (yes, really). But there's wisdom in the rhythms of pilgrimages to Athos. Spartan lodgings, communal meals and meditative walking paths hit a reset button for the men who journey here. And it isn't as sombre as it sounds: the monks make their own *tsipouro* (grape brandy) and share it

Olive farmers enjoy breakfast in the mountains above the town of Plomari on Lesvos.

EUROPE

TURKEY

Whether lounging in the hammam or clinking backgammon pieces, Turks found balance long before 'mindfulness' was coined. Their mix of secularity and superstition creates a space for mysticism in the modern world.

POPULATION
81 million

Turks consume
more tea per
capita than
anyone else

SHOPS IN
ISTANBUL'S
GRAND BAZAAR
> 4000

Turks have the work-life balance nailed, finding time to drink tea and visit the hammam between selling carpets in the bazaar and driving taxis like maniacs around Istanbul. Despite the encroachment of modern life, family remains important to the average Turk, and they take every opportunity to make the most of their sun-blessed country, filling the ferries leaving Istanbul for the Princes' Islands on summer weekends and enjoying *köyü kahvaltı* (village breakfasts) in bucolic garden restaurants. It's all part of the fatalistic attitude summarised by that ubiquitous Islamic expression, *insha'allah'* (god willing), which encourages people to live in the now. On the border of Europe and the Middle East, Turkey reconciles its contradictions by mixing mosques with the secular republic established by Atatürk, as well as superstitious beliefs, such as the blue *nazar boncuk* (evil eye) talisman on every door.

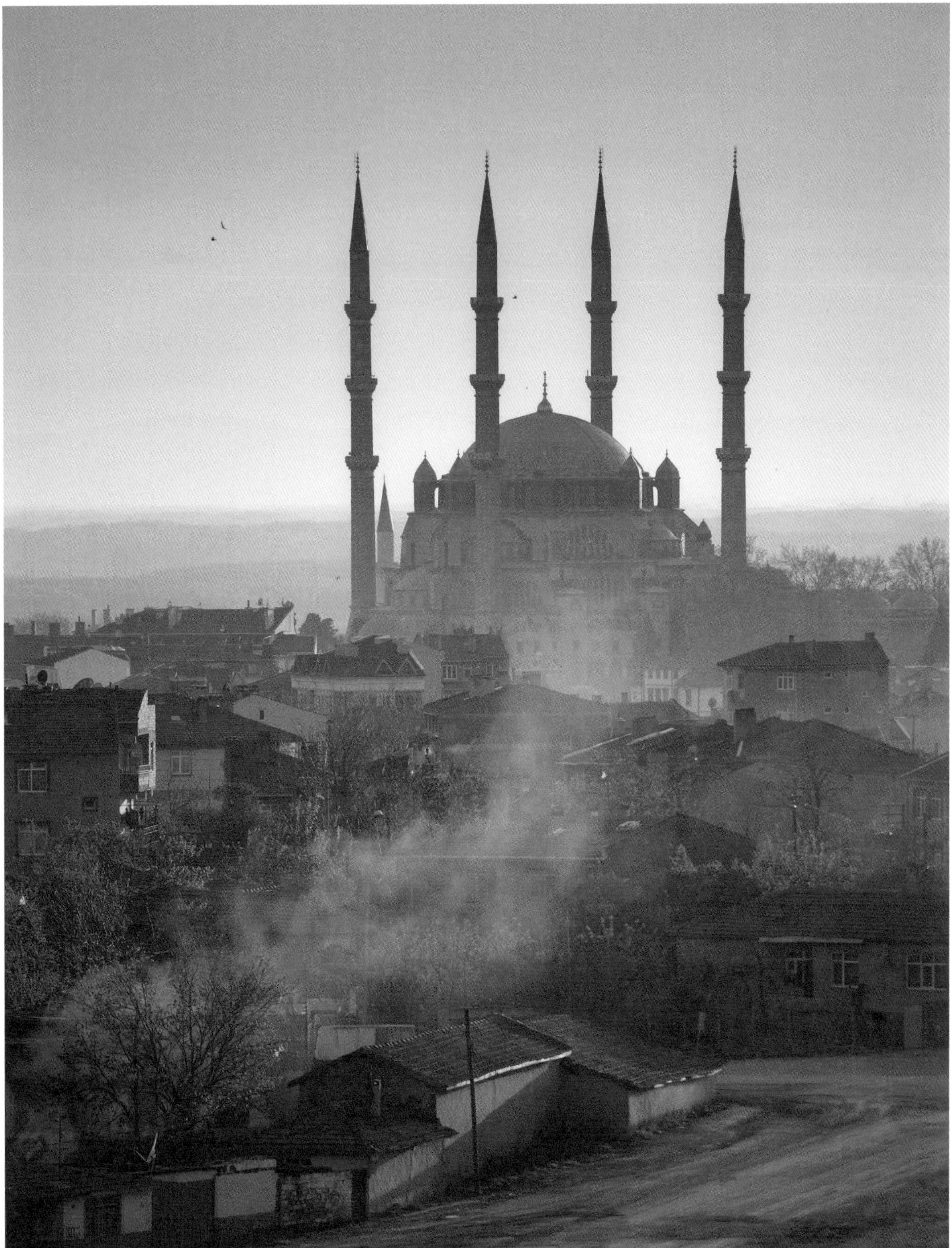

EUROPE

© Matt Munro/Lonely Planet

© MuratGungur/Shutterstock, © Mark Read/Lonely Planet

Clockwise from top: A market square in Istanbul beside the Bosphorus; the Rustem Pa Sa Mosque is famous for its İznik tiles; a game of *tavla* (backgammon). **Previous page:** The Selimie Mosque in Edirne.

TOP INSIGHTS for LIFE

SPINNING FOR SERENITY

The whirling dervish ceremony or *sema* is a classic image of Turkey. It features white-robed dancers – inspired by the mystic teachings of a 13th-century Sufi poet and religious leader – spinning serenely to achieve oneness with god. The dervishes are said to attain a beatific state, receiving Allah's blessings and communicating them to earth through their upturned right and downturned left hands. Learning to whirl like a pro takes months, but it's a meditative experience to just watch the *sema* at a *tekke* (dervish lodge).

STEAM AWAY STRESS

Steaming stress away in a hammam is a time-honoured ritual for Turks, having developed out of Roman baths via the Byzantine, Seljuk and Ottoman Empires that all called Turkey home. Local houses once lacked full bathrooms, with residents relying instead on these public bathhouses, which foreign fans nicknamed Turkish baths. The domed structures, with star-shaped skylights illuminating the steam below, often form part of a *külliyye* (mosque complex), reflecting Islam's emphasis on personal cleanliness and generating revenue for the mosque. Wash yourself or sign up for a soapy scrub and a massage by an attendant.

RELAX TO THE MAX

Keyif means relaxation, and for Turks that means hitting the *çay bahçesi* (tea garden) to catch up with your friends and, more importantly, yourself. Ideally enjoyed at least once a day, a restorative *keyif* session involves a few tulip-shaped glasses of sweet black *çay*; locals leave the *elma* (apple) tea to tourists, but they are partial to a *nargile*, or water pipe, stuffed with sweet-smelling apple tobacco. An alternative is the *kahvehane* (coffee house) for a cup of tar-like *Türk kahve* (Turkish coffee), with the option of having your fortune read in the sludgy residue, and a game of *tavla* (backgammon) is essential.

A TEA & A BATH

There are as many hammams and *çay bahçesi* as moustaches in Turkey, but you'll find particularly stunning restored Ottoman bathhouses and tea gardens with a view in Sultanahmet, Istanbul's Unesco-protected Old City. The 16th-century Ayasofya Hürrem Sultan Hamamı and Derviş Aile Çay Bahçesi are right between the Aya Sofya (Hagia Sophia) and Blue Mosque.

EUROPE

AZERBAIJAN

Best known for oil, caviar and a dazzling F1 Grand Prix, Azerbaijan also has a deep-rooted sense of hospitality and family values synthesising Turkic, European, Persian and Russian influences to forge its own identity.

POPULATION
10 million

'ENDANGERED LANGUAGES' IN AZERBAIJAN
11

OFFICIAL NATIONAL HOLI-DAY DAYS
16

Don't be fooled. Although a nation state with this name has only existed since 1991 (plus between 1918 and 1920), Azerbaijan has a long, rich and complex history. Those seeking easy stereotypes will have to dig deeper to understand this proud, sophisticated, deeply hospitable place, where the main mother tongue has much in common with Turkish, but the capital's elite often speak Russian, and several villages have their own unique languages. The predominant religion is Shia' Islam but unlike in neighbouring Iran, there is no pressure whatsoever for women to cover their hair (those you see wearing a hijab are typically Arab tourists). Bars and pub-cafes abound here and the tourist board encourages travellers to visit the many wineries that produce Azerbaijan's rapidly improving new vintages. Azerbaijan sees itself not only as the 'Land of Fire', but also as a land of tolerance.

227

EUROPE

© Karen Su/Getty Images

© wangbin6007/Shutterstock

From top: The Unesco World Heritage site of Momine Khatun Mausoleum in Nakhchivan; making hay while the sun shines in İvanovka. **Previous page:** Azerbaijan's capital Baku, with its distinctive Flame Towers, glows by night.

TOP INSIGHTS for LIFE

A DIVERSE NATION

Azerbaijan is an overwhelmingly Muslim country, but the brand of Islam here often incorporates local superstitions and folk beliefs, and the state remains proudly secular, making considerable efforts to stress its acceptance of diverse cultural outlooks. Female suffrage was approved in 1919, nine years before it was fully introduced in the UK. Qırmızı Qəsəbə is one of the world's only all-Jewish towns outside Israel. The unique Christian community of Nic links its faith and language back to the once-widespread culture of Caucasian Albania. Several villages in more remote mountain regions maintain their own distinct languages. And at İvanovka, Russian Molokans – non-conformists who were essentially banished from Russia in 1834 – still run their village along the lines of a Soviet collective farm.

TALYSH CENTENARIANS

Fresh air, hard work and an occasional vodka are what locals in the Talysh region of southernmost Azerbaijan credit for their unusually high chances of living past 100. Doubts cast on the accuracy of 19th-century birth records mean that the region's most famous supercentenarians no longer appear in 'verified' longevity statistics. But even if the authorities had made a mistake of a decade or two, Azerbaijani shepherd Shirali Muslumov's 168-year tally would still leave him as by far the longest-lived individual since the Old Testament.

FAMILY FIRST

Society is structured around the centrality of family and Azerbaijan is among the world's 12 most 'generous' countries in terms of national holidays. On top of these, several mourning days provide time to reflect on national tragedies – and there are all too many of them. When a family member dies, not only is time off work automatically granted to relatives, but whole roads are closed (even in busy cities) to erect temporary memorial tents. Weddings tend to be lavish affairs and also merit days off.

AZERBAI-JANI ART

Peruse classic Azerbaijani paintings on www.azgallery.org or more contemporary work through www.yarat.az. Listen to the classical music of Uzeyir Hajibeyov, the mugham of Alim Qasimov, or the jazz-fusion of Isfar Sarabski. Read the classic cross-cultural love tragedy Ali & Nino (better than the film) or Nizami's much older equivalent Leyla and Majnun, whose heroine inspired Eric Clapton's classic song.

EUROPE

GEORGIA

Artistic and fiercely proud, Georgians live in one of Europe's easternmost outposts, an ancient Christian nation where life revolves around wine, feasting and lusty celebrations of their lot.

POPULATION
4 million

BOTTLES OF
WINE EXPORTED
IN 2018
86.2 million

NOBLE-PRINCE-
LY (*THAVADEBI*)
FAMILIES
70

Georgia's rich tapestry of legends provides the structure for a passionate culture that embodies the life-affirming spirit of the Caucasus. This is where Jason and the Argonauts sought the Golden Fleece, and where the demi-god Amirani was chained to a mountain for disobeying God. The old capital Mtskheta is where pilgrims brought the 'seamless robe' that Jesus had worn on the day of crucifixion (though Trier and Argenteuil make their own claims). After Armenia, Georgia – known to its people as Sakartvelo – is the world's second-oldest Christian nation, after St Nino converted a Georgian king to the faith in 327 CE. That the miracle-working saint fashioned her crucifix from grapevines hints at the distinct Georgian-ness of the Christian message here: the region has a vinicultural tradition that stretches back millennia, and wine plays a vital role in customs and rituals.

EUROPE

Clockwise from top: Sunbeams pierce the window of the ornate Gelati Monastery, near Kutaisi; vineyard workers in the Alazani Valley; a monk at the winemaking Alaverdi Monastery pours a sample. **Previous page:** A family gathers for a feast of wine and food in Racha.

TOP INSIGHTS for LIFE

WHERE WINE BEGAN

Georgia is the birthplace of wine (*kvino*). Full stop. End of story. That belief has long been an article of faith for most Georgians. What's more, recent archaeological evidence suggests that they might have been right all along, as viniculture here goes back at least 8000 years. The country is brimming with wineries and Georgia's full-bodied, deep-red Saperavi wines are structured gems equivalent, perhaps, to a rich South American Malbec. But much more culturally important are the natural, amber-coloured *qvevri* wines made, aged and stored in large egg-shaped earthenware vessels – a unique method of winemaking recognised by Unesco as part of the world's cultural heritage.

FEAST & REMEMBRANCE

Wine is also served with abandon at feasts known as *supra*. These gatherings embody Georgians' remarkable ability to express emotion in all its forms. Locals joke that 'Russians drink to forget, but Georgians drink to remember' and a *supra* is far more than a drunken free-for-all. Led by a *tamada* (toastmaster), participants down glasses at moments appropriate to passionately delivered toasts on themed subjects. Expect joy for the living, tears for the dead, love of freedom, praise for brotherhood, and spontaneous bursts of song, quite possibly with the whole family singing in multi-layered harmonies.

GOD'S OWN LAND

Soon after He'd created the Earth, God decided to divide it up between its many peoples. That day, however, the Georgians were out drinking. By the time they arrived to claim their part, none remained. Unfazed, they mentioned that they were only late because they'd been drinking His health. God not only repented but rewarded them with the most beautiful and fertile region of all (previously earmarked for Himself). This local myth underpins a deep but non-jingoistic pride in the everyday that has helped Georgians psychologically through many difficult historical epochs.

TRY GEORGIAN SUPRA FOOD

Order Tiko Tuskadze's gorgeous pictorial cookbook, *Supra*, and whip up some Georgian cuisine while listening to beautiful polyphonic singing, a unique art form recognised by Unesco. Better still, jump on a plane and head to the wine region of Kakheti. Combine food and wines at Pheasant's Tears, or mix history, wine and classical music at the new Tsinandali Festival.

AFRICA AND THE MIDDLE EAST

AFRICA & THE MIDDLE EAST

MOROCCO

In Morocco, the mighty Atlas Mountains meet the serene Sahara, the sweeping coastlines contrast with the teeming medinas, and the charismatic culture remixes the influence of Europe, Arabia and Africa.

POPULATION
34 million

% OF POPULA-
TION WHO ARE
MUSLIM
99

Casablanca has
the only Jewish
museum in the
Arab-speaking
world

Morocco's diverse terrain is home to people from a hugely diverse background: the original Berber tribes of the region, known as the Amazigh, have, over millennia, absorbed Africans from the south, nomads from the desert, Jews from Egypt, Yemen and Spain, and Arabs from the east. This confluence of cultures is expressed today in the music and the cuisine of Morocco. Life here rests on two great cornerstones: the first is Islam, which permeates every aspect of behaviour, from the calls to prayer punctuating the day, to the language which invokes Allah in almost every sentence, to the way people interact with each other; the second essential element for understanding the Moroccan way of life is the importance of family, which leads naturally to great hospitality; guests get the royal treatment, and the wider community becomes an extension of the inner circle.

© Michael Heffernan/Lonely Planet

© thanosquest/Shutterstock, © Julian Love/Lonely Planet

Clockwise from top: A blindfolded storyteller at Djemaa El Fna in Marrakesh; shoes on sale in Fez's medina; mint tea – or 'Berber whisky' – is a Moroccan institution. **Previous page:** The old medina in Fez.

TOP INSIGHTS for LIFE

SHARING AND CARING

In the medina, every neighbourhood has its own mosque, fountain, *medersa* (religious school), hammam and even a public oven for baking bread. This creates a community where everyone knows everyone else, and there's an enormous sense of sharing and caring. The baker recognises each family's loaf, the man tending the hammam fire acts as matchmaker, women exchange gossip in the hammam, and so on. As people leave the medieval medinas behind and move to the cities, however, this intimacy is in danger of being lost, even in Morocco.

"Trust in Allah, but tie up your camel." - *Moroccan proverb*

BERBER WHISKY

Sometimes referred to as 'Berber whisky', mint tea is drunk all day, every day, throughout Morocco. The serving ritual involves spooning gunpowder green tea into a silver pot, then adding fresh spearmint and boiling water. After this concoction has brewed, it's poured from a great height to create a head of froth, then sweetened with heaps of sugar, traditionally chipped off a conical sugarloaf. Mint tea is offered everywhere in Morocco, from the humblest dwelling to the richest riad, as a sign of hospitality that can't be refused (although you could cut down on the sugar!).

SAY THIS FIRST

- *Inshallah* God willing. Add this after every statement, as in 'I'll see you on Tuesday, insha'allah'. If you don't, it might never happen.
- *Hamdullah* thank God. Don't forget to thank God for everything, as in 'I bought some lovely apples in the souk, hamdullah.'
- *Bismillah* in the name of God. Say this as a blessing before eating, or when setting out on a journey (even getting into a taxi).

SAVE A TRADITION

Are any traditions in your community in danger of disappearing? Which would you save? The Al Jazeera film about the storytellers, *A Marrakech Tale*, follows the fight to preserve traditional oral storytelling, documenting efforts to hand it down from one generation to the next. If you're in Marrakesh or Fez, head to Café Clock to watch the storytellers in action.

GET SQUEAKY CLEAN

While a trip to the hammam is no longer a necessity now that most houses have bathrooms, it's still a cherished custom. Armed with a bucket, gooey brown olive oil soap and a rough exfoliating glove, men and women head for the hottest steam room to open up their pores, then scrub their skin until it's pink and glowing. Relaxation and perhaps a massage follow in a cooler steam room. Women might also use *ghassoul* clay on their skin and hair. Along with female family members and friends, a bride visits the hammam before a wedding to ensure perfectly smooth skin for the application of henna designs on hands and feet.

IF IT'S COUSCOUS, IT MUST BE FRIDAY

Influenced by Arabia and Spain, Moroccan cuisine is famous for its delicate spicing and melding of sweet and savoury, such as beef with prunes or *b'stilla*, a pigeon pie sprinkled with icing sugar. *Seksou*, or couscous, is a must for Friday lunch and for weddings and parties. The huge pyramid of couscous is studded with tender vegetables (often so soft that all the family can eat them, from babies to toothless octogenarians), and conceals a piece of meat in the centre. This communal dish is placed in the middle of the table, slathered with sauce, and then everyone uses a spoon to eat from the section in front of them.

TELL ME A STORY

Hikayat, or traditional storytelling, is an ancient art, and part of Morocco's predominantly oral culture. Storytellers once roamed from place to place, performing in town squares such as Djemaa el Fna in Marrakesh, telling tales that entertained but also offered listeners a moral lesson. This tradition was in danger of dying out until one of the last storytellers – Haj Ahmed Ezzarghani – started training young male and female apprentices, who now keep the custom alive through their association, Hikayat Morocco (hikayatmorocco.weebly.com). They now tell the stories in English as well as in Arabic, so that visitors can also understand and enjoy them.

The colourful souk
in Marrakesh.

SOUTH AFRICA

In a complicated world, South Africans derive a sense of well-being from the simple things in life, like getting out into nature and standing around the braai (barbecue) — activities best combined.

POPULATION
55.3 million

OFFICIAL LANGUAGES
11

OLDEST PERSON'S AGE IN 2019
115

South Africa doesn't often make headlines for being a place of Zen-like enlightenment, but there is much to learn from the country's inhabitants. The fact that the rainbow nation has avoided meltdown, given its history of warring Brits, Boers, Zulus and Xhosa, is a testament to its people's philosophical outlook. Their humanity is referred to as *Ubuntu*, a word that evokes images of Archbishop Desmond Tutu and the 'White Zulu' himself, the late musician Johnny Clegg. In practice, most South Africans embody this concept by simply going to church, regularly visiting *ouma* (grandma) and sharing what they have with others. South Africans of all races are an old-fashioned bunch, with Christianity and family forming the twin pillars of life. There are even two words for family in Afrikaans, *gesin* (immediate family) and *familie* (extended clan), and churches fill on Sunday mornings.

AFRICA & THE MIDDLE EAST

© jamespenry/Getty Images

© Icswart/Getty Images, © Michael Heffernan/Lonely Planet

Clockwise from top: A Stellenbosch vineyard in the late afternoon sun; on a game drive in Kruger National Park; a monument at Nelson Mandela Capture Site in Howick. **Previous page:** Cape Town stands in the shadow of Table Mountain.

TOP INSIGHTS for LIFE

GLUE OF THE NATION

The Nguni word *Ubuntu* roughly translates as 'humanity'. Nelson Mandela remains its foremost exponent, having somehow persuaded the people of a country riven by apartheid to love their neighbours and tear down racial barriers. The great statesman also gave a shining example of this philosophy in action when he put on a Springboks shirt and congratulated Francois Pienaar's white-dominated South African team for winning the 1995 Rugby World Cup, a moment subsequently immortalised in the film *Invictus*. *Ubuntu*, then, is the glue that binds together one of the world's most multicultural nations, encouraging people from radically different walks of life to understand and respect each other.

FUN GATHERING

If an Afrikaner with bloodshot eyes tells you they had a *lekker kuier*, it means 'fun gathering' and you know they've partied hard. South Africa doesn't have pub culture on the same level as the likes of the UK, and many locals prefer to get together at home. A *braai* (barbecue) is normally an important part of proceedings, with slow-burning wood favoured by chilled-out Capetonians and charcoal used by faster-paced Joburgers. This love of *lekker* food and good company holds true across society; *braais* are known as *shisa nyama* in black African townships, but the ingredients are essentially the same, with the addition of the odd 'smiley' (sheep's head).

ALWAYS IN MOTION

Descended from the nomadic San bushmen, white settlers from Europe and the Bantu from Central Africa, South Africans have movement wired into their psyche. A constant theme in their history, it explains why they love to unwind by going walkabout in the country's epic landscapes. Many South Africans live for the feeling of warm earth beneath their bare feet. Mountain walking, road tripping and wildlife watching are all about this need to roam amid Mother Nature.

HEAD FOR THE WILDERNESS

Hit the road and head for the wilderness if you want to understand South Africans' yearning to explore and enjoy the natural world. Ideally, you should have the top down, the wind in your hair, the sun on your face and *Spirit of the Great Heart* by Johnny Clegg, music's greatest exponent of Ubuntu, on the car stereo.

KENYA

'If you want to go fast, go alone,' goes an African refrain, 'but if you want to go far, go together.' It's a sentiment that Kenyans from all walks of life appreciate.

POPULATION
48.4 million

NATIONAL MOTTO
Harambee ('Let us all pull together' in Swahili)

Nairobi is the world's only capital containing a national park

A local nickname for Nairobi translates as 'city in the sun' – a fitting moniker for a place where the commonest form of employment is known as *jua kali* (Swahili for 'fierce sun'), a catch-all term for anyone who makes a living – often on the roadside – producing goods out of scavenged materials. Experts in the art of making do, these grassroots entrepreneurs conjure up everything from barrows out of tin to fashion items out of rags.

About a quarter of Kenyans now live in urban areas, and while city dwellers in general have become relatively homogenised (predominantly Christians or Muslims), the country still boasts scores of traditional ethnic groups. The Samburu, Turkana, Kikuyu and Maasai and many others have maintained lifestyles and beliefs that have changed little over the centuries. Yet for Kenyans from all backgrounds, a sense of togetherness remains paramount.

© Jordon Sharp/Shutterstock

© Peter Grunert/Lonely Planet; © muendo/Getty Images

Clockwise from top: Market stalls on the side of Nairobi highway; colourful kangas are a statement piece in more ways than one; a Maasai guide at the Twala cultural Manyatta project. **Previous page:** A Maasai stands in Lewa Wildlife Conservancy, eastern Kenya.

TOP INSIGHTS for LIFE

TRADITIONAL TEXTILES

For many Kenyan women, *kangas* (a sort of Swahili sarong or sari) are not only versatile items of clothing, but also a powerful means of communication. Worn by women from virtually every walk of life, they bear slogans (almost always in Swahili and printed in block capitals) that communicate messages in marketplaces, villages and other public areas. The messages can be positive affirmations ('THE FRUITS OF PATIENCE ARE THE SWEETEST') or, often, a code designed specifically for a lover or rival ('LIKE IT OR NOT, THAT IS UP TO YOU').

"Don't follow a person who is running away." – Kenyan proverb

WASTE NOT, WANT NOT

Whether in the city or in the countryside, little is wasted in Kenya. Urban waterways might be clogged with rafts of discarded flip flops, but if you pick one up you're likely to see that even a $1 pair has been stitched, stapled or otherwise mended several times over. While Nairobi can scarcely be described as a beacon of sustainable living, most Kenyans are, of necessity, experts in reusing and recycling whatever they can. The country has one of the largest percentages of informal workers in Africa, and there are entire industries dedicated to transforming one person's trash into another person's treasure.

A SOCIAL SAFETY NET

Most Kenyans still live in scattered rural settlements but, as the dream of urban life lures more people to the cities, community bonds and family ties have become an increasingly important social safety net. Within many ethnic groups – the Kikuyu (the country's largest), Samburu, Turkana and, of course, the famous Maasai – a person's age is also hugely significant. For example, a man might expect to count on members of his own group (ie fellow 'warriors' who underwent initiation at the same time) as if they were his brothers.

JUA KALI-STYLE UP-CYCLING

We're often too quick to dispose of unwanted belongings. But rather than trashing them and buying something else, consider some *jua kali*-style upcycling instead. Could a dented saucepan become a hanging pot for plants? Could a once beloved skirt find a new life as a set of placemats or a cushion cover? It's not only sound environmental practice, but also good exercise for your mind.

MADAGASCAR

About the size of Texas or just a little bigger than France, Madagascar is not only home to a unique set of animals, but to a people and a culture unlike anywhere else.

POPULATION
25.7 million

ANNUAL RICE CONSUMPTION
120kg per person, more than China or Japan

More than half the population have animist beliefs

Everything about Madagascar is curiously different. The country abounds with animals found nowhere else, such as the ring-tailed lemur and nocturnal aye-aye. Plants range from rare orchids, including the lucrative vanilla, to prized rosewood and majestic baobabs. The landscape embraces lush rainforests, a stupendous coastline and bizarre karst outcrops of *tsingy* rock formations. And the people are just as unique as the place. They migrated from Indonesia to this great red island off the east coast of Africa about 2000 years ago, and Arab traders and Africans migrants have since added to the mix. But how can one of the poorest countries in the world have anything to say about living well? Here, 70% of people live below the poverty line, disease is rife and doctors are scarce. And yet the Malagasy maintain a fascinatingly distinct culture, dancing to the beat of their own *salegy* music.

AFRICA & THE MIDDLE EAST

© Vaclav Sebek/Shutterstock

left & right: © Justin Foulkes/Lonely Planet

Clockwise from top: The Avenue of the Baobabs glows gold in the sunlight; a group of women and girls in Toliara; a diademed sifaka with her baby in Andasibe-Mantadia National Park. **Previous page:** The fishing village of Andranokoditra, deep within Madagascar's Pangalanes Canal system.

TOP INSIGHTS for LIFE

EVERY LAST GRAIN

Rice is eaten at every meal, every day, in doughnut-like cakes for breakfast, with vegetables for a good lunch, and perhaps *ravitoto* for dinner – with puréed manioc leaves, meat and spices. Absolutely nothing is wasted: *ranovola* ('silver water') is a common drink made from the toasty, burned bits of rice left at the bottom of the pan. Add water, boil until golden, and you have a nourishing drink that's served in carafes or enamel kettles. In *hotelys*, or small roadside restaurants, it's free of charge.

> *"However little food we have, we'll share it even if it's only one locust."* – Malagasy proverb

CELEBRATING THE ANCESTORS

Respect for the family and ancestors is shown in the custom of *famadihana*, a practice of the central highland tribes of Madagascar. Every seven years, the bones of a beloved family member are removed from the tomb, wrapped in new silk shrouds and carried in grass mats around the tomb. The ancestor is told all about what has happened in the family since their death or the last time they were removed. Happy celebrations follow. People often spend more on tombs than on their homes, since life is transient but death is eternal.

FOLLOW THE FADY

So special are they, it's vital that what is left of Madagascar's rainforests is preserved for the health of the planet. Fortunately, the Malagasy are embracing better methods of farming and conservation, and some of their ancient *fady*, or taboos, help the cause. For example, it's *fady* to kill an indri because legend has it that a boy was saved from certain death by one; golden sifaka, another species of lemur, are also protected by *fady*; in some areas of the forest it's *fady* to cut trees, too, while land around tombs should never be disturbed.

RETURN TO VILLAGE LIFE

Immerse yourself in Malagasy village life for a reminder of what underpins our wellbeing: the family, interaction with the community and respect for the environment. You could stay in a home at Ambodimanga near Andapa, helping out with chores and learning to cook rice Malagasy-style, or spend a day in a fishing village near Morondava with the Kivalo Ecotourism Project.

SEYCHELLES

Few countries in the world can boast natural beauty like the Seychelles, whether on land or at sea – and respecting this spectacular environment is ingrained in the islanders' psyche.

**POPULATION
97,000**

**WHITE-SAND
BEACHES
> 100**

**43% of the
country is covered
in parks and
reserves**

There are just 97,000 inhabitants scattered across the 115 islands of the Seychelles, yet more than 40% of the country is protected, which hints at how seriously locals take the task of safeguarding this idyllic archipelago. With two national parks and seven marine parks, as well as several other protected areas under government and NGO management, the country has earned a reputation as a paradigm for ecotourism. Immediacy to nature is a given for every Seychellois, who feels strong ties to their environment, whether it be the lush forests covering the interior or the superb beaches lapped by peacock-blue sea. Mix that with a carefree attitude, a laid-back tempo, a healthy diet and warm temperatures year-round (and no cyclones), and you have the definition of paradise on Earth. In short, this is the perfect place to decompress and reconnect with your inner self.

© Westend61/Getty Images

left & right: © Justin Foulkes/Lonely Planet

Clockwise from top: A catamaran anchored off Anse Georgette beach on Praslin; a fisher tends his nets on La Digue island; grilled red snapper at the weekly market in Mahé. **Previous page:** A jungle of coco de mer palm trees in the Vallee de Mai Nature Reserve.

TOP INSIGHTS for LIFE

SAVOUR THE FLAVOUR

Just as you'd expect, inhabitants of these lush islands surrounded by the ocean enjoy a diet rich in fresh seafood (*pwason*) and tropical fruits. The Seychellois are devout seafood lovers, reputedly eating fish as much as the Tahitians, Japanese and Icelanders. Open-sea species such as marlin, tuna and swordfish feature prominently in traditional cuisine, served grilled or fried with a portion of rice (*diri*), and followed by a plate of tropical fruits for dessert – simple, fresh and healthy, which helps to account for Seychellois' relatively long life span (an average of 75 years).

> *"A pygmy's shadow is greater with the setting sun."* – Seychellois proverb

FEEL ZWA DE VIV

You'll never forget that feeling of the Seychelles. *Zwa de Viv* – literally 'Joy of Living' – is so pervasive in the archipelago that it's infectious. It will definitely make you feel relaxed without you even noticing it. Here time moves at a crawl, the atmosphere is supremely laid-back, and the warm welcome and smiles you'll see are some of the most authentic in all of the Indian Ocean. Nothing is taken too seriously and nobody is in a hurry – which gives theses islands their time-warped vibe, and acts as great therapy, rejuvenating mind and body in a few days.

LIFE'S A BEACH

Wherever you go in the Seychelles, you're never more than 20 minutes from a beach. And what a beach! The sand is a sugar-fine powder, granite boulders sculpted by the sea frame the shore, and the warm water is the colour of blue topaz. Seychellois are justifiably proud of their country's dreamlike setting and usually spend their weekends finding a cool, sandy spot to enjoy a picnic with the family, sing, dance or play soccer. Don't be shy and come around – more often than not you'll be invited to join the party!

EXPLORE A PRIMEVAL FOREST

Spend an afternoon exploring the Vallée de Mai on Praslin Island. This primeval, emerald-tinged forest, which remained totally untouched until the 1930s, is the only place in the world where the rare coco de mer palm grows in its natural state. It's also a birding hot spot, with several endemic species. Criss-crossed with hiking trails, this slice of Eden is a fantastic place to commune with nature.

TANZANIA

Tanzania's close-to-nature, spiritually connected lifestyle, its abundance of healing spices and fresh produce, and its long, languid coastline have nurtured a down-to-earth culture deeply rooted in traditional wisdom.

POPULATION
55.4 million

ORGANIC CLOVE FARMERS
> 100

% OF POPULA-TION WITH NO RELIGION
< 1

Tanzania doesn't top the lists of global lifestyle indexes. And yet, most travellers who have spent time in East Africa's largest country will tell you that getting to know Tanzanians, with their egalitarian world view and welcoming attitude, is one of the highlights of any visit. *Busara*, which roughly translates as 'life wisdom' in Swahili, abounds here, rooted in a connection with the spiritual world that characterises the outlook of so many Tanzanians, no matter what their religious denomination, and in the widespread regard for traditions. Elders, especially, are deemed to have *busara* in abundance, and are correspondingly respected and cherished, as is the extended family unit. More than anything, it is this life wisdom that enables Tanzanians to face adversity with equanimity, to smile in the face of hardship, and to know that, God willing, all will be well.

© pierivb/Getty Images

© Sun_Shine/Shutterstock, © Roger de la Harpe/UIG/Getty Images

Clockwise from top: A ceremony at Maasai Mara National Park; baobab trees in the Ruaha National Park; a *tingatinga* painting workshop in Stone town. **Previous page:** Women sell snacks through the windows of a train during a stop in the village of Kisaki.

TOP INSIGHTS for LIFE

NATURE'S RHYTHMS

In a country where more than two thirds of the population live in rural areas, nature determines life's rhythms. Away from the cities, traditional ways hold sway, with rites of passage, respect for elders and a strong sense of *ujamaa*, or community, providing a framework. *Kumekucha* ('it has dawned') is a common greeting used to mark the start of a new day and even in urban areas, *Shikamoo* (literally, 'I embrace your feet') is the necessary expression of respect when meeting someone senior in age. If you're ill, there is sure to be a natural remedy close at hand; the neem tree alone – known as *mwarobaini* or 'tree of 40' – is said to offer antidotes for up to 40 ailments, while Zanzibar's famous cloves, with their relaxing aroma and therapeutic oil, are used on the islands in traditional massage.

HAVE FAITH

With over 90% of Tanzanians professing a belief in God and almost equal numbers saying they believe in witchcraft, connections with the spiritual world play an important role in daily life. Whether it is Hindus beginning the day with offerings, Muslims massing for Friday prayers or Christians singing jubilant *kwaya* music on Sundays, Tanzanians' strongly-held beliefs shape their world view and help them weather life's often adverse circumstances.

TIES THAT BIND

Tanzania occupies the land where some of our earliest ancestors emerged, and family ties remain all-important here. Tanzanians are expected to attend weddings and other family celebrations, and sending a loved one off with a proper funeral is considered essential. The notion of family is broadly defined and includes an often bewildering array of relatives. The key thing is that your relatives are there for you when needed, and that extends to offering financial support. And at least once a year, Tanzanians journey back to their home village, where they probably have a plot of land and a small *shamba*, or farm, waiting for their retirement.

GO BACK TO BASICS

Buy some chickens to wake you before dawn with a rooster's crowing. Plant a vegetable garden. Watch the sun set. Visit your family. Respect nature. Perhaps the biggest lesson we can learn from Tanzanians is to stay close to natural rhythms, find something to believe in, and respect ancient wisdom embodied in generations-old traditions.

ETHIOPIA

Ethiopia is overwhelming. Not only because of its epic landscapes and deep history, but because it has a spiritual dimension that infuses every aspect of travel.

POPULATION
104 million

**ESTIMATED AGE
OF THE HOMINID
SKELETON 'LUCY'**
3.2 million years

**% OF AFRICA'S
ACTIVE
VOLCANOES IN
ETHIOPIA**
25

Being the only African country to have escaped European colonialism, Ethiopia has retained much of its cultural identity and its story is one of Africa's most exhilarating – it's not dubbed 'the cradle of humanity' for nothing. The fossilised skeleton of the hominid known as 'Lucy' was discovered here in 1974. And unlike so many other places in Africa, the ancient occupants of this land left behind extraordinary monuments to faith where you'll feel transported to another era. Then there's the otherworldly scenery, which runs the gamut from the skyscraping Simien Mountains to the bubbling volcanoes of arguably the hottest and most inhospitable place on Earth, the Danakil Depression – where better to tap the raw, reinvigorating power of nature? In the end, though, it is the Ethiopians themselves, with their unique way of looking at life, who will exert the strongest positive influence on you.

AFRICA & THE MIDDLE EAST

© Harri Jarvelainen Photography/Getty Images

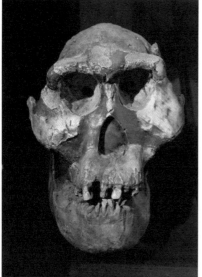

© Sergey-73/Shutterstock, © Anya Newrcha/Getty Images

Clockwise from top: The crater of Irta'ale Volcano is home to a permanent lava lake; Dassenech women perform a traditional dance; the fossilised skull of the hominid 'Lucy', discovered in Ethiopia in 1974. **Previous page:** A priest blesses pilgrims outside Bet Giyorgis church.

TOP INSIGHTS for LIFE

ROCK-SOLID FAITH

Ethiopia has no shortage of extraordinary places of worship. Nothing prepares you for the first time you see the Unesco-listed rock-hewn churches of Lalibela. For centuries, their origin has eluded everyone except locals, who firmly believe they were carved by angels. It's still a thriving centre of pilgrimage, which you can explore on foot. Among the dimly lit passageways and tunnels of the medieval churches, robed priests and monks still pass; from hidden crypts and shadowy grottoes comes the sound of chanting; and in the deep, cool recesses of the interiors, the smell of incense and beeswax candles wafts in the air. Let this spiritual energy flow over you.

RITES OF PASSAGE

When it comes to human cultures, Ethiopia has an embarrassment of riches. In the Omo Valley, ancient customs and traditions have remained almost entirely intact. A highlight of any trip is witnessing one of the many festivals that are an integral part of the culture, including age-old ceremonies marking rites of passage. Nothing is staged for tourists. The emotional impact upon those who experience such events can not only provide indelible travel memories, but also help you gain new perspectives. The best way to immerse yourself in these local cultures is to spend a couple of nights in a village and adopt a slower pace of life. You'll leave rejuvenated.

RAW NATURE

Picture this: 20 mountains peaking above 4000m as well as one of the lowest points on the Earth's surface – the infamous, volcano-studded, sulphur-spewing Danakil Depression, which lies more than 100m below sea level. In between these extremes are lush highlands, stirring deserts, sweeping savannah, towering escarpments, vast lakes and high plateaus, which feature the added allure of charismatic species such as gelada monkeys and Ethiopian wolves. In other words, plenty to make you power down and disconnect from the modern world.

SCALE A VOLCANO

You'll never forget your first glimpse of Irta'ale Volcano in the Danakil Depression. It has been in a state of continuous eruption since 1967 and its small crater is one of the only permanent lava lakes on the planet. After the three- to four-hour climb, one thing is sure: you'll be rewarded with the most surreal landscapes you've ever imagined. It's a mystical experience.

EGYPT

In a land that has more history than most,
Egypt has refined the art of living in the present
and letting the future take care of itself.

POPULATION
99.4 million

DEITIES IN
ANCIENT EGYPT
> 14,000

CALORIES
BURNED DURING
1HR OF BELLY
DANCING
250-300

With a history of strong religious belief, it is perhaps fitting that today's urban citizens of Egypt often put their faith in mosque clinics rather than government hospitals. In rural areas, homeopathic and herbal remedies that date back to ancient times (such as the application of *aloe vera* for burns) are still in use. In 2019 the Egyptian government introduced a new comprehensive health insurance system but it is likely to take 15 years to fully imple-

ment, and somehow has to keep pace with Egypt's burgeoning population. Given the strains on the system, it's little wonder that most Egyptians also invest faith in higher authorities when it comes to their wellbeing. They're in good company: their ancestors believed in the power of prayer while simultaneously relying on empirical evidence to treat disease. Indeed, some of the oldest medical literature appears in hieroglyphics from the time of the ancients.

Clockwise from top: Mosque-Madrassa of Sultan Hassan in Cairo's historic district; Khan el-Khalili souk in Cairo; a belly dancer with finger cymbals. **Previous page:** Dhows on the Nile in Aswan.

TOP INSIGHTS for LIFE

GAIN PERSPECTIVE

You don't have to be an Arabic-speaker to notice how often the phrase 'insha'allah' laces an Egyptian conversation. Loosely translated as 'God willing', it is used to hedge against the heresy of trying to predict the future. In practical terms, the concept helps to assuage anxieties about what lies ahead and puts all life's great challenges (and indeed death) into perspective. Often labelled in the West as 'fatalism' and easily misunderstood as an abnegation of responsibility, it is cherished locally as a therapeutic acceptance of human limitation.

"Fear does not prevent death, it prevents life." - Naguib Mahfouz, Egyptian writer and Nobel Prize winner

SHAKE THAT BOOTY

Once looked upon with suspicion (and secret admiration) by Western male travellers, Oriental belly dancing contributed to the siren trope that portrayed Arab women as seductive but slightly sinister. Thankfully, a postcolonial sensibility has brought a better understanding of Egypt's indigenous dance culture, and it is now celebrated worldwide not just for its extraordinary beauty but also its potential as a rigorous workout.

THE EVIL EYE

The first time a wide-open blue eye stares back at you, it can be disconcerting; then you'll notice them everywhere – hanging above a door, dangling from a car mirror and strung around the necks of babes. Dating back at least to the pharaohs, who were buried for protection with the Eye of Horus, the *nazar* (or eye amulet) has endured as a prevalent symbol in modern Egypt. Widely believed to ward off evil spirits, it relates to the concept of 'evil eye' – a curse arising out of *hassad*, or envy provoked by the good health and fortune of others. For those who take the concept to heart, the placebo effect of deflecting possible ills may have its own potency.

DANCE LIKE AN EGYPTIAN

If you want an exhilarating way to lose weight, try an hour of belly dancing. Easy to learn but hard to master, belly dancing is a great way to tone muscles, improve balance and promote fitness. Online courses are available or visit Egypt to contextualise the dance and fall in love with the music.

AFRICA & THE MIDDLE EAST

ISRAEL

Spiritual wisdom infuses this ancient land. Its modern-day people draw strength from sacred temples and ruins, and seek repose by the Dead Sea and sparkling Mediterranean coast.

POPULATION
8.4 million

% OF ISRAELIS
WHO EAT
HUMMUS
WEEKLY
93

The Dead Sea is
the lowest body of
water on Earth

Monuments of the Jewish, Muslim, Christian and Baha'i faiths are enclosed within the troubled borders of Israel. The natural landscape, too, inspires contemplation: Israel has vast deserts and bone-white coastal caves sculpted by the Mediterranean, and the Dead Sea. Millennia-old rituals inform daily life. Israel's Jewish believers lay hands on the 2000-year-old Western Wall and embrace the quiet that descends at twilight on Fridays for Shabbat. From introspection and communal worship blossom rich intellectual lives. People in Israel are lovers of bookshops and coffee-fuelled debate, and creative endeavours are everywhere, from start-ups to musical ensembles. A Middle Eastern diet provides brain food including low-cholesterol staples like hummus, falafel, olives and pita bread. The uniting factor among devout and secular, and Israel's myriad faiths? Beach culture.

AFRICA & THE MIDDLE EAST

Clockwise from top: Sociable street dining in Tel Aviv; a falafel sandwich – Israeli street food at its finest; sweets on sale at the Carmel Market in Tel Aviv. **Previous page:** Beach life in Tel Aviv, with a backdrop of the town of Jaffa.

TOP INSIGHTS for LIFE

AUDITING THE SOUL

In the Jewish spiritual practice of *cheshbon nefesh*, deeds are examined with the precision of an accountant balancing their books. Traditionally undertaken in anticipation of Rosh Hashanah (Jewish New Year) and Yom Kippur (the Day of Atonement), the process is powerful and effective because it's personal. Note down successes and failures, measuring them against the previous year's deeds. The goals of family and peers aren't part of the equation; practitioners seek to better themselves.

BEACH CULTURE FOR ALL

When the cult of bodily perfection rouses anxiety, look to coastal Israeli cities. On Alma Beach in Tel Aviv, head-scarfed women and bikini-clad sun worshippers are united in one pursuit: matkot, a paddleboard pastime (similar to beach tennis) that creates an agreeable soundtrack of thwacks. Matkot often has neither a clear point-scoring system nor a winner, unfolding purely for enjoyment. Come as you are, and be active.

DAY OF REST

Most Jewish Israelis observe Shabbat, where sundown on Friday ushers in a day of prayer and rest. When entire communities participate, there's a powerful change in atmosphere. In West Jerusalem, bells are rung in marketplaces to herald the end of commerce. Families and friends gather to share food that has been prepared in advance. Forgoing social media carries mental health benefits, so it helps that electronic devices are powered down for the duration.

BAHA'I WISDOM

Israel's northern coast is a cradle of the Baha'i faith. Religious leader Bahá'u'lláh is buried in the city of Akko, while the terraced flower gardens of Haifa are a monument to his predecessor, the Báb. According to the faith, structures like race, class and gender obstruct our ability to recognise humanity's oneness. Applied to interactions with other people, this tenet of Baha'i belief is transformative, urging us to be open and to challenge internal prejudice.

RITUAL BATHING

Immersion in a *mikveh* (ritual bath) punctuates milestones of Jewish life. The healing power of water feels intuitive, especially if you've ever sought out a long bath after a hard day, but heighten the experience with elements of Jewish tradition. Find a natural pool and take a breath to fully submerge your head – re-emerging often brings an exhilarating moment of clarity.

AFRICA & THE MIDDLE EAST

JORDAN

A country that has welcomed four major waves of refugees in 50 years knows a thing or two about the psychological benefits of being, as per Bedouin tradition, a nation of givers.

POPULATION
10.5 million

% OF BEDOUIN
LIVING A
NOMADIC LIFE
10

Dead Sea mud
contains 26
essential minerals,
12 of them unique

Ask many people in Jordan where they come from and they may well say 'the desert'. Bedouin roots, and a connection to the values of a traditional way of life, run deep in the veins of many Jordanians, finding modern expression in their famed sense of hospitality. If this sounds easy to say but not so easily proved, then the immigration figures over the past half century speak for themselves; wave after wave of migrants from embattled neighbouring states have sought and been given refuge in this tiny desert kingdom. We all know that giving feels good, but it's not without its stresses. To overcome the tensions of urban overcrowding, Jordanians can rely on two ancient antidotes: a walk in the wilds, along the country's ancient Nabataean and Roman byways, or taking a bath. The latter is a communal affair (generally segregated by gender) and often involves mud.

© Joe Windsor-Williams/Lonely Planet

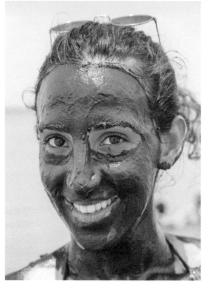

© Tom Mackie/Lonely Planet, © Justin Foulkes/Lonely Planet

Clockwise from top: A Wadi Rum Bedouin tent at night; a desert camp on the Jordan Trail in Wadi Feid; mud from the Dead Sea is applied to the skin as a natural spa experience. **Previous page:** Salt on the shore of the Dead Sea.

TOP INSIGHTS for LIFE

DESERT ROOTS

The Bedouin are not the only ones to understand the benefit of nights spent under desert stars: many modern Jordanians enjoy going back to basics (living, loving and laughing) in the camps of Jordan's expansive deserts. Wadi Rum, made famous in the Western imagination by Lawrence of Arabia, offers visitors an opportunity to sample the soul-salving effects of desert life. Some Bedouin here are still nomadic, raising livestock, sleeping under *beit ash shaar* (goat hair Bedouin tents) and thriving in balance with nature.

"A journey of a thousand miles starts with one step." – Arabic proverb

GLORIOUS MUD

Since ancient times the Dead Sea and the thermal waters of the Jordan Valley have been valued for their health-giving properties. People continue to come from all over the world to bathe in Jordan's medicinal waters, following in the footsteps of King Herod, who sought relief from psoriasis near Wadi Mujib. Today the resorts along the Dead Sea shore benefit from health tourism, attracting visitors with their luxurious spas, marble-edged pools and expert masseurs. The key component of the Dead Sea experience is mud: black ribbons of glossy deposits that are liberally applied and then baked onto the skin under the Rift Valley sun.

PATH OF PROPHETS

The 650km Jordan Trail links the temperate north of Jordan with its desert south, leading through nature reserves famous for their biodiversity and following the path of kings, Roman regiments, Nabataean traders, crusaders and prophets; it even passes close to the point where Musa (Moses) allegedly looked wistfully across Wadi Araba at the promised land. Hiking the trail represents not just a physical challenge but a therapeutic journey through a shared history.

FIND YOUR INNER BEDU

While deserts lend themselves particularly well to introspection and spiritual reflection, they are not the only environments in which to appreciate the value of a pared-down existence. Finding one's inner nomad can be accomplished by throwing off the shoes of today's accelerated life and walking barefoot (metaphorically at least) in any natural space.

LEBANON

A cultural matrix in the Middle East, Lebanon survives – and often enchants – in the eye of a geopolitical storm thanks to a combination of worldly sophistication, memorable cuisine and mutual tolerance.

POPULATION
6.1 million

Lebanon's oldest vineyards date back to 5000 BCE

The cedar tree – the national emblem – symbolises strength, resilience and eternity

Lebanon is a complex jigsaw of Shiite and Sunni Muslims, Orthodox and Catholic Christians, and Druze, Alawite and Maronite communities all crammed, together with more than 1.5 million Syrian and Palestinian refugees, into a space a third of the size of Belgium. The stylish, hedonistic capital, Beirut, is home to true bon vivants – poised, literate, multilingual – but even the humblest villager can claim to be a gourmand in a land where the influences of Arabic and Mediterranean cuisine arrive at a healthy, palate-pleasing intersection. Counterpoints abound but are at their most remarkable in the fertile Bekaa Valley, where the odd Hezbollah gift shop intersperses world-class vineyards. In spite of a troubled history, Lebanon draws strength from this cultural diversity, and many citizens see themselves as the inheritors of a far older tradition – that of the wine-making, seafaring Phoenicians.

© ramzihachicho/Getty Images

© JPRichard/Shutterstock, © HelgaBragina/Shutterstock

Clockwise from top: Stylish Beirut by night; a traditional Lebanese *maqabalat* lunch; Al Bass archaeological site in Tyre, Lebanon. **Previous page:** A colourful cafe scene in central Beirut.

TOP INSIGHTS for LIFE

SPOILED DAD

While it has a great deal in common with that of other Middle Eastern and Mediterranean countries, Lebanese cuisine triumphs where Arabic street food meets French gastronomy, creating the region's most refined *maqabalat* (mezze-like selections of shared starter-style dishes). Most archetypal is *moutabal*, a flavour-packed vegan dip made from roast aubergine with tahini, garlic, lemon and spices, and often sprinkled with pomegranate. Eating the creamiest versions can be a full sensual overload that is said (in gender-traditional relationships) to help a man reflect with gratitude upon the culinary prowess of his female relatives, hence the dish's alternative name: *baba* (father) *ghanoush* ([gets] spoiled).

PARIS OF THE EAST

Aside from the dark days of the 1980s, Beirut has long been seen as one of the most sophisticated cities in the Middle East, a place where the jet set can go skiing in the morning and lounge on the beach in the afternoon. Cultural contacts with France remain strong: French rock 'n' roll icon Johnny Hallyday even played one of his farewell tour gigs amid the Unesco-listed Roman ruins at Baalbek. Beirut's art scene and designer boutiques regularly grace the pages of publications like *Vogue*, the city boasts a remarkable range of high-end beauty clinics, and the advanced medical infrastructure includes hotel-standard private hospitals, which attract wealthy invalids from across the Arab world.

POETRY, PLEASE

Al-zajal is a Unesco-recognised form of semi-improvised folk poetry covering themes of love, tolerance and inter-communal dialogue, along with nostalgia and politics. Although versions of *zajal* are known across the Arab world, the form is most associated with Lebanon, where performers are likely to include at least some reference to the beauty of their native land.

SAVOUR THE TASTE OF LEBANON

Order a selection of Lebanese snacks, *moutabal*, hummus, *fattoush* (salad with crispy flakes), *kibbeh* (crunchy pine-nut falafels) and *manakish* (Lebanese 'pizza'). Savour them over a lingering glass or two of Chateau Ksara wine while pondering passages from Khalil Gibran's *The Prophet*, one of the most popular non-religious spiritual books ever written.

UNITED ARAB
EMIRATES

Though it's anchored by Bedouin traditions, the United Arab Emirates pairs its heritage with infinite ambition and utopian ideals for its future; not even the sky is the limit here.

POPULATION
9.7 million

Appointed its first
Minister of State
for Happiness and
Wellbeing in 2016

**AVERAGE HOURS
OF SUNSHINE
PER YEAR**
> 3500

Don't be fooled by the hypermodern skyscrapers: the Emirati soul still belongs to the desert. The Bedouin, a collective term for the nomadic tribes that spread across the entire Middle East, provide the foundation of Emirati customs, which are shared with other Gulf countries so closely that national borders sometimes seem like arbitrary lines in the sand. Tribal and family bonds are paramount to wellbeing, but the Islamic ideals of treating strangers and guests with genuine hospitality underpin visitors' interactions with Emiratis, who will appear with plates of soft and sticky dates and a *dallah* (a traditional metal pot with a long, thin spout) of free-flowing Arabic coffee before they are even asked for. Emiratis make up just 10% of the population of the country today, but this area has long been a hub for travellers and traders who add other nuances to the character and customs of the nation.

AFRICA & THE MIDDLE EAST

Clockwise from top: Falconry is a vital part of the UAE's national identity; henna designs are imbued with meaning and significance; Sheikh Zayed Grand Mosque is the largest mosque in the country. **Previous page:** A textile souk in Dubai.

TOP INSIGHTS for LIFE

MEETING IN THE MAJLIS

Often oversimplified in translation as 'sitting room', *majlis* is an important social space where people meet to discuss current affairs and share news, and it's also the name for councils that are an essential part of Emirati politics. Communities and their leaders gather to resolve issues in these large rooms, seated on long cushions on the carpet-covered floor. Participants brew and share Arabic coffee as the elders and sheikhs apply their wisdom to concerns raised. All members of the community are allowed to join in, regardless of age, which promotes transparency from leaders and helps children grasp cultural customs.

BIRDS OF A FEATHER

For thousands of years, the Bedouin of the Arabian Peninsula have used falcons to hunt in the desert. Falconry is still a highly regarded sport here, representing the traditional cherished Arab values of courage, prestige and integrity. Now recognised on Unesco's list of intangible cultural heritage, the practice requires patience as the falconer develops an intimate bond with his bird, which is trained using special methods passed down through generations. So dear are falcons in the UAE that it became the first country in the world to issue them with passports.

BLESSING THE BRIDE

Arab weddings are huge celebrations that often last for a week. One of the rituals of a wedding is the *laylat al henna*, or henna night. A few days before the ceremony, the bride and her female family members and friends gather to celebrate. Traditionally, a married older relative decorates the bride's hands, arms and feet, and it's said that the henna artist passes on the success of her own marriage. Daughters often request the designs their mothers wore at their weddings, and the patterns are imbued with meaning: butterflies symbolise transformation, flowers and palms bloom with happiness, and birds are the messengers of new love. The loops and lines are believed to carry *baraka*, positive energy that brings blessings and protects against evil.

TEACH YOURSELF WITH UAE 101

To get up to speed with Emirati culture before you arrive, check out *UAE 101: A Guidebook to the Emirati Culture*. Written by two neighbours, an Emirati and an Italian, this book highlights local traditions, folklore, food, drink and nuances of the country and its people.

AFRICA & THE MIDDLE EAST

OMAN

Grateful for the advantages of modern healthcare available under the current Sultan's enlightened reign, Omanis still nip back to grandma for herbal alternatives plucked from the desert fringe.

POPULATION
4.6 million

INDIGENOUS DATE VARIETIES
> 40

AVERAGE LENGTH OF AN OMANI GREETING
3 minutes

In Oman, there is no contradiction in the government promoting preventative medicine in a modern clinical setting while funding a centre for herbal medicine: there is room for both modern and traditional regimes in Omani culture, and it is disingenuous to sing the praises of one without remembering the other. This is a country, after all, where just 50 years ago there was only one hospital, and in 1998 medicine was still being de-

livered to mountaintop communities by helicopter. So wellness is understood not just in terms of improved infant mortality rates and longer life expectancy for both men and women, but also through the application of age-old practices, such as the eating of dates and drinking of camel's milk, and carefully nurtured cultural norms focused on the country's famous hospitality, courtesy and good grace.

© Justin Foulkes/Lonely Planet

© Matyas Rehak/Shutterstock, © Kertu/Shutterstock

Clockwise from top: Oman's vast and otherworldly Empty Quarter; a traditional mud village in the mountains among date palm trees; frankincense has grown in Oman for millennia. **Previous page:** A man surveys Wadi Ghul, the 'Grand Canyon of Arabia', from the top of Jebel Shams mountain.

TOP INSIGHTS for LIFE

THE DATING CULTURE

Those in the know will have only one (or three, five, seven...) at a sitting, as some say Prophet Mohammed gave his blessing for eating only odd numbers. We're talking dates – the nutritious, easily digested fruits of the desert, known throughout Arabia for their health-giving properties. In Oman, dates have been a vital part of the diet for centuries and no official occasion takes place without a serving of *nakhl* (dates) and a glass of *qahwa* (cardamom coffee).

"The use of date palms are as many as the number of days in a year."
– Old Arabic saying

TRIBAL TRAVELS

Utter the word 'holiday' in the Omani workplace and many staff have left before the word is complete. Some misinterpret this as work-shyness but that conflicts with the Herculean achievements, since 1970, of the Omani Renaissance. Many Omanis return home every weekend, completing mammoth treks across the desert (in 4WD vehicles on excellent roads) to be with family members, investing their urban wealth in the tribal patch for the wellbeing of all.

GIFT OF KINGS

Grown for thousands of years in southern Oman, touched by the magic of the monsoon, the *Boswellia* tree produces a resin famous for its pungent aroma. In common with the other two gifts of kings, frankincense is believed to have anti-inflammatory properties and it wafts through the doorway of every Omani household.

GOOD GRACE

Witness an accident, and it may be surprising to see all parties (including the police) spend five minutes shaking hands, knocking noses or asking after each other's children. Keeping an even temper and a sense of good grace permeates all Omani social interaction and is calming to the soul.

GRACEFUL IN ADVERSITY

Here's a treatment for high blood pressure: the next time you are gripped by road rage, imagine getting out of the car and shaking hands with your potential adversary. Ask after his or her wellbeing, family and neighbourhood. Finally, check on the latest news and having established there is none, try to lob in an insult. After sharing good grace, it's almost impossible!

© Claus Hessner//500px

ASIA

ASIA

IRAN

Home to one of the world's oldest continuous civilisations, Iran has a lesson or two about living well, as this land of artists, poets and travellers has been a point of cultural exchange for millennia.

POPULATION
83 million

**% OF POPULA-
TION UNDER 30**
60

The world's
largest hand-
woven Persian rug
was 5630 sq m-

One of the cradles of humanity, the land that is Iran has been inhabited uninterrupted for longer than anywhere else on Earth. Echoes of the ancients resound in the mountainous landscapes, the peaceful deserts, the lapping waves on the coast and even in the busy cities, where you'll find a treasure trove of Islamic architecture amid the shouts of merchants. Traversed by ancient trade routes, Iran has long been a cultural crossroads, influenced by East and West, and its Greek, Arab, Turkic and Mongol occupiers. Today it's the warm welcomes, friendliness and openness of Iranians that make for memories which will stick long after arrival. Be prepared to be peppered with questions, plus genuine offers to come over for tea and dinner from the get-go, which you should take: these invitations afford a close-up look at the rich weave of Iranian life.

ASIA

Clockwise from top: Nasir-al-Mulk Mosque dazzles with its stained glass and elegant carved pillars; weaving a Persian rug in a carpet workshop; harvesting saffron in Ferdows, Khorasan province. **Previous page:** Taking a rest in Naqsh-e Jahan Square.

TOP INSIGHTS for LIFE

IRAN'S RED GOLD

Iran is the largest producer of saffron, the most expensive spice in the world. The painstaking harvest has to be done by hand, and it takes 167 flowers to produce a single gram of the 'red gold'. Besides using it in cooking, Iranians believe that saffron helps relieve depression. In some parts of the country, it's also used before the new year celebrations to create yellow ink, which calligraphers use to write verses of the Quran on a porcelain plate. The plate is then washed, removing the colour, and the water is given to those who are ill to drink, in the hope it will bring health and good fortune in the upcoming year.

"Do not feel lonely; the entire universe is inside you." – Rumi, Persian poet

PERFECTLY IMPERFECT

Perisan rugs are perhaps the most recognised symbol of Iranian art, known for their beautifully complex designs and high level of craftsmanship. However, many rugs contain deliberate errors, introduced into the weave to acknowledge that only Allah is perfect. They're usually difficult to spot and can be as minor as a different colour used in the petal of a single flower.

DELICATE DANCE OF TAAROF

One of the most confusing social interactions for visitors to Iran is *taarof*, a system of formalised politeness and social ranking that is fundamental to understanding local culture. This delicate dance begins with an offer, perhaps of food from a host or from a diner to pay a bill, which should then be repeatedly turned down, usually two or three times, before accepting is permissible. This back and forth gives the person making the offer the chance to save face if they cannot actually make good on it. If you accept without preamble an offer that is *taarof*, the shocked look on the other person's face will soon reveal your mistake.

READ ANCIENT IRANIAN POETRY

Many ancient Iranian texts have been translated into English. Try the *Rubáiyát of Omar Khayyám*, an epic poem written in 1120 CE, which is one of Iran's most popular works internationally. Various collections of poems by Rumi, a 13th-century poet, scholar and Sufi mystic, are also easy to find; in fact, Rumi is the best-selling poet in the US!

UZBEKISTAN

Uzbekistan lies at the heart of the Silk Road, where the East met the West — and the result is a rich fusion that manages to be more than the sum of its parts.

POPULATION
30 million

RECIPES FOR UZBEK PLOV
> 1000

Laying Uzbek bread upside down is believed to bring bad luck

Uzbekistan thrives through embracing its own diversity, which extends not just to its geography but also to its people. This Central Asian country runs from the snow-capped Tian Shan Mountains to the arid Kyzylkum Desert, but the population is even more varied than the terrain: Uzbeks are the majority group here, but you'll also find ethnic Russians, Tajiks, Kazakhs, Karakalpaks and Tatars. There has been a Jewish population in Bukhara

for thousands of years, and there's evidence of Buddhism, Zoroastrianism and Hinduism at ancient archeological sites. Most people now practise Islam or Orthodox Christianity, but there are pockets of Zoroastrians, as well as shamans, agnostics and atheists. Living well in Uzbekistan means respecting other people's beliefs and working side by side with your neighbours. No one can survive alone in the desert, and no one gets rich on his own.

Clockwise from top: Chorsu Bazaar in Tashkent; Uzbekistan's national dish, *plov*; a stack of freshly baked *non* bread at the Kolkhoznyy Rynok bazaar in Bukhara. **Previous page:** Kalon mosque and minaret, Bukhara.

TOP INSIGHTS for LIFE

THE MORNING PLOV

This rice-based national dish is the highlight of any special occasion, be it a birth, circumcision, wedding or funeral. The ceremonial cutting of the carrots (yes, really) takes place the night before, and the finished dish, which is cooked overnight, is served immediately after the sunrise prayers. It's a communal meal, as not only does everyone eat from the same dish, but every member of the community is expected to partake, regardless of their wealth or status.

"If your country prospers, you prosper." – Uzbek proverb

HARMONIOUS LIVING

A *makhalla* is a residential district, but also a system of rules governing how to live with your neighbours in order to maintain good relations. Social cohesion, cleanliness, and care and respect for elders are key, as is the law of *shafat*, which dictates that if you wish to sell your house you should offer it first to family and neighbours, rather than to strangers, in order to protect the interests of your community.

WARRIOR DISCIPLINE

Closely related to judo, *kurash* is a traditional form of wrestling; the word means 'attaining a goal by fair means' (in essence, if you must fight to resolve your problems, do it in a regulated way). The sport dates back 3500 years and, in times gone by, was considered important for the physical and mental training of troops. *Kurash* has very strict rules, and is believed to encourage respect for your rival.

TEA FIRST

The *chaikhana* (teahouse) is the centre of every Uzbek community. It's where people meet to conduct business, arrange marriages and discuss politics and philosophy. You can pop in for a game of chess or backgammon, too. A porcelain bowl of steaming green tea is the symbol of hospitality, but – counter-intuitively – the less tea you're poured, the more you're esteemed as a guest (as you'll come back for more).

TASTE FOR THE BAZAAR

Eat your way through Chorsu Bazaar, Tashkent's main market, situated on a Silk Road crossroads. Seasonal produce comes straight from farms; the smell of fresh *non* (round, flat bread) wafts from giant bakeries; and everyone around you is thinking and talking about food. With your appetite whetted, pop over to the Central Asian Plov Centre for a dozen varieties of Uzbekistan's national dish.

ASIA

TAJIKISTAN

Although this country of snow-capped peaks and glacial lakes is less than a century old, its hardy inhabitants have maintained their mystical beliefs and ancient ways for millennia.

POPULATION
8.6 million

% OF COUNTRY THAT IS MOUNTAINOUS
> 90

Tajikistan contains the world's largest glacier outside the polar regions

More than any other nation-state to emerge from the fall of the USSR, Tajikistan is a geographical artifice. However, although the idea of a Tajik republic was only dreamed up in 1924, the region itself is an ancient cradle of cultures. The term Tajik (or Taj or Dari) had been used for centuries to describe Persian-speaking populations across vast swathes of Central Asia and the Middle East. Today, 'ethnic Tajiks' make up around 80% of the popula-

tion of Tajikistan, which also includes Persian-speaking, Sufi-influenced Sunnis plus the Pamiris of southeastern Tajikistan, where several local languages are spoken and the predominant religion is the Ismaili-Shiite form of Islam. In remote rustic villages and post-Soviet urban sprawls, each strand of Tajik society retains its own inspiringly spiritual understanding of life tempered by the harsh realities of an unforgiving, high-mountain existence.

© Nickolay Vinokurov/Shutterstock

© Eric Lafforgue/Alamy Stock Photo, © AlexelA/Shutterstock

Clockwise from top: Tajik girls work together on *chakan* embroidery during the celebration of Nowruz (New Year); the mausoleum of polymath Mir Sayyid Ali Hamadani in Kulob. **Previous page:** The Pamir Highway once formed one link of the ancient Silk Road.

TOP INSIGHTS for LIFE

MANIFEST MYSTICISM

Mystical forms of Islam underpin many aspects of Tajik life, having quietly survived the officially atheist Soviet era and more recent crackdowns on non-registered religion. The great Sufi poet Rumi (1209–1273) is said to have hailed from Tajikistan's Vakhst Valley, while Mir Sayyid Ali Hamadani, the 14th-century polymath who brought Islam to Kashmir, is buried in Kulob, a Tajik city whose women are famous for focusing their meditations on a form of embroidery known as *chakan*. Some styles of Tajik music also resonate with a Sufi-esque philosophy, notably *falak* with its themes of divine love.

COSMOLOGY IN A SINGLE ROOM

From the outside, a typical Pamiri house appears forgettable; a low-rise affair of crumbly mud-bricks whose garden setting seems its one salvation. Yet inside a surprise awaits: an intricate layout incorporating an architecture whose numerology is a complex representation of a spiritual universe. The most obvious feature is the *chorkhona* (central skylight), four layers of progressively smaller, box-shaped eaves. Each is turned through 45 degrees and represents an element of pre-Islamic Zoroastrianism – earth, water, air and fire. Pillars, meanwhile, represent key figures of Muslim history, with a conspicuously linked pair that stand for brothers Hassan and Hussein (the second and third Shiite Imams).

PASSION TO LEARN

Located at over 2100m above sea level and with a population of barely 30,000, Khorog (Хоруғ) in Gorno Badakhshan (southeast Tajikistan) is a remarkably remote spot that can take two days to reach by jeep from the capital, Dushanbe, yet the town has a thriving university and some of the highest levels of English language proficiency in the whole of Central Asia. Education and many other development projects here receive particular assistance from the foundation of the Aga Khan, seen as a spiritual leader by Ismaili Muslims, if better known in the West as a France-based racehorse-breeder.

DIVE INTO TAJIK CULTURE

For deep insights into every aspect of Tajikistan's culture, pick up Middleton and Thomas's chunky *Tajikistan and the High Pamirs*. Alternatively, learn about the Aga Khan's efforts to sustain Tajik's unique musical traditions (www.akdn.org/where-we-work/central-asia/tajikistan), or delve into the teachings of Ismaili Islam at iis.ac.uk.

ASIA

KYRGYZSTAN

The Kyrgyz are Central Asia's classic horseback nomads with a culture inspired by ancient heroic epics, and informed by an instinctive understanding of nature and the cycles of life.

POPULATION
5.8 million

% OF COUNTRY
COVERED BY
MOUNTAINS
> 90

WEIGHT OF A
TYPICAL YURT
TENT
450kg

In Central Asia, there's no sight more archetypal than a seasonal mountain-steppe encampment of yurts fronted by a Kyrgyz horseman wearing a kalpak hat. From a tip-tilted, front-folded tricorn base, the kalpak rises in a tapering tower of thick felt embroidered with an arabesque and topped with a tassel. It's completely impractical when driving a car, but on horseback forms an utterly distinctive badge of Kyrgyz identity that offers a degree of insulation from both summer heat and winter chill. Of course, by no means all Kyrgyz are nomads these days, and towns have their obligatory concrete carbuncles and traffic jams. However, more than anywhere else in the ex-USSR, Kyrgyzstan has managed to emerge from decades of collectivisation with elements of its nomadic traditions and philosophies intact, inspired by a history of self-dependence and the ingrained lessons of a rich oral folklore.

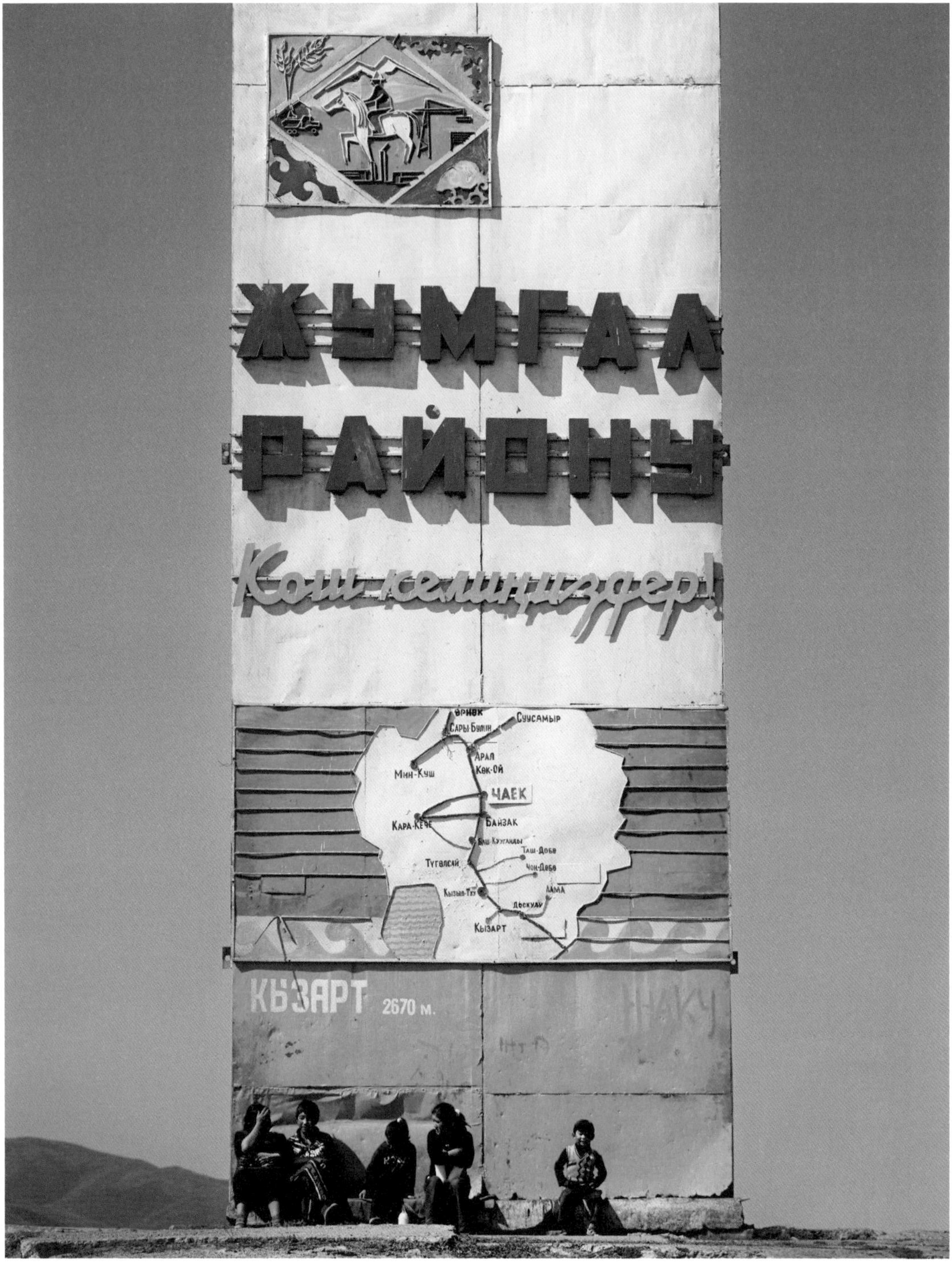
Жумгал району
Кош келиңиздер!
Суусамыр
Арал
Көк-Ой
Мин-Куш
ЧАЕК
Байзак
Кара-Кече
Таш-Дөбө
Чон-Дөбө
Кызарт
2670 м.

ASIA

© Katiekk/Shutterstock

© Eric Lafforgue/Lonely Planet. © Fredy Thuerig/Shutterstock

Clockwise from top: A game of *kok boru* near Lake Issyk-Kul; dinner is served in a yurt at Song Kul lake in Kyrgyzstan; Kyrgyz national dress includes *kalpak* hats, worn by boys and men above the age of six. **Previous page:** A welcome billboard at Lake Song-Kol pass.

TOP INSIGHTS for LIFE

YURTS & FREEDOM

Nothing better symbolises the Kyrgyz freedom of spirit than the yurt, the felt-covered 'tent' of the nation's semi-nomadic shepherds, which are common summer sights on many a *jailoo* (upland pasture). Unlike the flatter-roofed gers of Mongolia, Kyrgyzstan's yurts rise steeply to a central nose topped by the *tündük*, a circular smoke hole latticed by two trios of willow-stems. This is the star-framing view you have when lying in the centre of the yurt gazing up. As a pattern, it's so important to the Kyrgyz soul that a stylised version appears on the national flag.

"Go out light – come back heavy." – Kyrgyz proverb

HEROISM AS AN IDEAL

Collected in the world's longest known epic poem (in terms of lines, if not words), the multiple legends of Manas encapsulate the core beliefs that forge the traditional Kyrgyz identity. Recited in sing-song rhythms by revered *manaschi* ('divinely inspired' performers), the tales evoke a spirit of heroic independence, clan loyalty and a careful balance between brutality and hospitality. Independent Kyrgyzstan celebrated the epic's '1000th anniversary' in 1995, the purported 'tomb' of Manas is found at Talas, and Bishkek's airport is now named after him. Even during the Soviet era, Kyrgyzstan's best-known author Chingiz Aitmatov dared to suggest that *jigits* (warriors of Manas) rather than Bolsheviks were the local male role models.

EQUESTRIAN SOUL

Aptly enough for a traditionally nomadic shepherd culture, the Kyrgyz have a special place in their hearts for horses. The Kyrgyz language has a wealth of names for horses of different ages and statures, while in epic poems horses often understand languages and speak like humans. The national equestrian sport, *kok boru*, is a fearsome form of polo and the classic beverage of the highland pastures is *kumys* (fermented mares' milk).

JOIN THE NOMADS

If you have the time, don't hesitate to make a midsummer trip to the mesmerising lakeside at Son Kul where it's possible to stay in yurt camps with authentic semi-nomads. Otherwise, read the award-winning books of Chingiz Aitmatov, whose work includes plentiful reference to Kyrgyz traditions and environmental worries, often cautiously juxtaposed with the difficult realities of Soviet life.

ASIA

MONGOLIA

A nomadic nation with a culture based on honour and respect, Mongolian pride shines through every aspect of life, from the welcome they give guests to the value placed on traditions.

POPULATION
3.1 million

AVERAGE TEMPERATURE IN JANUARY
-26.5C

Mongolia is the most sparsely populated country in the world

Mongolia is changing – over the past two decades the capital Ulaanbaatar has transformed from a sleepy backwater to a thriving cosmopolitan centre. Many rural Mongolians, however, still live a traditional lifestyle, herding livestock and living in gers (yurts). Whatever direction their lives are taking, nearly everyone in this nation of three million souls takes time to enjoy life, pursue a dream or simply relax through meditation. Religion and spirituality are key factors to happiness here and most Mongolians make regular visits to the local monastery to pray for their family's wellbeing. Many also turn to shamans to create harmony in their home by communicating with spirits and ancestors. When they're not working, Mongolians spend time riding horses, hiking in the mountains, camping by lakes and reciting one of the many folk songs that have been passed down through generations.

From top: A Mongolian boy herds his flock of sheep on horseback; a Mongolian ger camp at Khovsgol Lake, in Khovsgol Nuur National Park.
Previous page: A shaman performs a traditional ritual in a forest near Ulaanbaatar.

TOP INSIGHTS for LIFE

SUCCOUR FOR STRANGERS

Travel across the steppes can be long and arduous, especially on horseback. Historically, it took several days to travel between towns, so Mongolians had to rely on the hospitality of strangers for food and shelter during the journey. While travel is easier now, deep-seated traditions still exist; it's perfectly normal to stop at a ger and receive tea and snacks from your host without further question. The conversation comes after the refreshments. Parents will even send their children out to nearby campers armed with milk curds and yoghurt. Typically, the guest only needs to relay the news from the last town they visited, but if a traveller has something to offer the host in return, better still.

RESPECT THE LAND

Unlike some cultures, Mongolians have never sought to dominate nature. Instead, they treat the environment with the same respect one might accord a parent, knowing that it provides the clean water, grass and soil on which their survival depends. Mongolians prefer not to dig in the earth at all; when it's absolutely necessary, they'll call in a holy man first to appease the spirits of the disturbed land. When they reach the top of a hill or pass, they will circle an ovoo (stone cairn) three times out of respect for the local deity, and place pebbles as an offering. Leaving nature undisturbed even means that sticks, rocks and other artefacts found on a hike should stay where they are, no matter how tempting a souvenir might be.

LIQUID DIET

Mongolians eat a lot of soup, believing that the sweat produced by the act of eating it cleanses the system and relaxes the body. Meat soup, in particular, is thought to be good for building strength and boosting immunity. Mongolian milk tea, made with salt, is another important part of every meal, as it aids digestion. Finally, there is airag, an alcoholic drink made from fermented mares' milk, which some believe may have health benefits if drunk in moderation.

LIVING WITH LESS

Mongolians who visit Western countries are often baffled by the large quantity of stuff people pack into their homes. It couldn't be more different back home. Your possessions need to be scaled down when you live in a ger, which leads to a lifestyle that is less materialistic and more focused on essentials. Mongolians are masters of decluttering, an important skill in a world where we have too much.

CHINA

A 5000-year-old culture with tremendous culinary and artistic traditions, China has contributed some of the world's most lasting philosophical concepts and mindfulness practices, from feng shui to filial piety.

POPULATION
1.38 billion

**COUNTRIES
WHICH SHARE
A BORDER
WITH CHINA**
14

There are 12
animals in the
Chinese zodiac

As one of the world's oldest and most influential cultures, China has plenty to teach the world about living a long, healthy and mindful life. Of course, the country's borders have been fluid through the centuries, changing with the rise and fall of different dynasties, each of which has contributed its own traditions and practices to the mix. The flow of information and goods across the world along the Silk Road transported many of these practices abroad (like eating noodles), and saw others arrive from afar (like Buddhism). The Chinese concept of time as a flowing river and the nation's adherence to Confucian ideals have produced a collectivist culture that values the harmony of the group. Many of the country's quintessential religious and artistic practices support this idea, and underpin an age-old wellness culture that encompasses movement, mindfulness, spirituality and nutrition.

Clockwise from top: Morning *qigong* practice along the old city wall of Xi'an; the use of chopsticks is said to aid digestion by encouraging eating in smaller bites; the art of calligraphy has been practised in China for four millennia. **Previous page:** A scooter rider in Beijing.

TOP INSIGHTS for LIFE

YIN AND YANG

The concept of yin and yang originated in ancient Chinese philosophy in the third century CE. It encompasses the idea that everything is connected; that the universe is an infinitely complex system of opposing, counterbalanced forces – light and

"With a smile, you play with the brush and ink, and sickness becomes lighter." – Lu You, Song dynasty poet

dark, day and night, good and evil, and so on – as visualised in the familiar symbol of a circle split into swirls of white and black, each of which bears a dot of the other colour. Following this principle, all elements are seen to play an equal part in the greater flux of existence, and only through leading a balanced life can one achieve happiness.

GO WITH THE QI

Feng shui (meaning wind-water) is a form of geomancy that purports to use *qi*, the mysterious, underlying life force in the Chinese religious philosophy of Taoism, to create a sense of harmony with the environment. Though it is mainly known around the world now as a way to decorate your home in a balanced way, *feng shui* is still practised across many other aspects of Chinese life, from when to get married to where to go on holiday based on the astrological energies at a particular time.

RESPECT YOUR ELDERS

The teachings of the great philosopher and politician Confucius have arguably had the biggest influence on modern Chinese culture. Among other tenets, the Confucian system of social order stresses the importance of filial piety, or respect for elders and ancestors, leading to a more harmonious society where we learn from history, and where the young and old are cared for in equal measure.

CHOP CHOP

The lore and purported health benefits

CHOP-STICKS 101

1. In your dominant hand, rest Chopstick A between the knuckle of your ring finger and the crook of your thumb, stabilising it with your middle finger. This serves as the anchor chopstick.
2. Grasp Chopstick B in a pinch with your pointer finger and thumb. This serves as the moving chopstick.
3. Using Chopstick A as an anchor, close Chopstick B around the chosen morsel, pinching it into Chopstick A. Lift to mouth, eat, repeat.

PRACTISE YOUR PENMAN- SHIP

You don't have to speak or read Chinese to feel the benefits of learning calligraphy. A traditional Chinese calligraphy class in your home country will give you the best feel for the benefits of this whole body-mind practice. However, learning any type of calligraphy or repetitive painting can have similar stress-busting effects, including controlled breathing that lowers the heart rate.

of using chopsticks (*kuaizi*) also dates back to Confucius, who felt it was immoral to eat meat or have knives at the dining table. He cultivated the use of chopsticks instead, and they remain the primary utensil in China and across many parts of Asia today. Some scientific studies have suggested that using chopsticks actually aids digestion, too, as it encourages slower eating and taking smaller bites.

LIFE FORCE

Qigong is a system of postures, movements, breathing and meditation practices designed to improve and channel qi. Similar to yoga, *qigong* combines exercise with mindfulness to help the practitioner explore the connections between the body and spirit. Today, *qigong* is used in health, spirituality and martial arts training, and practised as a form of exercise and relaxation around the world.

BE AN ANIMAL

Chinese astrology is based on a 12-year cycle. Each year is associated with a natural element (earth, fire, wood, metal and water) and an animal. According to mythology, 12 animals raced to reach a banquet

held by the Jade Emperor and were ordered in the zodiac according to their arrival times at the party. People born in a certain year are said to take on the characteristics of its associated animal, and the fortunes of the year ahead can purportedly be predicted by its animal and element. The cycle repeats every 12 years and, during the year of 'your animal' (*benmingnian*), some people use *feng shui* and superstitious practices like wearing red undergarments to ward off bad luck.

DIFFERENT STROKES

Calligraphy, or *shufa*, has been practised in China for at least 4000 years. Calligraphy masters note that in order to achieve precision, the whole body must be balanced, with good posture and controlled breathing, resulting in a focused, meditative state. Calligraphy is still popular in China, and you will sometimes see elderly calligraphers brushing characters onto the pavement in water – their works quickly dry and they start again, a nod to the Buddhist principle of non-attachment.

Hutong residents play *mahjong*, a tile game invented in China during the Qing dynasty.

SOUTH KOREA

South Koreans take a unique approach to nutrition and strive to lead mindful, conscientious lives, benefitting from one of the most robust wellness industries in the world.

POPULATION
51.4 million

ANNUAL
CONSUMPTION
OF KIMCHI
22kg per capita

AVERAGE AGE
OF FIRST-TIME
MOTHERS
31.6

The influence of intimate contact with China and Japan is evident in Korea's system of values, which draws on broader Asian philosophies like Buddhism, Confucianism and Taoism. Wellness is a huge part of Korean life; health practices such as eating naturally probiotic foods to combat the bitter winters, hiking through the country's soaring mountains and visiting its sophisticated bathhouses, all have ancient roots. Alongside these longstanding good habits, South Korea is one of the world's most technologically advanced societies, placing a high value on education and an environmentally-friendly lifestyle. Despite the fast pace of life here, it is easy to find respite swimming along the country's lengthy coastline or practising meditation during a stay at a Buddhist temple. Through it all, South Koreans manage to keep their sense of balance by cultivating mindful relationships and maintaining social harmony.

ASIA

Clockwise from top: South Korean soldiers demonstrate taekwondo in Gyeryong-si; Ewha Womans University in Seoul, the world's largest female educational institute; Korean kimchi promotes good gut health. **Previous page:** A cycle path beside the Han River in Seoul.

TOP INSIGHTS for LIFE

EAT YOUR PICKLES

Koreans have been pickling vegetables since the Three Kingdoms period (57 BCE–668 CE), using an early understanding of fermentation and salt to preserve radishes and cabbage for the peninsula's harsh winters. Kimchi today is most often made by fermenting Chinese cabbage with red chilli powder, garlic, ginger and salt, though there are hundreds of varieties made from just about anything imaginable. The lactic-acid bacteria present makes kimchi a probiotic food that promotes good gut health.

"Don't drink the kimchi soup first." – Korean proverb

JOIN A JJIMJILBANG

Jjimjilbang, or Korean bathhouses, are more than just spas – they are 24-hour wellness wonderlands offering massage, soaking tubs, swimming pools, saunas and ice rooms, rooms infused with herbs or spices purported to have different health benefits, and even sleeping rooms. It is not unusual for Koreans to visit a *jjimjilbang* for a rockin' Friday evening out and stay the night!

NUNCHI SKILLS

Korean social life is based on the concept of *nunchi*, a subtle type of emotional intelligence that involves interpreting other people's feelings, body language and social standing. Those who possess *nunchi* are quick to gauge the mood in the room, instinctively know what other people are thinking, and can anticipate what they need. Through the power of empathy, they maintain social harmony.

A MOTTO FOR ALL

The country's unofficial national motto, *Hongik Ingan*, translates as 'living and working to the greater benefit of all mankind'. This collectivist mentality has shaped most aspects of Korean life since the Joseon dynasty, and is a foundational philosophy for its national sports, including the martial art of taekwondo.

CHEER UP YOUR GUT

The Korean addiction to pickled vegetables is good for gut health, with most medical traditions now agreeing that probiotics (the 'good bacteria' in fermented foods) aid digestion and nutrient absorption. Sampling kimchi at any Korean restaurant is a good start, but even if spicy fermented cabbage doesn't appeal, it's easy to add foods like yoghurt, gherkins, kefir, kombucha and miso to your diet.

ASIA

JAPAN

Despite a ferocious work ethic, Japan is one of the world's healthiest countries, boasting high life expectancy, thanks in no small part to unique perspectives on living well that remain revered and relevant.

POPULATION
126 million

Nine out of 10
people live in
urban areas

**VENDING
MACHINES**
> 5.5 million

All too often Japan is stereotyped as a place where the importance of work supersedes all else, bringing with it high levels of pressure and plenty of stress. Yet the reality is far more nuanced, and perhaps because of the cultural centrality of work, Japanese people place great value on communing with nature, on quietude, on stillness, on the calming forces that come from both within and without. A walk in a park is never just a walk.

A stand of bamboo has a spirit worth listening to. A soak in an onsen is a meditative ritual. The shifting of the seasons prompts reflection not just on the flowers or the changing leaves, but one's place in the world, one's own longevity. These tenets come from deep traditional values, some religious, some cultural, but they have allowed the Japanese to elevate the search for wellness into a branch of the sublime.

ASIA

© brize99/Shutterstock

© Ippei Naoi/Getty Images, © Idubphoto/Getty Images

Clockwise from top: A *sunamushi onsen* (black-sand spa) in Ibusuki; a cup of antioxidant-rich matcha tea; forest hiking near Shiratani Unsui Gorge.
Previous page: The Naruko Gorge in autumn.

TOP INSIGHTS for LIFE

A REASON FOR LIVING

Translated loosely, *ikigai* is 'the reason one gets up in the morning', or one's sense of personal value – in other words, why you do what you do. And while this may vary widely between individuals, there's something universal about the need to identify the foundation for one's actions. This sense of purpose seeps down into nearly everything in Japanese life – hence the task one is doing, be it grand or menial, will be done well, with attention and care. Many Japanese postpone retirement because they feel valuable doing what they do, even if that is desk work.

> *"I can see clouds a thousand miles away, hear ancient music in the pines." – Ikkyū, Zen Buddhist priest and poet*

SOAK IT UP

While many countries have hot springs, nowhere else is the concept of soaking in warm (or even hot!) water revered the way onsen-dipping is in Japan. Whether one dips in a riverside, mixed-gender pool or books into a high-end onsen hotel, the basic process is the same: strip completely, wash carefully beforehand, then slip in for a good soak – often in meditative silence, letting the heat soothe muscles and melt away stress. Japan has a variety of different bathing experiences, too: waters range in pH and salinity, but there are also sand baths, and even green tea or sake baths. Each variation is said to relieve certain ailments, but whether true or not, one thing is undeniable: it just feels good.

AN IMPERFECT WORLD

The concept of *wabi-sabi* is complex and elusive, embracing the idea that perfection is unattainable, and that, therefore, something flawless cannot truly be perfect – thus, potters crafting tea ceremony bowls

BATHE IN A FOREST

Get out of the city (or suburb) and into a real, lush, life-affirming forest. Walk looking up, not down. Leave the path to find a spot that's quiet, perhaps even untrodden. Stop under a particular tree and stare through its branches into the sky. Breathe deeply, fully, freely. Repeat as often as needed.

GET INTO HOT WATER

When you visit Japan, search the web to identify a nearby onsen (www. onsenjapan. net). Wash carefully – it's a purification ritual not just for your body, but for your mind. Free yourself of stress as you enter the water. Focus on the moment, breathing the steam deep into your lungs. When you emerge, you'll feel relaxed on a deeper level than ever before.

that cost thousands of dollars will introduce tiny flaws, acknowledging that their work cannot be free from imperfection. A person admiring the stillness and beauty of a garden pool will think of wabi-sabi when the silence is broken by a frog jumping in with a splash.

THE BEAUTY OF BREAKAGES

The art of *kintsugi* involves repairing cracks – often those in shattered porcelain – not with something that disguises the break, but with gold. The concept that a vessel can be even more prized, even more valuable, after being broken is a wonderful way to look not merely at objects, but at the challenges of one's own life. How we repair the breaks is what makes us stronger, and our past more beautiful.

DIVE INTO NATURE

Shinrin-yoku, otherwise known as forest bathing, is a practice that involves connecting with nature to experience the sense of rejuvenation that follows a walk in the woods – in much the same way as one might step out of a hot shower or good

bath feeling refreshed and relaxed. Science has just started to confirm what intuition already suggests: a plethora of studies show a positive link between a walk in the woods (and getting out into nature generally) and the strength of the immune system.

THE ZEN OF TEA

When is a cup of tea not a cup of tea? When it's served as part of a Japanese tea ceremony, an experience that is part performance, part meditation, part recreational, and very, very Zen. First introduced from China through Hirado, an island in Kyūshū, green tea cultivation and the associated ceremony has now become one of the iconic images of Japan. Most Westerners assume it's a form of dining, but in fact, it's an entire philosophy: the way you enter the room; which flower you look at while waiting to be served; the posture and position of the server; the temperature, the taste, the artful sweets that decorate the plate.... Done right, it's an experience that is as carefully curated as a Japanese garden.

A potter at work in his studio, Kyoto.

PHILIPPINES

Filipinos believe that you are only thriving if your loved ones and community are too. This social and moral obligation makes all the difference when it comes to leading a happy, meaningful existence.

POPULATION
106 million

CONSUMPTION OF PORK PER CAPITA
14.2 kg

Over 400 million text messages sent per day

In Filipino culture, nurturing relationships is important; you can only blossom if you have strong family ties and healthy friendships. Around 86% of Filipinos are Catholic. Churches are public spaces which foster a strong sense of community. Doing good deeds is a religious obligation, but people are also sociable and hospitable by nature. Filipinos love nothing more than to laugh, dance and celebrate at splashy Christmas and birthday parties and fiestas, where communal traditions like eating *lechon* (roasted pig on a spit) still thrive. On these occasions, the power of fellowship shines through, as everyone shares in organising and serving. Families tend to live together here, in connected or adjacent houses, but the search for work means they can also end up great distances apart: statistics show that up to 10 million Filipinos work overseas. Despite this, they never forget the importance of home.

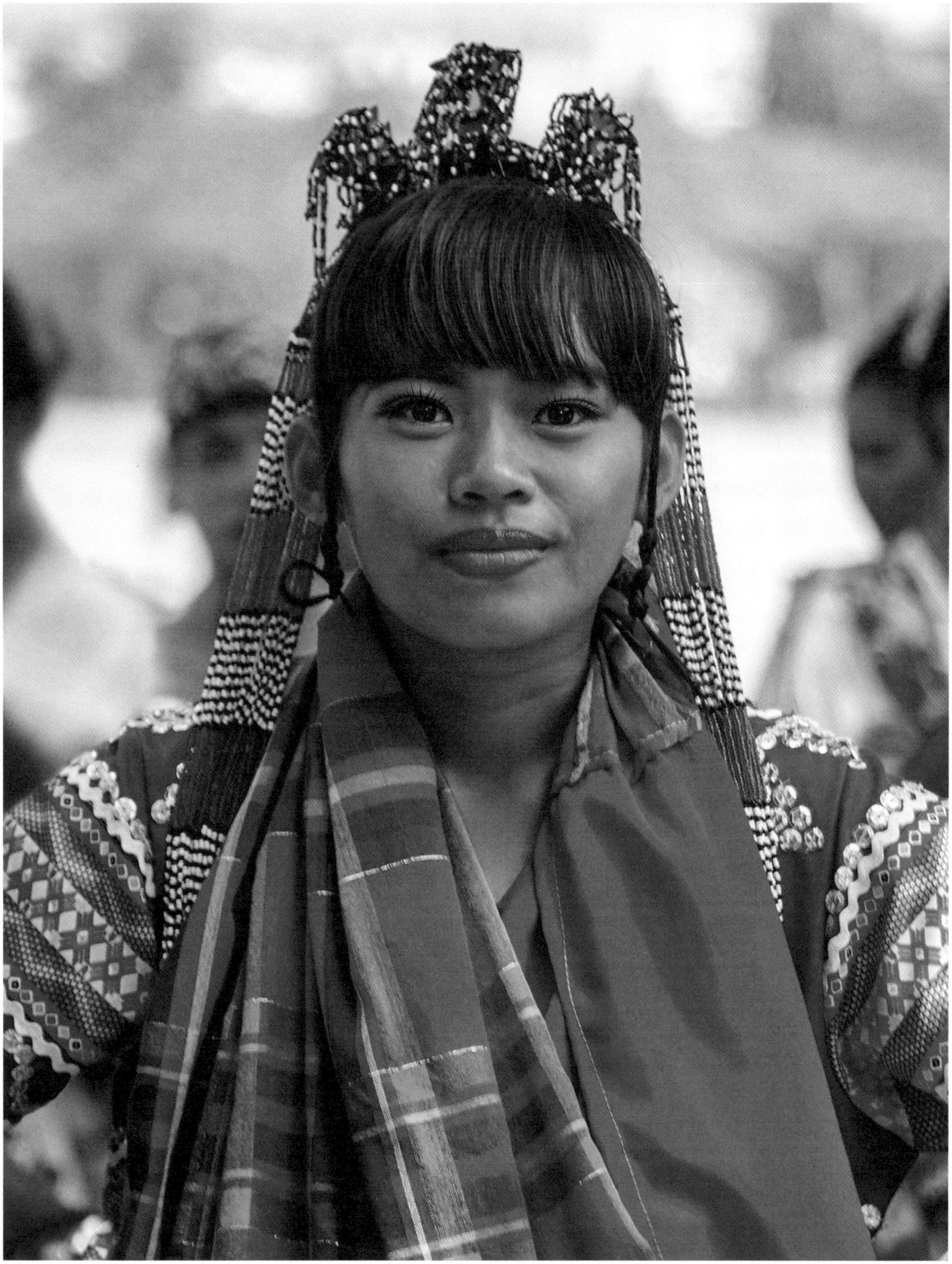

From top: A fruit market on the Philippine island of Palawan; a plate of *inihaw na liempo* (marinated pork belly served with spiced vinegar).
Previous page: A Filipina dancer at the Timpuyog Festival in Sarangani Province.

TOP INSIGHTS for LIFE

PLAYING NICE

Pakikisama is the notion that getting along with others is important. People should be fundamentally friendly and polite to one another, whether saying hello to someone on the street or inviting a neighbour over for coffee. As a Filipino, you don't need to agree with everyone, but you should be able to relate to them empathetically and put yourself in their shoes (what's known as *pakikiramdam*).

> *"A broom is sturdy because its strains are tightly bound."* – Filipino proverb

LEND A HAND

Bayanihan translates as 'community spirit', but its meaning goes beyond that – for Filipinos, it's the practice of doing a good turn for others without expecting anything in return. Underlying this is the belief that fostering a network of people around you makes individuals stronger, and instils personal joy. *Bayanihan* occur within a group – such as the way everyone helps to organise the barangay (village) fiesta – or individually, in the form of *pasalubong*, the tradition of bringing back gifts for friends and family after being away. Overseas Filipinos are expected to send money home, or boxes of presents, including household wares and toys. You are only doing as well as the people you love.

PAY YOUR DEBTS

Utang na loob is a 'debt to one's inner self'. It's the principle of reciprocity ingrained in Filipino culture – a person must always repay favours and demonstrate gratitude. It expresses itself as fierce loyalty to those who care about you, whether it be family, friends or the community. For example, you should never fight with your parents because you're forever indebted to them for giving you the gift of life. While the notion of being forever indebted may sound heavy, for Filipinos it is liberating to know someone always has your back.

THE GIFT OF GIVING

For Filipinos, the idea of coming home empty-handed is unthinkable. On your next adventure, why not send postcards to family and friends? They're the perfect *pasalubong* – inexpensive but meaningful, especially in the age of Facebook and emails. Knowing your loved ones will be surprised and touched by such a gesture is certain to feel good.

ASIA

INDONESIA

It's best known for Bali, but intrepid travellers are slowly realising that no matter where you go in the 17,500 islands of Indonesia, you're sure to be greeted with generosity and hospitality.

POPULATION
263 million

LANGUAGES
> 700

**POSITION ON
THE CAF WORLD
GIVING INDEX**
1st

Indonesia has been described as 'the world's most invisible country'. It is the fourth most populous on Earth, yet around 7000 islands – well over a third of the total – are uninhabited. The country's position on the Ring of Fire has bestowed it with some of our planet's most fertile – and spectacularly beautiful – landscapes. Most visitors to the world's biggest Muslim country tend to congregate on (predominantly Hindu) Bali, but Indonesia, which also contains vast, lesser-explored Christian archipelagos, defies any easy generalisation. An island-hopping trip from Aceh (Sumatra) in the west to West Papua (New Guinea) in the east would be like road-tripping from London to Cameroon, and the diversity en route would be just as mind-boggling. And yet, every community – regardless of religion or ethnic background – shares the common qualities of generosity and hospitality to travellers.

Clockwise from top: Bali's dramatically positioned Pura Luhur Uluwatu temple; novice monks lighting paper lanterns for Loi Krathong festival; fruits for sale at an Indonesian market stall. **Previous page:** Musicians playing Gamelan music in Bali.

TOP INSIGHTS for LIFE

HOME-GROWN DIET

With a young, growing urban population, fast food is eating into the traditional Indonesian diet, but in rural communities, most people still prefer home-grown produce. Their diet revolves around rice, sometimes served with chicken or fish (and very rarely red meat), plus fresh vegetables bought from the local market. Fruits, tubers and edible leaves are grown in family compounds, alongside an array of plants used in time-tested herbal remedies. Science has started to recognise the benefits of these plants, including *Moringa oleifera*, thought to have the power to bring the sick back from death's door. Studies show that moringa is high in protein, and rich in essential oils, vitamins and minerals.

CHERISH THE CHILDREN

You'll rarely hear a child crying in an Indonesian village; babies are hardly ever out of a loving relative's arms. (In Bali, a baby must not even touch the ground until it is three months old, as it is believed that the spirit of the earth will be too powerful.) Even as they grow older, any crying child will immediately receive a show of affection. They will rarely be punished, and the sternest reprimand they might hear are the words *tidak boleh* ('you may not' or 'it is not done'). In some cultures, this might result in spoiled adults...but the well-balanced, caring and generous nature of the average Indonesian seems to speak for the efficacy of the system.

RITUAL COST-BENEFITS

Rituals and festivals play a huge part in the life of most Indonesians. For many Balinese, in particular, a large proportion of a family's income is spent on offerings for the constant round of ceremonies. In Kalimantan and Sumatra, families plough their money into agricultural ceremonies, and in Sumba and Tana Toraja, funerals are so expensive that debts are often passed down through the generations. The heartfelt obligation that Indonesians feel toward their families and home towns binds communities that have remained strong through millennia.

A DAILY ACT OF CREATION

Every Indonesian is an artist or craftsperson of some sort. Children learn how to prepare offerings from an early age and carving, weaving or basket-making are passed down from grandparents. The concentration required for any act of creation is often seen as a form of meditation. Give some thought at least once a day to creating something you consider beautiful.

SINGAPORE

Sleek Singapore stands out from the crowd. Home to a pulsating blend of religions, races and cultures, this is a country hungry for success — and it has an appetite to match.

POPULATION
6 million

Submitted a
Unesco bid for
its unique hawker
culture in 2019

A national Tree
Planting Day has
been held since
1971

In just over 50 years since independence, this nation - geographically small but densely populated, with more than 8000 people per sq km - has morphed from a busy shipping port into a global financial powerhouse, and it's shown plenty of grit, discipline and determination along the way. In the safe, clean and future-facing Lion City, citizens work hard, embrace their multiculturalism with real zeal and herald their nationality with pride. Religious celebrations take place year-round for the country's main ethnic groups - Chinese, Malay, Indian and Eurasian - making for a packed calendar of festivals; and that, in turns, translates into a never-ending conveyor belt of delicacies. And it is here, on a plate, where the greatest source of Singaporean happiness seems to lie: the nation's unadulterated love of food has created one of the world's most mouth-watering culinary landscapes.

ASIA

© Phil Weymouth/Lonely Planet

© ZambeziShark/Getty Images, © Pete Seaward/Lonely Planet

Clockwise from top: Diners on a busy Chinatown street in Singapore; a street vendor in front of a traditional Chinese shopfront in Georgetown; dumplings at a hawker centre in Changhi Village. **Previous page:** Walkway inside the Flower Dome, in Singapore's Gardens by the Bay.

TOP INSIGHTS for LIFE

LET'S MAKAN! LET'S EAT!

The Little Red Dot's bustling hawker centres – open-air food courts – serve up succulent street food at bargain-basement prices. Often referred to as the nation's communal dining halls, this is where you'll find Singaporeans from all walks of life queuing together for their favourite grub. Seating is usually at round tables, sharing is encouraged, and conversations often turn to good-natured, but hotly contested, debates about which eating establishments are 'die, die, must try' – Singlish for 'to die for'. To get in on the action, follow your nose, join the longest line or ask passers-by for their recommendations.

THE GREEN DREAM

Up to 80% of Singaporeans live in small units in high-rise blocks, so getting out into nature on a regular basis is a top priority for the populace. The country aspires to be a 'City in a Garden', and as the concrete jungle gives way to skyscrapers that support whole ecosystems, and nature reserves and green corridors continue to sprout, that dream is slowly becoming a reality. Wander the Unesco-listed Singapore Botanic Gardens, which not only teems with flora and fauna but also with fitness fanatics, tai-chi addicts and families, or glimpse the future at the space-age Gardens by the Bay.

SIMPLE KNEADS

Singaporeans clock up some of the world's longest working hours, but they also try to find some 'me' time. For those with deep pockets, there are high-end hotel spas to try, but thrifty locals head to shopping centres where mid-range massage parlours and cheap-and-cheerful reflexology stalls abound. It's a motto of 'no pain, no gain' here as pressure points, supposedly connected to vital organs, are poked and prodded to get the circulation going. If you're short on time and cash, just head to a local park to find a reflexology path instead – slip off your shoes, walk across the knobbly rocks... and try not to scream.

TAKE A BIG BITE

Explore the national obsession with grub by sinking your teeth into the Singapore Food Festival. Held over two weeks in July, the festival celebrates the city's culinary scene with lashings of food-related events, including workshops, cinema screenings, and food crawls, plus STREAT, the festival's signature event showcasing some of the Lion City's most scrummy local dishes.

THAILAND

In the 'Land of Smiles', good humour and goodwill form the Buddhist blueprint for serenity — in this lifetime and the lifetimes yet to come.

POPULATION
68.6 million

TEMPLES IN THAILAND
> 40,000

LENGTH OF A MUAY THAI MATCH
5 rounds of 3 mins

The concept of karma reigns supreme in Thailand. Around 94% of people are practitioners of Theravada Buddhism, and the religion shapes many aspects of life, from daily almsgiving to the political system. Thai Buddhists believe that to be human is to suffer, but this outlook doesn't stop them from enjoying life. On the contrary; they're a friendly, fun-loving people – and a smile goes an awfully long way here. With more than 1400 islands and a quarter of the population living near the coast, the influence of the sea is profound, encouraging Thais to keep their problems in perspective; humans always make mistakes, but being mindful leads to better choices, bringing peace to ourselves and those around us. Showing respect is a crucial part of their culture, whether to teachers, elders or ancestors, and Thais see the wellbeing of the group as more important than the wellbeing of the individual.

© Catherine Sutherland/Lonely Planet

© Justin Foulkes/Lonely Planet, © a_volkov/Getty Images

Clockwise from top: Shan people planting rice in Mae Hong Son, northwest Thailand; a martial arts master performs a ceremonial dance before her fight at Muay Thai Festival in Ayutthaya; food stalls at Bangkok's Rot Fai Ratchada Night Market. **Previous page:** The Grand Palace, Bangkok.

TOP INSIGHTS for LIFE

GRIN & BEAR IT

Thailand is known as the 'Land of Smiles' for good reason. It's a serious faux pas not to turn your frown upside down. Thais are averse to being publicly disgraced to the point of losing respect – what's known locally as 'losing face'. So to avoid such humiliation, they act with the utmost self-restraint. Confrontation is best avoided, a principle echoed by Buddhist belief. It makes Thais masters of manifesting good vibes. Sometimes, all it takes is a smile or a joke to lighten up a tense or awkward

"Even a single moment of anger can ruin your peace of mind forever." – *Thai proverb*

situation. That's the life philosophy of *sanuk*. Translated, *sanuk* means 'fun', but it encompasses the notion of having a positive, playful attitude in all that you do – even work.

RELAXATION SQUARED

Thais approach life with the sentiment of *sabai sabai*. It translates as 'relax, relax', but it means something closer to 'don't worry, be happy' and reflects a laid-back island lifestyle. Don't take things too seriously; don't sweat the small stuff under the blazing sun. *Sabai sabai* can be as simple as enjoying a tranquil situation: a good massage (you'll see many massage parlours named this) or a rest under a shady coconut tree. It's also a perspective that helps to avoid conflict. After all, in Thailand, plans often change, schedules slip, the unexpected happens. So what's the best way to stop losing your marbles? That's right. *Sabai sabai*.

KEEP THE SPIRITS HAPPY

Thais are known for their belief in the supernatural. On streets and in homes around the country, you'll see colourful little shrines decorated with garlands, streamers and candles. These spirit houses, as they're called, are where the souls of the deceased find everlasting peace. Thais regularly

BIRTHDAY BENEVO-LENCE

Thais 'make merit' – perform good deeds – on their birthdays, as it's believed to bring health and happiness. Instead of accepting gifts this year, try asking for donations to a preferred charity or organising a volunteer outing. You may find that the Thai philosophy of sharing your blessings, instead of just counting them, brings deeper meaning to another journey around the sun.

SEE A MUAY THAI FIGHT

Don't miss the *wai kru ram muay* that begins every Thai boxing match. To twangy traditional music, fighters do the *wai kru* by circling the ring, praying in every corner. Afterwards is the *ram muay*, a beautiful dancing ritual comprised of slow movements and footwork personalised by the fighter, his teacher and their chosen deities.

outfit these shrines with fresh offerings of items like fruit, rice and open bottles of soda with a plastic straw, to appease their celestial masters. In Thai culture, it's important to pay respect to not just the living, but also the dead – otherwise, the spirits may cause chaos!

THE UNIVERSAL GREETING

In Thai culture, one gesture encompasses hello, goodbye and an apology all rolled into one: the *wai*. When greeting someone, especially in business or formal situations, you put your hands together in a prayer-like position in front of you. The more respect commanded by that person, like a monk or an elder, the higher up you fold your hands. Showing respect is a big part of Thai culture, and the *wai* is its simplest, most ubiquitous form. A lovely example is the *wai kru*; a ceremony in which a student shows gratitude to his or her teachers. Muay Thai fighters will do it in the ring before fighting, as well as traditional Thai dancers on stage before a performance.

SHARING IS CARING

In Thailand, the group is more important than the individual. The togetherness that fosters is especially evident in how people eat. At home and in restaurants, Thai meals are generally served on large plates meant for sharing. Whether a curry, fish or soup, people around the table help themselves. Rice can come in a big pot or each person gets their own portion. It may seem relaxed, but there are unwritten rules – for example, you shouldn't take more than a couple of spoonfuls at a time and elders should be served first. That sense of community is even reflected in the flavours themselves: Thai food is known for its balance of spicy, salty, bitter, and sweet. Harmony is everything!

A cook prepares for the lunchtime rush at a food stall in Chiang Mai.

VIETNAM

Ruled by the Chinese for a thousand years, and by the French for a hundred, much of the Vietnamese way of life bears traces of foreign influence, including the approach to health and wellness.

POPULATION
97 million

**Adult obesity
rate: 2.1% (one of
the lowest in the
world)**

LITERACY RATE
94.5%

With nearly 100 million people packed into a long and thin S-shaped land mass, Vietnam is a country of contrasts. After nearly a millennium of Chinese domination, and its more recent history as part of French Indochina, it gained independence in 1954. It's no surprise, then, that much of Vietnamese culture draws from these influences, from its use of traditional medicine to its Romanised alphabet, a rarity among Asian languages. While it's Southeast Asia's fastest-growing economy, nearly 40% of the population still work the fields, mainly in the Red River Delta to the north and the Mekong Delta in the south. And although there's a lot about Vietnam that is unhealthy (almost one in two adult males smoke, for example), it still manages to have one of the lowest adult obesity rates in the world, in part by drawing lessons from its unique heritage about how to look after body and mind.

ASIA

© Jethuynh/Getty Images

© Pascal Mannaerts/Alamy Stock Photo, © Wirestock Images/Shutterstock

Clockwise from top: Tea pickers on a plantation in Bao Loc; group exercise in public parks is a common sight in Vietnam; fire cupping is a popular Vietnamese treatment for a host of ailments. **Previous page:** Noodles for breakfast at a market in Hoi An.

TOP INSIGHTS for LIFE

LET'S GET PHYSICAL

Because most homes in Vietnamese cities are small, life spills out into open spaces. In the early morning, you're bound to find lots of people in the park walking, kicking a shuttlecock, or exercising at government-installed gym stations. The Vietnamese also love doing things in groups, so expect to find classes ranging from ballroom dancing to tai chi to Jane Fonda-esque aerobics. While membership is usually on a monthly basis, you can often pitch in a few dong and join the fun.

LIFELONG LEARNING

Vietnam has an extremely high literacy rate compared with South Asia's 72% average. This is all the more surprising since the rate was reportedly around 5–10% as recently as 1945. Some credit goes to the 17th-century Romanisation of the Vietnamese language, making it easier to read than the script-based languages of neighbouring Cambodia and Thailand, for example. In any case, Vietnamese culture prizes lifelong learning.

Everywhere you look, you'll find people reading online and off, from kids engrossed in Detective Conan mangas to senior citizens sat on a stool in front of their homes reading newspapers in the bright sunshine.

SUCK IT UP

When a Vietnamese person suddenly feels under the weather, traditionally, the culprit is 'evil wind' and a cạo gió session usually follows. Literally 'scraping the wind', a coin or sturdy spoon is used to slowly and lightly scrape the skin until red, bruise-like marks appear, helped along by some type of greasy, medicated oil. A similar procedure called giác ho'i uses glass cups that have been partially vacuumed either by a pump, or by a quick pass over a burning, cotton-tipped baton, and then placed on the skin. Fire cupping is thought to suck out the bad wind, leaving the patient looking like they lost a fight with a giant octopus, but ostensibly feeling better. While the techniques may have come from China, the Vietnamese claim these traditional folk treatments as their own.

ASIA

MYANMAR

Colourful, captivating and often conflicted, Myanmar offers philosophical riches and profound lessons from Buddhist life to those willing to dig deeper than the newspaper headlines.

POPULATION
55.6 million

**% OF POPU-
LATION WHO
CHEW BETEL NUT**
43

The annual value
of exports of
hair shaved from
ordained monks is
US$6.2 million

Myanmar's cultural heritage is often overshadowed by the country's troubled politics, but look beyond the media reports and you'll find a society that resounds like a temple bell to the teachings of Theravada Buddhism. The scriptures of the Pali canon inform most aspects of life in Myanmar – formerly Burma – and the quest for spiritual merit is not a once-a-week activity but a theme that runs through every day. Burmese children enter monasteries as novice monks and file out into the streets each day to collect alms, before reversing the roles, and handing out alms themselves when they return home. It's a way of life that teaches humility and patience, something tangible in the streets of this complex, remarkable country. Most travellers are surprised when they visit for the first time and discover, behind what makes the news, a society motivated not by desperation but by hope and optimism.

ASIA

Clockwise from top: Wooden canoes on Myanmar's picturesque Inle Lake; applying *thanaka* to the skin is a long-held Burmese tradition; *thanaka* wood used for cosmetic paste. **Previous page:** Young novice monks carrying alms bowls on a public jeep.

TOP INSIGHTS for LIFE

A LIFE OF MERIT

Burmese Buddhists take great pains to accrue spiritual merit as part of daily life, whether feeding pigeons – any one of which could be a reincarnated human soul – or offering donations of food to the nation's 600,000 Buddhist monks and nuns. The quest for merit has led to some enterprising solutions: at temples and monasteries, pilgrims pay a donation to release tame birds, who then fly back into their cages, ready to provide merit for the next pilgrim in line.

PROPITIATING NATS

The worship of *nats* – the spirits of saintly humans, animals, trees and plants and natural forces – is Myanmar's unofficial second religion, and every Burmese village is connected to the supernatural world through the spirits that inhabit its land, water and trees. Offerings of food, drink, flowers and even cigarettes are left daily in front of household shrines and village *nat sin* (spirit houses).

MONASTIC EDUCATION

At an age when most children are obsessed by trainers and game consoles, Burmese youngsters shave their heads and enter monasteries, owning little more than their sandals and robes, a begging bowl and a paper parasol. In exchange, they gain the spiritual richness that comes from the scriptures of Theravada Buddhism. Though most children later leave the *sangha* (monastic brotherhood), the values learned in the monasteries last for a lifetime.

NATURE'S FACTOR 50

Part beauty treatment, part sunblock and part natural coolant, *thanaka* is a national institution. Every Burmese family has a granite grindstone for converting wood and bark from the *thanaka* tree into a paste to be applied to the face and body, instantly marking someone out as Burmese. There's science behind this 2000-year-old tradition – *thanaka* is rich in antioxidants and anti-inflammatory and antibacterial compounds.

JOIN THE SANGHA

Meditation centres and monasteries across Myanmar accept foreign visitors as temporary novices, and the government even provides a special meditation visa to facilitate long stays for inner contemplation. In exchange, you'll have to shave your head and follow the same austere lifestyle as other novices – sleeping on wooden boards and waking before dawn to join other monks on the daily quest for alms.

ASIA

BANGLADESH

South Asia's least explored quarter, Bangladesh is a nation of hidden depths, with a complex cultural heritage that draws life lessons from Islam, Hinduism and Buddhism.

POPULATION
159.5 million

Nearly two-thirds of the population work as farmers

More than a quarter of people live on the coast

Sprawling around the waterlogged wetlands of the world's largest river delta, Bangladesh serves up a full platter of cultural riches, inspired by the changing seasons and its position at the threshold between Hindu, Buddhist and Islamic empires. Bangladeshis follow Islam but embrace yoga and Ayurveda. Despite the international border parked awkwardly between them, people in Bangladesh and Indian West Bengal identify as Bengalis ahead of anything else. The music, writing and art of this unique corner of the subcontinent blend themes of spirituality with rebellion, rejecting the orthodoxy in favour of personal freedom, and prioritising the individual relationship with the divine over rigid rules imposed by organised religions. Inspired by the *bauls* – an ancient sect of wandering minstrels – the national narrative is all about shared experience, and the sense of wellbeing that comes from spiritual love.

From top: A *baul* singer performs at a festival in Sirajdikhan; Kansat in northwestern Bangladesh plays host to the country's largest mango market. **Previous page:** A fisher throws a net in the river in Dhaka.

TOP INSIGHTS for LIFE

MUSICAL REBELS

Think of Bangladesh and it's probably not mystic minstrels that come mind – but the country's *bauls* represent one of Asia's most fascinating traditions. Following a life of intense spirituality, music and personal indulgence, these wandering poet-musicians draw strands of inspiration from Tantric Hinduism, Buddhism, Sufism and Islam. At the heart of the *baul* way of life is a belief that human love is the path to the divine, and that true freedom lies outside the constraints of organised religion and society.

BENGAL'S SWEET TOOTH

Nobody loves sweets like the people of Bengal, known historically as Gauda, kingdom of *guda* (cane sugar). Treats include delicious concoctions of curds, palm sugar, ground grains and pulses, rose water, fruit, nuts and spices, which instantly transport the eater to the kitchens of childhood. For Bengalis, a portion of *doi mishti* (sweetened curd) is like being wrapped up in mother's apron while the monsoon pours outside.

SEASONAL EATING

With six seasons to consider – *grishma* (summer), *barsha* (rainy), *sharat* (autumn), *hemanta* (late autumn), *shhit* (winter) and *basanta* (spring) – Bengalis take their seasonal food very seriously. They go mad for mangoes and jackfruit during the monsoon harvest season, and the Bengali New Year in April is celebrated with a national feast of *ilish macch bhaja* (fried Indian herring).

ARTISTIC AWAKENING

The British occupation awakened an explosion of artistic expression in Bengal, as artists, writers and thinkers pushed back against the imposition of colonial culture. Under the guidance of Rabindranath Tagore, Kazi Nazrul Islam and Raja Ram Mohan Roy, Bengalis deserted established notions about religion, society and marriage, turning the spotlight onto Bengal's rich precolonial heritage. This shared sense of Bengali solidarity even survived Partition – the national anthems of both Bangladesh and India were written by Tagore in his native Bengali.

WRITE A BAUL SONG

Baul themes weave through Bengali poetry like strands on a loom, and writing your own celebration of existence, spirituality and rebellion can be highly cathartic. A classic *baul* song celebrates freedom, divinity, the wonders of nature, the nature of existence and physical love. There are no fixed rules for melody or meter – *baul* songs are accompanied by a drone tone provided by the *ektara* (gourd lute).

ASIA

BHUTAN

Tiny, landlocked and remote, Bhutan is a font of knowledge on how to live well, and a standard-bearer for a world motivated not by money but by Gross National Happiness.

POPULATION
766,000

% OF COUNTRY
THAT IS
MOUNTAINOUS
98.8

Nearly three-
quarters of the
population live in
rural areas

Bhutan is best-known for two things: a US$250 daily fee for tourists and the concept of Gross National Happiness. In fact, the two are interlinked: the tourist tax pays for healthcare, education and impressive levels of government support, and the longstanding national policy of 'high value, low impact' tourism has helped Bhutan preserve its culture, customs and environment in a way neighbouring countries can only dream of. What is Gross National Happiness? According to locals, it's the pursuit of wellbeing, defined by family, health and a life full of Buddhist karma, rather than materialist measures such as Gross National Product. This quest takes surprising forms – the enthusiastic contemplation of death, for example, and the veneration of the phallus as a symbol of fertility – but it also informs everything from the country's national health service to its world-leading environmental policies.

ASIA

Above: Monks dancing at Pangri Zampa monastery, Thimphu. **Previous page:** Monks stroll through the ornate courtyard of Tango Goemba monastery, originally founded in the 12th century.

TOP INSIGHTS for LIFE

THE PURSUIT OF GNH

When picking an economic strategy for a nation, it takes a certain philosophical outlook to make happiness one of the key measures for success. But that was the decision made by king Jigme Singye Wangchuck when he launched his plan to bring Bhutan into the modern age in 1972. To this day, Gross National Happiness – measured via national surveys about lifestyle, wellbeing and karma – is one of the government's key markers of progress.

CARBON-NEGATIVE LIVING

While world leaders haggled over slight reductions in emissions, Bhutan quietly got on with becoming the world's first carbon negative country – that is, absorbing more carbon than it produces. Respecting nature plays a huge role in Bhutanese culture, and protecting flora and fauna is seen as a religious duty. Bhutan also aims to become the world's first fully organic country in 2020, adding to its long list of environmental credentials.

DIVINE MADNESS

You only have to be in Bhutan for a few moments before you notice the phalluses painted on the walls. This primal fertility symbol is often depicted in graphic detail – a celebration of the importance of sex and family in this deeply traditional society. Credit for the custom goes to the 16th-century lama Drukpa Kinley, the Divine Madman, who subverted the austere traditions of Tibetan Buddhism in favour of a joyful celebration of sex, alcohol, and indulgence, winning many new converts to the faith.

CONTEMPLATING DEATH

Across Bhutan, hillsides bear fluttering gardens of shroud-white *dhar* (pole-mounted prayer flags), erected in honour of departed loved ones. Traditionally, 108 flags are raised for the dead in ceremonies on the 7th, 14th, 21st and 49th day after death. It's a powerful reminder of the fragility of human existence, in a culture where people deliberately contemplate death five times a day to remove the fear of mortality.

ASSESS YOUR GNH

Measuring happiness in terms of cash, property and career is a Western construct. To recalibrate your perception in terms of Gross National Happiness, sit down and re-evaluate your life in Bhutanese terms. Are you healthy, educated and well governed? Do you make good use of your time? Are you part of a community? Is the environment you live in rich in cultural and ecological diversity?

ASIA

NEPAL

A land of mountains, monasteries and mystery, Nepal has long drawn travellers in search of answers to life's big questions – whether trekking, wildlife-spotting or temple-hopping, few leave empty-handed.

POPULATION
9.7 million

% OF COUNTRY COVERED BY MOUNTAINS
75

A quarter of the population live more than 2hr from the nearest road

There's something about mountains that makes you feel closer to god – or to your own insignificance in the face of nature's magnificence, depending on your philosophical outlook. As the home of eight of the world's 14 highest mountains, Nepal has a convincing claim to being closer to the heavens than almost anywhere else on earth, and its lofty position has certainly influenced the outlook of its people. Being confronted daily by both the wonder of nature, and its destructive power – in the form of earthquakes, avalanches, landslides and floods – Nepalis have a particularly introspective attitude to life. The teachings of Hinduism and Buddhism weave through daily existence like the incense smoke that drifts through Nepal's mountain temples, and beliefs frequently intertwine in a nation unified by the concept of karma and the positive benefits of good actions to aid all of humanity.

ASIA

© Kristin Ruhs/Getty Images

© OceanFishing/Getty Images, © Valdis Skudre/Shutterstock

Clockwise from top: Colourful Holi celebrations in Bhaktapur; the mountain village of Pokhara is overlooked by the mighty Annapurna Massif; lighting incense butter candles. **Previous page:** Tibetan flags at Annapurna Base Camp.

TOP INSIGHTS for LIFE

EIGHT STEPS TO ENLIGHTENMENT

As the birthplace of Buddhism, Nepal has given the world perhaps its most authoritative guide to living a life free from suffering. Born a pampered prince in the kingdom of Kapilavastu, near modern-day Lumbini, Siddhartha Gautama was mortified by his first glimpse of human hardship, and devoted his life to shaking off the bonds of attachment to material things. By treading the eightfold path – right understanding, right thought, right speech, right action, right livelihood, right effort, right mindfulness, right concentration – his followers hope to unshackle themselves in the same manner,

"Do not dwell in the past, do not dream of the future, concentrate the mind on the present moment." – Siddhartha Gautama, the historical Buddha

escape a life of suffering and move on to nirvana, the ultimate state of spiritual wellbeing.

LET IT BE

If one phrase captures the Nepali attitude to life more than any other it's 'ke garne'. This much murmured motto literally means 'what to do?', but it's less an admission of defeat than a philosophy of accepting your fate, in a country where life is subject to the whims of shifting tectonic plates and monsoon rains. It would be foolish to rail against forces you can't control, the thinking goes, but by taking charge of your own thoughts and feelings, you can make the best of each moment, rather than being burdened by regrets and attachment to things lost.

WALKING AS PRAYER

In Nepal, trekking is more than just a means of getting from A to B – it's an act of deep religious devotion. Some of Nepal's most popular trekking trails trace ancient pilgrimage routes, tramped for centuries by Hindu and Buddhist devotees seeking

TREK TO SACRED LAKES

The climb to the sacred lakes at Gosainkund is one of the closest treks to Kathmandu, but it feels a million miles from the mobbed trails that snake around Everest and Annapurna. Start the pilgrimage from the city limits of Kathmandu or the Langtang Valley, and find space for inner reflection as you gaze at the snow-capped peaks reflected in Gosainkund's millpond-calm waters.

WALK EVERY-WHERE

If you avoid the internal combustion and live more like a Nepali, the carbon footprint of your transport will shrink dramatically. Speed is the driving force behind petrol power, but you can get almost anywhere on foot if you give yourself time. Start small – walk to work instead of taking the bus – and your heart, as well as the environment, will thank you for it.

enlightenment at divine peaks and sacred lakes. Perched at 4380m, the holy lakes at Gosainkund were reputedly hollowed out by the points of Shiva's trident, and legions of Hindu and Buddhist pilgrims throng the trails from Helambu and Langtang to prove their devotion during the festivals of Janai Purmina and Ganga Dussehra.

ALL PULLING TOGETHER

Befitting a nation where people are crammed onto small patches of farmable land at the bottom of rugged mountain valleys, Nepalis have a long tradition of working together, and nowhere is this more apparent than during Nepal's fevered festivals. Every year during Indra Jatra, Seto Machhindranath Jatra and Rato Machhindranath Jatra, vast wooden chariots are slotted together and stacked storeys-high with greenery, then hauled through the streets of Kathmandu and Patan by armies of devotees in an electrifying testament to this powerful community spirit.

SPIRITUAL ENGINEERING

Thanks to the influence of Tibetan Buddhism, the Nepalis are masters

of economy when it comes to the art of prayer. Even the humble prayer wheel is a superior piece of spiritual engineering – each spin is equivalent to reciting the mantra written repeatedly on the scroll inside thousands, or even millions, of times. Across Nepal, water-powered prayer wheels spin mantras ceaseless into the ether, while fluttering prayer flags adorning every monastery and mountain pass carry prayers of goodwill and compassion into the world with each passing gust of wind.

LOW-CARBON LIVING

Despite concerted efforts to drive roads into the Himalaya, Nepal remains one of the least connected nations on the planet. Huge swathes of the country can only be reached on foot, and millions of Nepalis live a low-carbon lifestyle that would shame the Western world. In the high Himalaya, yak herders move with the seasons, summering in high-altitude meadows in temporary shelters made from stacked stones, roofed over with bamboo collected from along the trails. It's a life of considerable hardship, but also a lesson in how little human beings actually need to get by.

Hikers cross a bridge in Shey Phoksundo National Park.

INDIA

The birthplace of three of the world's great religions, and crucible for countless philosophical movements, India has laid a path for the world to follow since at least 7000 BCE.

POPULATION
1.3 billion

OFFICIAL LANGUAGES
22

About a quarter of the population are vegetarian

The hippies who beat a trail to India in the 1960s were just the latest in a long line of spiritual travellers to be lured there. Early sailors and traders got hooked on the new religions exploding across the subcontinent, exporting Hinduism, Buddhism and Indian philosophy as far afield as Siberia, Cambodia and Indonesia. Elements of Indian mysticism, medicine and maths crept into Islam and even found their way into the English language, transported to the UK by stiff-upper-lipped colonial administrators who went rogue, smoking *charas* (marijuana) with holy men. Nowhere has had such an impact on the way the world views wellness and wellbeing. Without India, there would be no yoga or meditation, no Ayurveda or mantras, and possibly no vegetarianism. For all India's tensions, the attitude to life of its 1.3 billion people is what keeps the subcontinent from collapsing under the weight of its contradictions.

ASIA

© Manuel from Madrid/Shutterstock.

© nattanan726/Shutterstock, © gulfu photography/Getty Images

Clockwise from top: The practice of yoga began over 5000 years ago in India; lighting candles for Diwali, which literally means 'rows of lamps'; the painted face of a Sadhu man who blesses visitors to Pashupatinath Temple. **Previous page:** Candles as offerings on the Ganges River, Varanasi.

TOP INSIGHTS for LIFE

KARMA CULTURE

The principle of cause and effect is woven like a thread through Hinduism, Buddhism, Jainism and Sikhism, and through the very fabric of Indian society as well. The Indian concept of karma is vastly more complex than just 'do bad things, suffer bad things' – it's an all-encompassing perspective, which acknowledges that existence is an interconnected cascade of actions and outcomes, and that the

"There are many causes I would die for. There is not a single cause I would kill for." – Mahatma Gandhi

enlightened mind can navigate life like a sailor plotting a passage in the stars. At its heart is the idea that by looking inwards and improving yourself, you can improve the whole world.

YOGA FOR LIFE

Thanks to the phenomenal popularity of *hatha* (forceful) yoga – a system of stretches and postures designed to awaken spiritual energies – India's best-loved contribution to global culture has spilled out from sacred shrines and mountain retreats into classroom workouts and office boardrooms across the globe. In India, however, yoga is not an exercise regime but a life choice, intertwined with complex spiritual and philosophical beliefs that would test the commitment of most practitioners outside the subcontinent. Being able to execute a perfect downward dog is only scratching the surface.

DRIVE AWAY DARKNESS

The explosive festival of Diwali (Deepavali) is just the most exuberant expression of India's favourite metaphor: the use of light to expel spiritual – as well as physical – darkness. In Hindu philosophy, light is knowledge, darkness is ignorance, and evil entities are feared not for their monstrous appearance, but

BEGIN YOUR YOGIC QUEST

Yoga is a lifelong path, but all journeys start somewhere. Begin the quest for spiritual harmony and physical flexibility with a *hatha* yoga class, focusing on the *asanas* (postures) that facilitate the flow of spiritual energy. Later, there'll be time to delve into the philosophical and religious side of yoga, once you've mastered sun salutations, downward dogs and the cobra pose.

SHINE A LIGHT

Even non-Hindus can appreciate the meditative process of bringing light to darkness. Follow the example of devotees along the River Ganges, and make a biodegradable 'boat' from tree leaves to carry a flickering butter lamp with a natural fibre wick, then release it on a river or the sea at sunset, while you contemplate the symbolism of the light it carries out into the darkness.

for their power to drag people into ignorant ways of thinking, trapping the soul in the painful cycle of rebirths. Rituals such as *aarti* – the offering of fire to Hindu deities – come from this same compulsion to shine light onto spiritual things, driving away the darkness of material worries that stand as obstacles to *moksha*, or liberation.

AMAZING AYURVEDA

Europe's herbal balms and mustard poultices have nothing on the rich traditions of Indian Ayurveda. First recorded some 3500 years ago, the principles of Ayurveda blend elements of religion, herbal medicine and philosophy into a holistic whole. Health, according to its adherents, depends on the complex interaction of body, spirit and mind, and Ayurveda's vast cornucopia of treatments and therapies are just tools to bring the energies within the human body into balance.

THE PATH OF PEACE

When Mahatma Gandhi launched his campaign of *satyagraha* – non-violent opposition to oppressive colonial rule – he was playing from

a philosophical rulebook written four millennia before by the authors of the Vedas, India's most sacred texts. At the core of *ahimsa*, the path of peace, is the notion that all living things contain a spark of the divine, and that harming any of them will impede your own journey towards enlightenment. India's historic wars are testament to the fact that this idea is rarely practised perfectly, but the success of the Quit India campaign proves that even mighty empires can crumble in the face of peaceful protest.

MIGHTY MEDITATION

Thanks to the influence of Hinduism, Buddhist and Jainism, inner reflection is hardwired into the psyche of the Indian subcontinent. The earliest references to meditation come from the Indus Valley, making the practice almost as old as human civilisation; the people of the north Indian plains used it as a path to inner peace in the fifth millennium BCE, thousands of years before the Egyptians raised the pyramids. Without meditation, there would be no ashrams, no yoga and no self-realisation, and Buddha would never have achieved enlightenment.

Shirodhara is a form of Ayurveda therapy in which warm oil is poured on to the forehead.

ASIA

PAKISTAN

Thanks to centuries of trade and conquest, Pakistan has absorbed outside influences like silk in a vat of dye, adding unique colours to the Pakistani way of looking at the world.

POPULATION
208 million

% OF
POPULATION
WHO FOLLOW
SUFI TEACHINGS
60

% OF LAND
USED FOR
AGRICULTURE
25

With Pakistan's tumultuous politics, its cultural contribution is often overlooked, but pull back the curtain and you'll find a nation of thoughtfulness and introspection. Pakistan's soul is not to be found at its military marches and political rallies, but in the uplifting melody of qawwali devotional hymns at Sufi shrines, and the rainbow-coloured scenes painted on its trucks and buses. Travellers here soon realise that the country has more similarities with India than differences. Though viewed through an Islamic prism, Pakistan has its own exuberant festivals, sites of pilgrimage and mystical ascetics, as well as its own rich traditions of art, architecture and expression. Known in ancient times as the Gateway of Asia, Pakistan has soaked up ideas from traders and conquerors, creating a culture that is devoutly Islamic but indelibly coloured by the teachings and philosophy of Hinduism, Buddhist and Sufi mysticism.

ASIA

© Adnan Ali/500px

© SM Rafiq Photography,/Getty Images, Nadeem Khawar/Getty Images

Clockwise from top: The Pakistan Monument in Islamabad symbolises the unity of the Pakistani people; a musician plays the South Asian *ektara* near Ranipur; a cheerful example of Pakistani truck art. **Previous page:** A painted arch at Wazir Khan Mosque in Lahore.

TOP INSIGHTS for LIFE

MELODIC QAWWALI

In the Pakistani provinces of Punjab and Sindh, the haunting sound of qawwali singing rises above Sufi shrines and *dargahs* (tombs) like a desert wind. This ancient form of devotional singing is heavy with symbolism. Some qawwalis speak of spiritual love for Allah, others talk of fleeting human love and the poignant frailty of human existence. It's both an admission and a celebration of the pleasure and pain of being alive.

GARDENS OF PARADISE

The word paradise is a western corruption of an ancient Persian term – *pairidaeza*, the garden that grows around a well or oasis. Accordingly, the rulers of medieval Pakistan filled their palaces with elegant gardens, an earthly mirror to the gardens of paradise waiting at the end of human existence. At Shalimar Bagh in Lahore, the Mughals filled 16 hectares with fountains, water features, and lace-like pavilions – a place where sultans and emperors could, just for a moment, escape the cut and thrust of conquest.

FREIGHT-TRUCK ART

Pakistan's freight trucks are mobile art galleries, adorned from bumper to bumper with hand-painted pictures of flowers, birds, revered saints, sports stars, movie stars and politicians, vignettes of unspoiled nature and idyllic village scenes. In the dusty foothills, these rainbow-coloured trucks add stabs of colour to the monochrome landscape – a celebration of life in a terrain almost devoid of it, like the hand-woven carpets in the tents of desert nomads.

ECSTATIC ISLAM

Pakistan is a majority Sunni state, but the provinces of Punjab and Sindh have a fascinating history of Islamic mysticism. The life of Pakistan's Sufi *fakirs* combines strict asceticism and the rejection of material possessions with the joyful celebration of spiritual love through uninhibited singing, dancing and music. It's a tradition with clear parallels to the Hindu *sadhus* and Sikh *udasis* of northern India, mixing agony and ecstasy in pursuit of a personal relationship with God.

LISTEN TO QAWWALI

The great singer Nusrat Fateh Ali Khan spread the love of *qawwali* singing far beyond Pakistan's borders, but nothing compares to attending an impromptu performance at a Sufi shrine. At the *dargah* (tomb) of Baba Farid at Pakpattan in Punjab, the air is filled with melodies at sunset – an experience both moving and life-affirming – as Sufi devotees give voice to their love for Allah.

ASIA

SRI LANKA

The pearl of the Indian Ocean shines brightly on the cultural map, with an island attitude coloured by the traditions and customs that three great religions brought to its shores.

POPULATION
22.6 million

% OF COUNTRY
COVERED IN
PARKS AND
RESERVES
26

% OF
GLOBAL TEA
PRODUCTION
19

Small but perfectly formed, the tropical island of Sri Lanka has soaked up a tide of influences from neighbouring cultures and fused them to produce its own unique way of looking at the world. The notion that mind, body and soul are bound together in a whole arrived with Hindu and Buddhist missionaries from neighbouring India, while Muslim sailors from the Arabian Peninsula and Southeast Asia brought a love of music, ornamentation and ceremony, as well as a taste for the finer things in life. Sri Lanka's complex cultures have not always lived in harmony, but all have left their indelible mark on the island's customs, food and language. The result is just what you would expect from a place exposed to the tradewinds of empire – a mélange of beliefs and practices that sometimes compete and sometimes complement each other, all contributing spice to the Sri Lankan perspective on life.

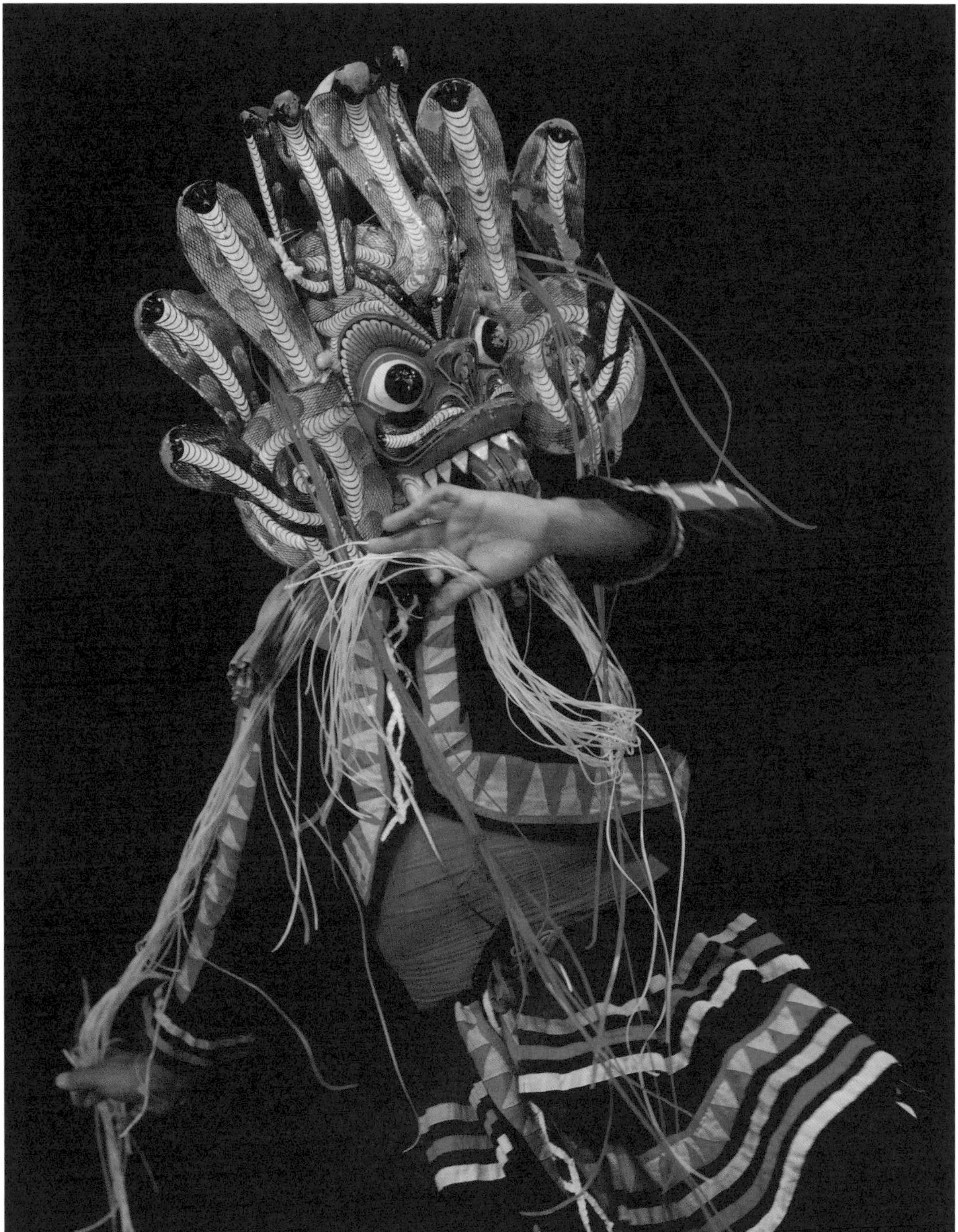

ASIA

Clockwise from top: The ancient hospital stupa ruin in the Medirigiriya Vatadage, built during the Anuradhapura era; a Sri Lankan stilt fisher; jars of potions and pills at an Ayurvedic centre. **Previous page:** A masked Kandyan dancer performs in Kandy.

TOP INSIGHTS for LIFE

HORTICULTURE AS PRAYER

Grown from a cutting taken from the sacred bodhi tree at Bodhgaya, India, where Buddha attained enlightenment, the Jaya Sri Maha Bodhi at Anuradhapura is perhaps the world's most remarkable example of transgenerational botany. Generations of Sri Lankans have lovingly tended this venerable tree since the third century BCE, when it was transported to Sri Lanka by the daughter of the Indian emperor Ashoka. During its lifetime, dozens of empires have risen and fallen on this teardrop-shaped island, but Jaya Sri Maha Bodhi still stands – a testament not to the power of armies but to the devotion and dedication of ordinary people with pruning shears.

"Living beings love happiness; cherish love for living beings." – From the epic poem *Mahavamsa*

THE WORLD'S FIRST HOSPITAL

Of all of Sri Lanka's many contributions to world culture, the altruistic concept of public healthcare is perhaps the most enduring. According to the *Mahavamsa*, Sri Lanka's ancient chronicle of royal life, King Pandukabhaya created the world's first hospital in the fourth century BCE, introducing the world to such novel ideas as wards, pharmacies and hospital meals. At sites like Mihintale and Medirigiriya, the ruins of ancient hospitals can still be seen, complete with medical stores, refectories, treatment rooms and troughs where patients were bathed in therapeutic oils. Initially, treatment was reserved for monks and royalty, but in line with the Buddhist principle of responsibility towards all mankind, the idea was quickly rolled out to the greater population.

A BEACON FOR ALL

Pilgrimages tend to be exclusive affairs, dedicated to a single religion, but in Sri Lanka's lush tropical

A WEEK OF WELLNESS

To immerse yourself in Sri Lankan traditional medicine, book into one of the island's many Ayurvedic resorts. Panchakarma – literally 'five actions' – is a programme of treatments administered over five days, from massages and herbal infusions to the drizzling of warm oil onto the forehead to relax the mind and awaken the third eye *chakra* (energy centre).

NURTURE A TREE

Cultivating a tree from a cutting is a bit like parenthood – a slow, determined process that will last most of the rest of your life. It takes effort and commitment, patience and dedication, but persevere and you may one day sit under a tree you planted in the springtime of life, with a tremendous sense of satisfaction and connection with the world.

interior, Adam's Peak – aka Sri Pada – manages to be all things to all people. Pilgrims of all faiths trek together by candlelight to reach a foot-shaped stone imprint at the summit, revered as the footprint of Buddha by Buddhists, as the imprint of Lord Shiva by Hindus, and as the first impression left by Adam when he deserted the garden of Eden by Muslims and Christians – all of which makes the mountain a rare beacon of inclusivity.

DESHEEYA CHIKITSA'S HEALING HERBS

As India has Ayurveda, so Sri Lanka has Desheeya Chikitsa, an ancient system of herbal medicine (*hela veda*) and therapeutic treatments handed down through generations, and fused with Ayurvedic ideas imported from India in the third century BCE. The Sri Lankan health department maintains dedicated teaching centres for the preparation of *deshiya kasaya* (ointments), *churna* (powders), *taila* (oils), *patthu* (pastes) and *guli* (pills), made from the medicinal plants and minerals found in abundance on the island and dispensed to patients to heal body, mind and soul.

DANCE THERAPY

Banished from the mainstream, the ancient ritual of *thovil* still takes place covertly in country villages, where shamans perform frenetic dances in terrifying masks to pounding drums in a bid to drive away the demons blamed for mental and physical illness. Spirits known as *yakku* (or *yakseya*) carry the can for everything from blindness to stomach upsets, but they flee in fear from the devil-dancers, effecting miracle cures. While there's no scientific reason for *thovil* to be effective, many Sri Lankans insist that it works, with the noise, colour and energy acting as a sensory placebo, prompting the body to heal itself.

READ IT IN THE STARS

Sri Lanka embraced *jyotishya*, or astrology, with gusto in the second century BCE, when King Dutugemunu decreed that every village in the country needed an official *nekatiya* (astrologer). Today, the movements of celestial bodies are used to determine the timing for all sorts of life events, from marriage to which auspicious letters should start a newborn's name and when to give a child their first haircut.

Musicians at the temple
complex of Mihintale,
revered as the birthplace
of Buddhism in Sri Lanka.

OCEANIA AND PACIFIC ISLANDS

AUSTRALIA

Home to the world's oldest living culture, and with one of the lowest population densities on earth, Australia puts the natural world at the heart of its attempts to live well.

POPULATION
23.5 million

ESTIMATED AGE OF ABORIGINAL CULTURE
> 60,000 years

More than a quarter of Australians go bushwalking

Aboriginal people have maintained a low-impact, ecologically sustainable and spiritually rich connection with the planet for longer than any other society. This careful act of stewardship kept Australia's environment and ecosystems in fantastic shape – a legacy that provides a sense of meaning and feeling of belonging to more recently arrived communities as well. When Australians seek to connect with the things that matter, they often head for the great outdoors. While most of the population lives in cities, green spaces thread through urban areas, almost all of which are on or near the coast, and kids grow up playing on the beach, tearing through the bush and falling asleep in tents. And while today's land management may not have the impressively low impacts of the past, books like Bruce Pascoe's *Dark Emu* are ensuring that ancient wisdom slowly filters through into modern practices.

© Ferdinand Henke/EyeEm/Getty Images

© Kinson C Photography/Getty Images, © Matt Munro/Lonely Planet

Clockwise from top: Socialising around a glowing bonfire in Exmouth, Western Australia; a Kuku Yalanji tribesman paints his body in Daintree National Park; a lifeguard surveys the surf at Bondi Beach. **Previous page:** A red sand road in Francois Peron National Park.

TOP INSIGHTS for LIFE

SACRED SMOKE

Often the first step in visiting traditional country, Aboriginal people use a sacred smoking ceremony to cleanse, heal, ground and introduce newcomers to the land. Freshly picked leaves, bark and/or fungus, selected for their healing properties, are placed on a fire, creating a thick and fragrant smoke through which newcomers are invited to pass. The ingredients chosen vary from place to place, but it's important that they are grown locally because the ceremony is about making yourself known to the country and breathing that country into yourself – to cleanse and connect you, and to pay respect to the traditional owners and their ancestors.

"We burn things that are aromatic and beautiful. It's a spiritual application of smoke. Ours is to glorify Mother Earth: without her, we're no one." – Bruce Pascoe, Australian writer and historian

CARING FOR COUNTRY

Whether it's bushwalking, wild swimming or yarning by the campfire, Australians love to 'go bush'. Many go much further, volunteering to work in environmental care, wildlife rescue and bush rehabilitation projects. These projects foster a strong spirit of community and a greater understanding of the natural world. They also give people a powerful sense of connecting with nature, both the natural environment and their own internal nature. For Aboriginal people, whose connection with the land is a defining part of their identity, 'caring for country' is a spiritual responsibility. They often describe a sense of rejuvenation when they're on their homeland, a place of which they have intimate ecological knowledge – and that knowledge now inspires

DESIGNATE A WILD ZONE

The first principle of permaculture is to 'observe and interact', and observing nature's garden is a great place to start. Permaculture designers always designate a wild zone that is left free from human interference. No matter how small, this area can provide invaluable insight into the workings of nature in your particular corner of the planet.

389

many of Australia's modern-day landcare practices.

SURF'S UP

There are an estimated 2.5 million surfers in Australia and it's easy to see why. With a population overwhelmingly living just a short distance from the coast, most Australians can hear the siren call of the waves every day of their lives. They're drawn to ride the pounding surf by a heady mix of beauty, danger and communion with the ocean. The moments of quiet reflection interspersed with sudden injections of adrenalin surfing offers keep Australians zipping into their wetsuits at the crack of dawn well into their sixties and beyond.

MAGIC GUM TREE

Australia's most famous family of trees, the strongly scented eucalyptus, has been used for healing a variety of ailments for thousands of years. Credited with all manner of antibacterial, antiseptic, decongestant, anti-inflammatory and insect-repelling properties, eucalyptus oil can also be dripped into the washing machine or mop bucket to freshen things up with a clean bush scent. When struck down by a cold, Australians often drape their heads in a towel over a bowl of steaming water containing a few drops of eucalyptus oil or a handful of gum leaves, which is said to clear the sinuses and soothe respiration.

WORKING WITH NATURE

Developed in Tasmania in the 1970s by Bill Mollison and David Holmgren, permaculture ('permanent agriculture') is a system of 12 ecological design principles that have had a huge impact on how we live within our environment. The system takes a DIY approach to the design and maintenance of productive ecosystems, placing an emphasis on working with nature rather than attempting to control it. The principles are applied to everything from growing food to generating energy, building homes and even organising and educating communities. Despite emerging half a century ago, it couldn't be more relevant than now, as the adoption of permaculture principles results in zero waste, clean environments and increased biodiversity.

An indigenous landowner recounts dreamtime stories and traditions in Mimbi Caves, Western Australia.

PAPUA NEW GUINEA

PNG is not dubbed 'the Land of Mysteries' for nothing. Whether they're cultural or natural, these mysteries will help you reconsider your values, venture out of your zone of comfort and broaden your mind.

POPULATION
7 million

**INDIGENOUS
LANGUAGES**
> 800

There can be up to
100 dance groups
at an annual
cultural festival

PNG is a unique land steeped in culture, tradition and mystery. True to its claim of being one of the last frontiers on Earth, the extraordinary wilderness, unique landscapes, strong heritage, living traditions and intricate history beckon to be explored, not only as a curious visitor, but as an open-minded adventurer. PNG's remoteness has preserved a traditional lifestyle, with many Papua New Guineans still residing in small villages and surviving on farming. Here time moves at a crawl, far from the hullaballoo of the Western world. Culture comes alive in a kaleidoscope of colours and atmospheres at the various shows that occur across the country annually, providing an insight into the fascinating customs of the local tribes. In brief, travelling around PNG is guaranteed to provoke a culture shock and bring life-changing experiences on an emotional, cognitive and spiritual level.

© Michal Knitl/Shutterstock

© szefei/Getty Images, © RuthMariePhoto/Shutterstock

Clockwise from top: Living the good life – traditional stilt houses on the Sepik River; weaving a traditional *bilum* (string bag) by hand; Papua New Guinea is home to 40 species of the magnificent bird-of-paradise. **Previous page:** Women near Mount Hagen wearing ceremonial costume.

TOP INSIGHTS for LIFE

LAND OF FESTIVALS

Pounding drums, masked warriors, feathered headdresses, face paint and mesmerising dances are just a few things you'll see at some of the most fantastically colourful festivals, shows and sing-sings on the planet. The best part is, as a visitor, you're encouraged to mingle with the dancers while they get prepared and even while they perform on stage – usually a soccer field, with no physical separation between the performers and the public. This is a unique opportunity to – literally – come face to face with uplifting traditional cultures, experience new rituals and feel connected with tribespeople.

BACK TO BASICS

Most Papuans live in remote areas. One of the great ways to experience PNG firsthand is to stay in a village (preferably on the Sepik River), share meals with locals and sleep in stilt homes. By day, guides will show you the local highlights – reefs, beaches, waterfalls and rare birds. Plastic is unknown in these rural settlements.

The nearby bush or rainforest provides traditional foods such as wild nuts, ferns and fruits, as well as material for leaf-house and canoe construction, rope and basket making, and firewood. You may be allowed to witness ceremonies that are normally closed to tourists – adult initiation rites, bride-price exchanges and pig-killing festivities. A rare privilege.

UNDERSTANDING KASTOM

When it comes to social interactions, PNG is a totally different world. Everything is defined by the *kastom* (custom), a code of conduct and living that encompasses rites, rituals and social interaction between and within clans, and maintains the all-important link with ancestors. The exchange of gifts, such as yam or pigs, is an important element of the *kastom*, as it creates a much-revered network of mutual obligations. Visitors are not expected to follow these rules, but respecting the *kastom* will bring you lots of positive attention and will make you feel part of the community.

SPOTTING BIRDS OF PARADISE

Save a day for some birdwatching. PNG is home to an astonishing variety of spectacular birds, including the iconic birds-of-paradise. The male Raggiana bird-of-paradise decorates the flag of PNG and the 10-kina note. An outing at dawn in the forest with a Papuan guide who will share his knowledge of the jungle is a magical way to commune with nature.

OCEANIA AND PACIFIC ISLANDS

FIJI

Fiji brands itself as the quintessential Pacific island paradise, and while the brochures don't lie about the beauty of its beaches, traditional culture still proudly holds sway away from the resorts.

POPULATION
927,000

ISLANDS IN
FIJIAN
ARCHIPELAGO
> 300

Fiji is thought to
have the highest
player-population
ratio of any rug-
by-playing nation

What could be more Fijian than a white-sand beach fringed with gently swaying coconut palms? This is a nation that has them by the dozen, and it welcomes all with a friendly '*Bula*' (hello). Beyond the beaches, Fiji boasts crumpled mountains clad in tropical rainforest, while below the waves the technicolour reefs are so dizzying that Fiji is unofficially known as the soft coral capital of the world. But it's more than just a tourism marketer's dream. Village life is still the central pillar of Fijian culture, laced with codes of respect, hospitality and mutual support. Whether it manifests itself as going to church or a Hindu temple, enjoying a feast cooked under banana leaves in a traditional *lovo*, or pit oven, leading the fight against climate change, or just loudly cheering on the beloved national rugby team, Fiji's culture is rich and welcoming.

© chameleonseye/Getty Images

© chameleonseye/Getty Images, © ChameleonsEye/Shutterstock

Clockwise from top: A Fijian man weaves palm tree leaves into a basket; cooking up *kava*, the national drink of Fiji; a rail of cheerful *bula* clothes at a Fijian market. **Previous page:** A kayak on the golden sands of Waya Island, Kadavu.

TOP INSIGHTS for LIFE

PASS THE KAVA

Few things are more Fijian than sitting in a circle with a group of friends drinking *kava*. It's made from the powdered *yaqona* root and mixed in a large wooden ceremonial bowl – a ritual reserved for chiefs and priests. A coconut shell of the muddy and mildly narcotic drink is passed around the circle to a series of claps, with a strict order of serving for guests. Rounds are repeated until the bowl is empty, or refilled – and *kava* sessions can go on until the small hours, as the world is put to rights over buzzing conversation. It's the ultimate form of Fijian social bonding.

"Each bay has its own wind." – Fijian proverb

DRESS FOR SUCCESS

Fijians love to dress up. While there's no formal national costume, styles often revolve around the *bula* shirt and dress, which are made of exuberantly coloured material covered with tropical-themed prints.

The Fijian custom of *kalavata*, which entails everyone wearing clothes of the same coloured and patterned material, helps to establish a sense of shared identity; you'll frequently see family members dressed in the same manner to celebrate special occasions. Even big offices in the capital Suva often have a day a week where everyone is encouraged to wear their *bula* clothes.

BEARING GIFTS

Traditional village practices still hold sway in large parts of Fiji. Many of them centre on rituals around gift giving, which help to reinforce social ties. Any visit to a village starts with *sevusevu*, the presentation of a gift that acts as both a passport to entry and an invitation to visit. Village life here is highly communal and mutually supportive, reflected in the custom of *kerekere*; here, a friend or relative in need can ask for help, which the giver must offer freely and without any expectation of repayment.

LIVE BY ISLAND TIME

Life isn't a rush in Fiji. The languid Pacific air means that schedules are never set in stone. 'Fiji time' is something of an elastic concept, where everything happens at its own unhurried pace. It's a good reminder to switch off from your digital personas once in a while, and enjoy modern life at a slightly more relaxed pace.

NEW ZEALAND

Blessed by its isolation in the South Pacific, New Zealand is a friendly, multicultural country where visitors are always welcome — if they pay respect to the land.

POPULATION
4.5 million

New Zealand was the first nation to grant women the vote

OFFICIAL LANGUAGES
English, Te Reo Māori and NZ Sign Language

Despite being a relatively small nation, New Zealand has played a significant role on the international stage since its inception as a self-governing British colony. Giving women the right to vote before any other democratic nation; going nuclear free in the mid-1980s; and, more recently, recognising the legal personhood of the Whanganui River, New Zealand has often taken the lead with its progressive politics. After signing the 1840 Treaty of Waitangi, settlers' relations with its indigenous Māori were far from ethical, but there's been great strides towards reconciliation and education in the last few decades. The profound Māori relationship with land and kin underpins the national psyche, and Te Reo Māori has melded with the English language to create a uniquely Kiwi parlance. Finally, there is the national sense of humour, which doesn't allow anyone to take themselves too seriously.

Clockwise from top: The dormant volcano Maungawhau (Mt Eden) overlooks Auckland; a chef forages for bush asparagus on a Maori food excursion in Taumarunui; a carving of a Maori warrior. **Previous page:** A traditional Maori *hongi* greeting in Rotorua.

TOP INSIGHTS for LIFE

GUARDING THE LAND

The concept of *kaitiakitanga* (guardianship or protection) underpins life in New Zealand (something that hasn't always been the case). As *pākehā* (non-Māori) New Zealanders have wised up to the damage done by introducing invasive animals and plants to the country, and the world realises the interconnectedness of the global

"New Zealand is not a small country but a large village." – Sir Peter Jackson, Kiwi film-maker

climate, there has been a renewed focus on managing New Zealand's environment for the future, as its indigenous people always did. Traditionally the local *iwi* (tribal group) took responsibility for caring for the land, maintaining a healthy ecosystem to grow and forage for food, and only taking what was needed.

THE TIAKI PROMISE

When visitors arrive in New Zealand today they're asked to take the Tiaki Promise, a modern-day example of *kaitiakitanga*. It's a commitment to care for the country, for present and future generations. Travellers pledge to respect the land, sea and nature (ie, tread lightly and leave no trace of your visit); travel safely and show care and consideration for all (this applies to driving carefully, too); and to respect New Zealand's unique culture by travelling here with an open heart and mind.

PRINCIPLE OF MANAAKITANGA

New Zealanders are exceptionally friendly to visitors... as long as they do the right thing. This spirit of welcome is another Māori value that has helped shaped the national psyche since first contact with colonists (although the locals did not always take kindly to their invaders). 'Poverty Bay' near Gisborne is so named because Captain James Cook's visit here afforded him nothing

LEARN THE LINGO

Language creates reality, so to get a better understanding of the Māori worldview, learn some Te Reo Māori from a downloadable language app like Drops. Once spoken only by Māori people, this melodic language is now taught and celebrated by New Zealand's *pākehā*, too.

after his crew shot at *iwi* chiefs who had arrived on the beach to greet him. If the crew had taken a different approach, the principle of *manaakitanga* (hospitality) would have seen the locals sharing their riches with the interlopers.

THE POWER OF BACKSTORY

Your backstory is important when building new relationships: to the Māori, this is not simply your family tree, but your extended family's connections. Even better, you should be able to recite your *whakapapa* (genealogy) in the proper order: building each layer on top of the last until you reach the present. Underlying *whakapapa* is the understanding that we're all bound together in some way. How do you know who you are if you don't know your history? The popularity of TV shows like *Who Do You Think You Are?* suggests that *whakapapa* is as important for people elsewhere as it always has been for the Māori.

MORE THAN BLOOD TIES

In traditional society, *whānau* (extended family) was three or four generations plus other related families all living together in a self-sufficient unit. But *whānau* is a more complex concept than just simple blood relations; it has an emotional and spiritual dimension that non-Māori people might think of as 'my people'. *Whānau* share values, but they also have responsibilities to each other and the broader collective. In a modern world gripped by a sense of isolation and loneliness, adopting the Māori fellowship of *whānau* may be the antidote we're all looking for.

NUMBER 8 WIRE MENTALITY

New Zealand's *pākehā* are responsible for the Number 8 wire mentality. The concept comes from Kiwi farmers' ability to fix just about anything with whatever was at hand (such as the eponymous thin wire used to construct fences). Today it can mean any situation that requires creativity and ingenuity, and often entails making something from very little. This mindset might also help to explain why a country with only 4.8 million people has produced a disproportionate number of notable people, from mountain climbers to film-makers.

Maori rock carvings at Mine Bay, Lake Taupa.

FRENCH POLYNESIA

Prioritising a chat and a laugh with family and friends is what makes life go around in gardenia-scented French Polynesia, so set your clock to island time.

POPULATION
290,000

AVERAGE ANNU-
AL TEMPERATURE
27°C

TIARE TAHITI
GARDENIAS
HARVESTED PER
YEAR
110 million

Perhaps the warm, soft air creates a friction that slows everything down in French Polynesia: cars trundle along the roads at 30km per hour, often with the driver hanging the door-side arm casually out the window; at schools, supermarkets, or anywhere else where people gather, they prioritise saying hello and having a chat over whatever task is at hand. The wellbeing of island-dwellers depends largely on everyone getting along. That's not always possible, of course, but a focus on the healing power of laughter, a limited sense of what it means to own something, and literally stopping to smell the flowers (or better, wearing them) help tremendously in this far-flung South Pacific archipelago. When you learn to live at this laid-back pace, the speed of city life suddenly seems ludicrous – and you'll probably find friends to laugh about that with you.

© Darrell Gulin/Getty Images

© Seaphotoart/Shutterstock, © Michael Runkel/Getty Images

Clockwise from top: Garlands of perfumed flowers are ubiquitous across French Polynesia; kayaking in the clear waters of Tikehau in the Tuamotu Archipelago; a Pacific double-saddle butterflyfish swims among the coral. **Previous page:** A paradise on earth: the silken sands of Mo'orea Island.

TOP INSIGHTS for LIFE

TAKE IT SLOW

If anyone moves too fast in French Polynesia they will likely be told 'haere maru' (take it slow), with a smile. In the islands, there's always time – time to be with your loved ones, time to enjoy a drive, time to tend the garden or just hang out in the water with a beer by the beach. If you rush, you'll miss out. Simple things are the most important in life, so don't let them pass in a blur.

FLOWER POWER

The national flower of French Polynesia, the tiare Tahiti gardenia, is given to visitors as soon as they step off the plane; tuck it behind your ear and you'll fit right in. Garlands and crowns of gardenias and myriad other blooms are made for special occasions or worn just for the sake of brightening up the day; in fact, flowers are so ubiquitous here that they perfume the very air.

C'EST A NOUS

In pre-European times, there was essentially no concept of ownership here. There is much more of that today, but there's still a strong sense that many things are communal. One person might own a car, for example, but any member of their extended family will borrow it without a second thought. Mention that you like an item in a person's home, and they might give it to you on the spot, sometimes adding 'c'est a nous' (it's ours). There's no point being too attached to an object, especially when someone might borrow it tomorrow anyway!

LIGHT & LAUGHTER

You'll hear the sound of laughter regularly in French Polynesia – emanating from people's homes, coming from the streets. If you talk to locals, every few sentences will contain a joke, so you'll soon be joining in the chorus. Making others laugh is the parallel goal of all conversations, alongside communicating whatever needs to be said. This vein of humour gives life a certain levity, halves stress and makes your whole body feel better.

PACE YOURSELF

Give yourself lots of time to get somewhere. Walk or bike instead of taking the car, take the scenic route or just drive in the slow lane. Notice details; smell flowers and perhaps pluck one to take along; go into a shop or business you've never gone into; enjoy each moment to its fullest. When there's time, even the most mundane journeys can be uplifting.

INDEX

Published in November 2020 by Lonely Planet
Global Limited CRN 554153
www.lonelyplanet.com
ISBN 978 18386 9044 1
© Lonely Planet 2020
10 9 8 7 6 5 4 3 2 1
Printed in Malaysia

Written by: Carolyn Bain, James Bainbridge, Ray Bartlett, Greg Benchwick, Joe Bindloss, Claire Boobbyer, Celeste Brash, Jean-Bernard Carillet, Paul Clammer, Harmony Difo, Megan Eaves, Mark Elliott, Mark Everleigh, Mary Fitzpatrick, Bailey Freeman, Bridget Gleeson, Gemma Graham, Ashley Harrell, Skye Hernandez, Sophie Ibbotson, Anita Isalska, Ria de Jong, James Kay, Lauren Keith, Michael Kohn, Emily Matchar, Etain O'Carroll, Stephanie Ong, Monique Perrin, James Pham, Helen Ranger, Nora Rawn, Brendan Sainsbury, Regis St Louis, Polly Thomas, Tasmin Waby, Kerry Walker, Jenny Walker, Luke Waterson, Nicola Williams, Barbara Woolsey.

Managing Director, Publishing: Piers Pickard
Associate Publisher: Robin Barton
Commissioning editors: Dora Ball, James Kay
Editors: Jessica Cole, James Kay, Polly Thomas, Monica Woods
Art Direction: Daniel Di Paolo
Layout Designer: Lauren Egan
Print Production: Nigel Longuet
Front cover depicts the *Cristo Redentor* by Paul Maximilien Landowski
Cover Illustration: Eiko Ojala

Australia	Ireland	USA	Europe
The Malt Store, Level 3, 551 Swanston St, Carlton, Victoria 3053 T: 03 8379 8000	Digital Depot, Roe Lane (off Thomas St), Digital Hub, Dublin 8, D08 TCV4	Suite 208, 155 Filbert Street, Oakland, CA 94607 T: 510 250 6400	240 Blackfriars Rd, London SE1 8NW T: 020 3771 5100